Risk Management in Project Finance and Implementation

Risk Management in Project Finance and Implementation

Henri L. Beenhakker

QUORUM BOOKS
Westport, Connecticut • London

Library of Congress Cataloging-in-Publication Data

Beenhakker, Henri L.
    Risk management in project finance and implementation /
Henri L. Beenhakker.
        p.   cm.
    Includes bibliographical references and index.
    ISBN 1-56720-106-7 (alk. paper)
    1. Capital investments.   2. Industrial development projects—
Finance. 3. Risk management. I. Title.
HG4028.C4B43   1997
658.15'2—dc21   97-8856

British Library Cataloguing in Publication Data is available.

Library of Congress Catalog Card Number: 97-8856
ISBN: 1-56720-106-7

First published in 1997

Quorum Books, 88 Post Road West, Westport, CT 06881
An imprint of Greenwood Publishing Group, Inc.

Printed in the United States of America

The paper used in this book complies with the
Permanent Paper Standard issued by the National
Information Standards Organization (Z39.48-1984).

10 9 8 7 6 5 4 3 2 1

To

Caroline, Barbara, Mark, and Britta

Contents

Contents

Figures and Tables

FIGURES

TABLES

Preface

Proper risk management requires knowledge in a wide range of areas, including available forms of project finance, possible government interventionism, ways to quantitatively measure risk, game theory, hedging techniques, options, and capital budgeting. The main purpose of this book is to familiarize the reader with a multifaceted approach to risk management that involves the interaction among these various disciplines, as well as to advance new theory. The discussion is self-contained; no prior knowledge of these disciplines is assumed.

The text is written in a style that economists, engineers, and financial analysts will find familiar; this is because risk management often requires interactions among these professionals. It is designed as a reference as well as a textbook. Each chapter begins with a summary so that managers, who may lack the time to read the entire book, can quickly decide whether the material offered in a given chapter is related to their particular decision problems.

The inclusion of a little calculus was unavoidable, since the book emphasizes the general nature and proper use of mathematics as a decision-making tool. Nonetheless, the text is written for use by business managers and investment analysts who lack a sophisticated mathematical background; subjects requiring more advanced mathematical training are dealt with in the appendices. Concepts that are likely to be new to many readers have been explained carefully, and many numerical examples have been included. The book can, therefore, also be used as a text in business schools and departments of economics or industrial engineering. It is particularly recommended for educators who wish to bridge the gap between the worlds of practice and education, and thus to enhance the connection between what students learn in school and what they will need to solve real-life management problems. The chapters are written in a modular, self-contained manner so that they may be read in any order.

Risk management efforts are often hindered by incomplete data pertinent to the evaluation of an investment proposal. Such a lack is no justification for abandoning a rational approach, however. Approximations and guesses frequently have to be made in addressing real-world problems. It is important, of course, to determine what is being approximated to so that errors of judgment are not compounded by subsequent errors of assessment. Special care has been taken to point out the assumptions underlying certain developments in the area of risk and return.

The book is organized as follows. Chapter 1 examines various finance structures and new international-financing techniques. The success of the project finance structure depends on the satisfactory allocation of risk among the interested parties; that is, the sponsors and lenders and, to a greater or lesser extent, the contractors, suppliers of raw materials or equipment, operators, product purchasers or end users, insurers, and government agencies. With the movement toward the globalization of markets, it is important to be aware of interventionist government policies (the subject of Chapter 2). We can reduce project risks by analyzing the impact of these policies. Chapter 3 discusses sources of risk and uncertainty and procedures to measure risk. It also explores how the concepts of game theory, which have been largely neglected by investment analysts, can be applied to determining strategies that maximize an investor's minimum possible gain and reduce risk.

Chapter 4 addresses the important question, "What can we do to reduce the risk of either a project or the firm as a whole?" This discussion of hedging begins by considering forward contracts. Next, a slightly more sophisticated instrument, the futures contract, is analyzed. The potential problems related to hedging, duration matching of assets and liabilities, forward rate agreements, and interest rate and currency swaps are analyzed in Chapter 5. Options, which are special contractual arrangements giving the owner the right to buy or sell an asset at a fixed price anytime on or before a given date, are the subject of Chapter 6. Options can serve to reduce the risk of price fluctuations; however, there is a price to be paid for the reduction in risk.

Chapter 7 deals with warrants and convertibles. A warrant gives the holder the right, but not the obligation, to buy shares of common stock at a fixed price for a given period of time. A convertible is a financial instrument that gives the holder the right to exchange a bond for a common stock. Bonds with warrants and convertible bonds are normally associated with risky companies. With diversification, individual risky stocks can be combined to be less subject to risk than any of the individual securities. Chapter 8 analyzes the development of an efficient portfolio, that is, a portfolio in which each investment must be equally productive so that if one security has a greater marginal effect on the portfolio's risk than another, it must also have a proportionately greater expected return. Chapter 9 deals with determining the proper discount rate for use in calculating the present value of cash flows, which is termed the opportunity cost of capital. It also discusses the links between risk and the cost of capital, as well as the effect of corporate and personal taxes on the value of a firm.

Students in my courses on financial management and investment decision making at Johns Hopkins University have made many useful suggestions for improving the book from the students' perspective. I am also most grateful for the comments on an earlier version of this text that I received from teachers, financial analysts, and managers. In particular, I wish to thank Britta Beenhakker and Myriam Gardon for preparing the tables and improving the first draft of the text, and Jaroslava Miler for the graphics work. Finally, I wish to thank my wife, Caroline, for her forbearance and tireless support.

CHAPTER 1

Risk Minimization in Project Finance

Ride the horse in the direction that it is going.

—Werner Erhard

We define *project finance* as a wide range of financing structures with one common feature—the financing does not primarily depend on the credit support of the sponsors or the value of the physical assets involved. The techniques of project finance apply to a wide range of ventures, from major infrastructure projects such as the construction of a tunnel or port to the development of natural resources such as oil and gas fields. Large-scale infrastructure projects account for a significant part of today's project finance activity. Many of these projects take place in countries of the developing world, while their sponsors are often from the industrialized world.

In dealing with project finance, those providing the debt put a large degree of reliance on the performance of the project itself; consequently, they concern themselves with the feasibility of the project and its sensitivity to the impact of potentially adverse factors. As a result, project finance is more expensive than conventional financing because of (1) the increased insurance coverage that may be required in view of, for instance, political risk and consequential loss; (2) the time spent by the lenders and their technical experts and lawyers in evaluating the project; (3) the charges made by the lenders for assuming additional risks; and (4) the costs of monitoring technical progress and performance during the life of the project. The reasons why borrowers opt for project finance include restrictions on borrowing, tax benefits, and risk sharing.

The success of the project finance structure depends on the satisfactory and economical allocation of project risk among the various interested parties, namely, the sponsors and lenders and, to a greater or lesser extent, the contractors, suppliers of raw materials or equipment, operators, product purchasers or end users, insurers, and government agencies. The extent to which any party will be willing to accept project risk depends on the return it expects to receive. Banks rarely enter into project financing without some form of commitment on the part of the project sponsors, which may simply take the form of an equity investment in the project. The security may consist of a mortgage of the physical assets and assignment of the rights to the cash flow from the project. However, the value of the physical assets comprising the project may be substantially lower than the monies advanced, making the project's economic viability crucial.

The economic feasibility study must show that, on the basis of projected cash flows, sufficient cash will be generated by the project to pay for all operating expenses, debt service, taxes, royalties, and other costs and still leave a surplus with which the project company can meet its target for return on equity. In addition, it is advisable to include a cushion for contingencies such as changes in market demand, fluctuations in exchange and interest rates, and inflation. To carry out the technical feasibility study (design, construction schedules, operating proposals, and so forth), most major banks have in-house technical experts. Although these experts can play a major role in protecting the bank's interests, lenders often will also employ an independent engineer for assessment and monitoring of the project.

1. COMMON MISCONCEPTIONS AND ERRORS

The assumption that lenders do not require a high level of equity investment from the project sponsors is one misconception that can make negotiations between project sponsors, lenders, and governments difficult. Another misconception about project finance is that lenders should, in all circumstances, consider the project as the exclusive source of debt service. Other examples of misunderstanding and error are described in the following paragraphs.

Underestimation of Construction and Development Risks

A complete assessment of contruction and development risks calls for evaluating the likelihood and implications of (1) shortfalls in expected capacity, output, or efficiency, (2) shortfalls in the expected mineral reserves, (3) cost overruns, (4) delays in completion, (5) underestimation of availability of land, building materials, energy, raw materials, workforce, management personnel, reliable contractors and/or transportation, and (6) force majeure. *Force majeure* refers to factors outside the control of the parties, such as fires, floods, earthquakes, wars, revolutions, and strikes. These factors are particularly important during the construction and development phase since they can affect contractors and suppliers. However, they can also play a role during the operating phase as they can affect the markets for the product.

Some of these risks can be minimized through:

taking out commercial insurance and securing support through export credit guarantee;

demanding contractors' bonds, and completion guarantees from suppliers, contractors, and subcontractors;

demanding cash deficiency agreements from the shareholders or sponsors of the project company;

entering into binding and enforceable long-term, fixed-price contracts for supplies, energy, and transportation with creditworthy and reliable counterparties; and

incorporating provisions in the underlying contracts with suppliers and contractors, for instance, so as to penalize delay, fix costs, and set performance and efficiency criteria.

With reference to insurance, in some countries regulations may dictate that coverage is effected through local insurance companies. If this is the case and the arrangement is not satisfactory, project sponsors and lenders may arrange for some or all of the risks to be covered through reinsurance offshore.

Contractors' bonds usually constitute unconditional on-demand payment obligations in favor of the project company and are usually in the form of either a bond, a guarantee, or a standby letter of credit. The types of bonds that may be required are:

1. performance bonds, which effectively guarantee performance by the contractor for a certain proportion (5 to 10 percent) of the contract price;
2. bid or tender bonds, according to which the bidders for a construction contract commit to take on the contract, if offered, on pain of forfeiting, for example, 1 or 2 percent of the contract price;
3. advance payment guarantees, which provide a guarantee on the part of the construction company to refund an advance payment in the event of failure to perform (in case the construction contract provides

for the project company to make an advance payment to the contractor to assist in buying the materials and equipment to start construction);
4. retention money guarantees, whereby the construction contract provides for the project company to retain a specified percentage of the progress payments in order to cover the rectification of any defects that are not immediately apparent; and
5. maintenance bonds, which are bonds designed to cover defects discovered after completion of the construction. Discovery must occur within the "maintenance period" specified in the construction contract.

A completion guarantee is a guarantee of performance of the project company's obligations to bring the project to the point of completion. It is particularly important for large-scale infrastructure projects characterized by (1) long construction periods, (2) capitalization of interest during the construction phase, and (3) high cost and high risk during the construction phase, in contrast to low unit cost and lower risk during the operation phase.

Deficiency agreements or working-capital maintenance agreements provide comfort similar to that provided by completion agreements, with the difference that they may remain in place beyond the completion date. They provide that the share holders or sponsors of the project company undertake with the lenders to ensure (by providing loan capital) that the project company will always have sufficient funds to complete or operate the project or, alternatively, to satisfy certain specific financial ratios that have been negotiated. A claim of breach of this nature would involve the lenders having to prove actual financial loss, which they would have no obligation to ameliorate.

Underestimation of Market and Operating Risks

To assess marketing and operating risks, we have to examine:

1. the existence of a local or international market for the product;
2. projections for prices for the product and, if applicable, tariffs and trade barriers;
3. the likely strength of any competition and similar projects being contemplated;
4. access to markets in terms of transportation and communications and in terms of commercial access in cases where markets are controlled by central planning authorities;
5. obsolescence if there is a risk that the technology used in the project or the product demand will be superseded; and

6. new technology, in which case the reluctance to support a project using untried technology must be weighed against the risk of being overtaken by more innovative competitors.

Some of these risks can be minimized through:

long-term take-or-pay contracts, as used in resource extraction or manufacturing projects;

the provision of guarantees as to a minimum off-take and price or agreement on an availability fee arrangement (capacity charge) with further fees then payable for power produced, as used in electricity generation projects;

throughput agreements, as used in pipeline projects;

tolling agreements, as used in refinery or utility projects; and

supply-or-payment agreements, which focus on suppliers of raw materials and/or energy.

Take-or-pay and take-and-pay contracts are long-term contracts guaranteeing periodic payments, in certain minimum amounts, for the supply of services or goods. The expressions are often used interchangeably; however, in a true take-or-pay contract, the obligation is unconditional and, therefore, payment must be made whether or not the services are actually rendered or the goods actually delivered. In a take-and-pay contract, payment is only made when the service is actually rendered or the goods are actually delivered.

Throughput agreements are often associated with the financing of a petroleum project in which large oil companies participate as the joint holders of an exploitation license. The coventures may then form a pipeline company to construct and operate an oil pipeline from the oil field to one or more refineries. The oil companies subsequently enter into a throughput agreement with the pipeline company under which they agree to pass sufficient oil through the pipeline at agreed tariffs so that the cash earned will be sufficient to enable the pipeline company to meet all its financial obligations. Often included is a "hell or high water" provision—which establishes an unconditional obligation regardless of any event affecting the transaction—so that if, for any reason, it becomes impossible to pass oil through the pipeline, cash payments will be made in an amount sufficient to enable the pipeline company to meet its commitments. The pipeline company assigns the benefit of the throughput agreement to its lenders so that they have the right to receive the payments and to enforce the agreement against the oil companies should the need arise.

Tolling agreements apply to projects, such as refineries and utilities, that offer a service whereby the tolling party's property is processed in some way by the project company and then returned. The tolling party is required to supply materials for tolling such that the fees will cover the project's debt service and operating costs under any circumstances.

Supply-or-pay agreements require the supplier either to provide the necessary input or to make payments in an amount sufficient to enable the project company to get the supplies from other sources. They are sometimes called *put-or-pay* agreements.

Underestimation of Financial Risks

The feasibility study should address the potential impact on the project of financial developments outside the control of the project sponsors. These developments may include (1) falls in the price of the product on world markets, (2) increases in world commodity prices, especially for supplies of raw materials and energy, (3) increases in interest rates, (4) fluctuations in exchange rates, (5) inflation, and (6) trends in international trade, protectionism, and tariffs.

These risks can be minimized in the financial package through:

including protection against a fall in the price of the product or an increase in the price of energy or raw materials through hedging facilities, such as forward sales, futures, and options (although their use may entail an additional financing requirement for margin calls);

including hedging facilities against exchange and interest rate risks by way of such means as currency and interest rate swaps and interest rate caps and floors; and

formulating the debt-service repayment profile by reference to a matrix of factors, including such factors as market prices, inflation rates, energy costs, and tax rates, as influencing the "dedicated percentage" of revenues allocated to the lenders or as determining the obligations of the project sponsors under the applicable take-or pay contracts, throughput agreements, or tolling agreements.

Underestimation of Political Risks

Lenders and borrowers take a political risk in any cross-border financing. Political risks may include:

1. a collapse of the existing political order in the borrower's country;
2. the imposition of new taxes or tariffs;
3. exchange transfer restrictions;

4. expropriation;
5. the introduction of quotas or prohibitions on exports of the project's production in cases of domestic shortages;
6. the introduction of controls to restrict the rate of depletion of the project's reserves;
7. the use of preemption rights on the part of the host government to purchase the production from the project in certain circumstances;
8. the introduction during the life of the project of more stringent environmental protection legislation, which could adversely affect planned production rates or operating costs;
9. the introduction of restrictions on the repatriation of profits and debt service;
10. the introduction of restrictions on access to supplies of raw materials or energy; and
11. deregulation or the lifting of tariff barriers in a case where the project was planned on the assumption that fixed prices and a regulation of access to markets would continue.

Political risks may be mitigated through:

taking out insurance against political risks on a commercial basis or with official bodies, such as export credit departments or multilateral development agencies;

familiarization with the tax and tariff laws in the host country;

collecting, controlling, and, if necessary, retaining the project's cash flows offshore to generate hard currency through, for example, sales contracts;

seeking assurances against expropriation or nationalization with guarantees that if these assurances were later proved false, proper compensation would be payable; and

checking and clarifying any licenses granted to the project sponsors.

If financing is arranged in parallel with the World Bank or international aid agencies, a formal arrangement of the lending structure may reduce the risk that the host government will interfere with the lenders' interests. Similarly, if the financing is syndicated to lenders from different "friendly" countries, the risk of jeopardizing trade and other relations with these countries may deter the host government from taking actions that are detrimental to the lenders' or sponsors' interests.

Political risks can be insured against by project sponsors, lenders, suppliers, and purchasers through private commercial agencies or governmental or multilateral agencies whose role is to promote exports, trade, or development in the host country. The agencies providing this coverage in the G-7 countries are as follows:

Canada	Export Development Corporation (EDC)
France	Compagnie Française d'Assurance pour le Commerce Extérieur (COFACE)
Germany	Hermes Kreditversicherungs AG und Treuarbeit AG Wirkschaftsprufungsgesellschaft (Hermes)
Italy	Sezione Speciale per l'Assicurazione del Credito all'Esportazione (SACE)
Japan	Export-Import Insurance Division of the International Trade Administration Bureau of the Ministry of International Trade and Industry (EID/MTI)
United Kingdom	The Export Credit Guarantee Department (ECGD)
United States	The Export-Import Bank (EXIM)

The available support differs from country to country; however, project sponsors, lenders, and other interested parties can apply for some degree of protection against war, insurrection (rebellion), or revolution; expropriation, nationalization, or requisition of assets; and the nonconversion of currency or imposition of discriminatory exchange rates. In addition, the insuring agencies will often provide coverage to guarantee exporters of essential suppliers to the project and performance by contractors.

One multilateral agency that provides insurance against political risks is the World Bank's Multilateral Investment Guarantee Agency (MIGA). Policies may be purchased either individually or in combination against losses arising from:

1. currency transfer resulting in the inability of investors or lenders to convert and transfer local currency into foreign exchange;
2. expropriation, that is, acts by the host government that reduce or eliminate ownership of, control over, or rights to insured investment, whether the acts are direct or indirect;
3. war and civil disturbance (including politically motivated acts of sabotage and terrorism) resulting in damage to, or destruction or disappearance of, tangible assets; and
4. breach of contract by a host government, provided the investor obtains an arbitrated award or judicial sentence for damages and is unable, after a specified period, to enforce it.

The World Bank (for public sector projects), International Finance Corporation (for private sector projects), and regional banks such as the European Bank for Reconstruction and Development, the European

Investment Bank, the Asian Development Bank, the African Development Bank, and the Interamerican Development Bank can be approached to support projects in developing countries.

The right to develop and operate a project is often based on a license or concession from the government of the country in which the project is to be situated. The license or concession is frequently issued under regulations that give the host government widely stated rights to revoke it should certain events occur. Where coventures are involved, there is also a risk to the lenders that the license may be revoked, not merely through an act or omission of the borrower with which the lender is concerned, but also through an act or omission of any other member of the consortium. In addition, a license may impose on the licensee obligations that must be performed by set dates, sometimes under the threat of forfeiture or revocation. Lenders are advised to examine the following potential issues:

1. assurances that the government will not seek to impose direct or indirect restrictions on production or depletion that risk affecting the projected cash flow adversely;
2. the host government's approval of any plans for development and operation of the project;
3. the host government's approval of the financing;
4. whether the lenders will be allowed to take a security interest in the license or concession, and if so, whether that security will be enforceable without further approval;
5. the lenders' ability to remedy breaches of the license before the government revokes it;
6. the terms on which any new license will be granted in case the original one is revoked;
7. the lenders' rights to take over and operate the project upon default and to transfer the license to another operator;
8. assurances regarding the rate of royalties and other charges to be imposed by the government; and
9. assurances regarding the tax treatment to be applied to the project.

Underestimation of Legal Risks

Projects are often carried out in countries where the legal system is less sophisticated than in the United States or Western Europe. Legal risks may pertain to (1) the rudimentary protection of intellectual property rights (patents, trademarks, copyrights), (2) the inadequate regulation of fair trading and competition, (3) problematic dispute regulation (unequal access to courts, unenforceable foreign judgments, and the inability to refer disputes to arbitration), and (4) limited rights to appeal.

Project lenders are well advised to become thoroughly familiar with the legal risks at an early stage by getting the relevant information from their local lawyers and to seek confirmation of the position from the host government's law agencies such as the ministry of justice and the attorney general's office, or equivalent. It is also noted that the local lawyers and judiciary may be unversed in the sorts of problems likely to be involved in project-related issues. In addition, the legal system may be slower, more expensive, and less predictable than lenders are accustomed to.

Underestimation of Environmental Risks

Environmental liabilities involve mainly the project operators, and indirectly, the project sponsors and lenders. An increase in costs to project operators can affect a lender's assessment of the profitability of a project. However, this is not the only consideration that lenders must take into account. Since project finance usually involves lenders taking mortgages and other security over the project site and assets, they should be aware that if they exercise their rights under the security to take over the project, they may well assume direct responsibility for the environmental impact of the project and its products.

In addition to fines and penalties for pollution, environmental costs may include:

1. costs of environmental impact assessments;
2. fees payable to regulatory and licensing bodies;
3. costs of taking out insurance to cover the risk on environmental damage;
4. costs of environmental audit programs;
5. costs of compliance with new packaging and labeling requirements;
6. loss of profits arising from forced shutdowns of the plant;
7. cleanup costs of polluted sites and civil liabilities for damage to property, health, or the environment;
8. costs of increased waste disposal, handling, and transportation; and
9. environmental taxes on the use of nonrenewable resources or the production of polluting products.

Some general steps that project operators, sponsors, and lenders can take to protect themselves are:

familiarization with the legal framework governing environmental liability in the host country;

obtaining experts to evaluate the information that is gathered;

making compliance with environmental standards a specific condition of financing;

having the documentation contain representations, warranties, and covenants on the borrower's part to ensure a focus on these issues and compliance with all applicable regulations and recommended practices; and

ongoing monitoring of the project, to include environmental assessments.

The Risk of Project Failure Is Shared Equally by Project Lenders and Sponsors

Lenders will not want to see a project abandoned as long as some surplus cash flow is being generated over operating costs, even if this level represents, to the project sponsors, an uneconomic return on the resources and the manpower dedicated to the project. Another common misunderstanding is that lenders assume political risks since they often seek assurances from the host government about the risks in the availability of foreign exchange and/or exploration. These risks are frequently covered by insurance or export-credit guarantee support, the costs of which are usually borne by the project and the project sponsors. The key to the successful negotiation of project finance is to arrive at a balance of risk sharing between the project sponsors and lenders that is acceptable to all parties. Lenders may require undertakings from creditworthy shareholders or coventurers ensuring that the project will at least reach the production stage, and if not, that the shareholders will satisfy the outstanding debt. In addition—or alternatively—lenders may wish to see the shareholders' equity committed to the project ahead of, or at least together with, their loans.

Project Loans Are Entirely Secured on the Assets of the Project

Although lenders normally take security on the project assets as well as cash flows, it should be recognized that the realizable value of such assets may be negligible, as, for instance, in the case of pipelines, tunnels, and roads that cannot be used for any purpose other than in connection with a particular project. Similarly, the value of a nonoperating power plant is likely to be significantly less than the cost of building it. The purpose of taking security in these cases is to permit a sale of the business as a going concern and/or to prevent third parties from interfering with the project. In fact, what makes project financing different from other forms of asset financing is that the value to third parties of project assets may well be minimal (unless they are assuming the running of the project). By contrast, an asset in the form of a building, locomotive, or ship always retains some residual value that the lender can realize by disposal, although it may be at a "forced," sale price.

2. THE PARTIES INVOLVED

The number of parties involved in project financing may be significant and may include the project sponsor, financial adviser, experts, project company, leasing companies, borrower, banks, agent bank, engineering bank, arranger, security trustee, lawyers, international agencies, host government, and insurers. (Naturally, project finance need not necessarily include all these parties.)

The project sponsor may be one company or a consortium of interested parties, such as contractors, suppliers, purchasers, or users of the project's facilities (as with a tunnel or airport) or products. Sponsors may include parties with indirect interests, such as owners of land through which a road is to be built and who expect the value of their property to increase as a result. The sponsor may often retain the services of a financial adviser, perhaps a commercial bank familiar with the country where the project is to be located. The financial adviser, who may be a lender as well, can advise on local conditions and suggest how to "sell" the project to win approval from lending banks. The financial adviser often prepares a document giving a profile of each of the project's sponsors and describing the nature and economic feasibility of the project, substantiated by the underlying assumptions about the project's costs, market prices and demand, exchange rates, and similar features. The adviser will, however, seldom accept responsibility for the project's economic and technical feasibility. Instead, the adviser or the project sponsor may retain experts of international repute to prepare, or at least vouch for, the project feasibility study. The experts will often have a continuing role in monitoring the progress of the project and act as arbiter in the event of disagreements between sponsors and lenders over the satisfaction of the performance covenants and tests, as stipulated in the finance agreements.

The project company is the entity that will operate the project once it has been completed. The legal form of the project company may depend on the legal framework of the host country, which may limit the ability of foreign entities to do business or require local participation in the establishment (which could also reduce political risks).

Concepts of limited liability, partnership, and common ownership in the host country may differ from those with which the sponsors are familiar, thus affecting relations between the sponsors as originally set out in the joint venture agreement or shareholders' agreement. The project structure may involve one or more leasing companies if capital allowances are available for the writing down of plant and machinery or other assets. The role of leasing companies is to acquire and lease to the project company some, or all, of the assets in return for a rental cash flow sufficient to cover the acquisition costs and also provide a commercial return. The borrower may or may not be the same party as the project company, depending on the availability of security and the enforceability in the host country of such things as claims, exchange controls, and taxes. There could be several borrowers, with each raising funds separately to cover its individual participation; borrowers may include the construction company, suppliers of raw materials to the project, the project company, or purchasers (off-takers) of the project's products.

The large scale of many projects often calls for a syndicate of banks which may be chosen from a wide range of countries in order to reduce political risks. If there are restrictions on the ability of foreign banks to obtain security over project assets, the syndicate may well include one or more banks from the host country, meaning that a prorated sharing clause can be arranged. A prorated sharing clause is a clause in a loan agreement whereby banks agree to share among themselves amounts received or recovered from the borrower and/or guarantors, prorated according to their participation in the financing. In some projects, commercial banks act as guarantors, standing behind "front" lenders whose loans are exempt from withholding taxes that would apply if the commercial banks were to lend directly to the borrower.

The agent bank is responsible for coordinating drawdowns and dealing with communications between the parties to the finance documentation. It is not responsible for the credit decisions of the lenders entering into the transaction. The engineering bank, which may be a syndicate of banks, is responsible for monitoring the technical progress and performance of the project and serving as liaision with the project engineers and independent experts. The arranger is the bank that has arranged the financing and syndication of the lending. The arranger will normally take the lead role in negotiating the loan conditions and security documentation. The security trustee is often the agent bank. Thus, the security is held by the agent bank in its capacity as security trustee. This may be particularly the case in a straightforward project financing involving a syndicate of lenders. In other projects, however, there may be different groups of lenders interested in the security and coordination of their interests, calling for the appointment of an independent trust company as security trustee.

The international nature of large-scale project financing necessitates the retention of an experienced international law firm. The lawyers should conduct a review of the legal, tax, and regulatory system in the host country and obtain local lawyers' opinions as a precondition to lending. Project sponsors are well advised to involve their lawyers at an early stage to ensure that the financing structure is properly conceived, the anticipated tax and other incentives or benefits are indeed available, and the necessary security arrangements can be implemented.

Many projects in developing countries are jointly financed by the World Bank. Other agencies involved in joint financing include the World Bank's private sector commercial-lending arm, the International Finance Corporation, the Asian Development Bank, the African Development Bank, and the European Bank for Reconstruction and Development. These agencies have their own policies and procedures on issues such as competitive-bidding procedures, security, and the enforcement and termination of financing, which may affect the structure of a particular transaction.

The host country may take an equity interest through a domestic agency, although it will seldom participate directly in a project finance as the borrower or owner of the project company. The host country may also be the main off-taker of the product or user of the service to be provided. In the case of build-operate-transfer (BOT) infrastructure projects such as toll roads or bridges, the host country will inherit the project at the end of a concession period. Naturally, the host country may also be represented by a municipality. The term BOT often refers to new construction concessions, while *rehabilitate-own-transfer* (ROT) is sometimes used to refer to concessions in which investments entail primarily rehabilitation rather than construction. The build-own-operate (BOO) process is similar but does not involve the transfer of assets. Finally, divestiture involves the transfer to the private sector of the ownership of assets and the responsibility for future expansion and maintenance. The host government's involvement may also be limited to granting operating licenses and/or incentives such as tax benefits or serving as the guarantor of foreign exchange availability.

To ensure that the risks have been correctly identified and countered calls for a close working relationship with insurance brokers and underwriters. Proper insurance coverage is particularly important for project finance since the security guaranteed by insurance is a crucial safeguard in cases where recourse to the borrower and/or sponsor is limited.

3. FEASIBILITY STUDY

An in-depth, technical, economic, and financial feasibility study is a sine qua non before any project can be sold to commercial lenders. The study must be presented in a convincing and authoritative manner. In regard to content, it must review all aspects critical to the viability of the project and involve the coordination of technical experts, financial advisers, and lawyers.

Although the issues to be considered depend on the type and scale of the project to be financed, the following is a general checklist of the major issues to consider:

the costs of acquiring the project site, construction, and development;

the availability and costs of services to the project site (water, energy, transportation, and communications);

access to supplies of raw materials and, in case of foreign sources of supplies, possible tariff or foreign exchange barriers to imports;

in cases of pipeline or processing projects, the likely throughput;

in cases of transport projects, the likely traffic flows by type of transport;

in cases of extraction projects, the extent and certainty of reserves;

the existence of accessible markets (domestic and/or foreign) for the product or service and the demand within these markets;

the availability of necessary technology, equipment, management personnel, and skilled and unskilled labor;

the availability and convertibility of currencies and the effect of foreign exchange controls;

the availability and transferability of operating licenses and other official permits;

projections of costs and returns and their underlying assumptions with regard to interest rates, inflation, taxes, exchange rates, delays, and other contingencies;

the effect of project delays, which are not uncommon in developing countries;

policy toward risk;

identification of the critical variables and preparation of a related sensitivity analysis;

proper financial ratios and other financial covenants;

preparation of an interest rate and debt service/repayment profile;

commissions and fees payable to experts;

the possibility of a breakeven deferment period;

the existence of potential for added value through, for instance, by-product sales or property development;

the availability of insurance against project and country risks;

the project's environmental impact and the need to comply with environmental protection legislation;

the legal status, power, and authority of the parties to perform their respective obligations under the project agreements and security documents;

the ownership and good title to the project assets;

the pari passu status of the borrower's obligations and the possible existence of local rules giving preferred status to certain creditors;

the likelihood of local courts awarding potential judgments in foreign currency;

the validity of the choice of law and forum for dispute resolution;

the enforceability of foreign judgments and arbitration awards; and

reporting requirements and project supervision.

4. RESTRICTIONS ON BORROWERS/SPONSORS AND LENDERS

A project's finance structure and organization may be affected by restrictions imposed on the borrower company or sponsor by:

its own articles of association or the laws of its home jurisdiction;

restrictive covenants such as borrowing limitations and cross-default clauses, as applicable under its existing financial documentation;

licensing agreements;

provisions of the joint venture agreement between the borrower and its cosponsors; and

restrictions on state entities' powers to borrow or give guarantees.

There are sometimes ways to circumvent some of these restrictions, as demonstrated in the following example. It is, therefore, always advisable to seek legal advice when confronted with such restrictions.

This example pertains to a country with restrictions on state entities' powers to borrow. The state entity is a fertilizer company (FCo). To overcome this problem a *trustee borrowing vehicle* (TBV) is established. Thus, the borrower is the TBV, which is created as a trustee for the FCo. A trustee is a person or organization to whom another's property (or the management of another's property) is entrusted. The TBV structure is presented in Figure 1.1 and operates as follows:

1. Banks finance the construction of the state-owned FCo by making a loan to the TBV, which in turn disburses funds to a construction company (CCo) in line with a construction contract between the FCo and CCo. This portion of the TBV structure is indicated with "A" above the arrows in Figure 1.1.
2. The FCo establishes an off-take agreement (a long-term agreement to purchase minimum amounts of the project's product at an agreed price) with an off-taker on a take-or-pay basis and instructs the off-taker to make all payments to the TBV. This is indicated by the letter "B" below the relevant arrows in Figure 1.1.
3. From the revenues, TBV pays debt service to banks and remits the surplus to the FCo. These transactions are indicated with a C below the relevant arrows in Figure 1.1; the thinner arrow indicates that the surplus may or may not exist.

Figure 1.1
TBV Structure

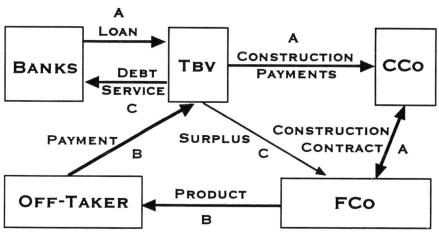

4. The FCo undertakes to pay the TBV an amount equal to debt service in the event that its payment directions to the off-taker are changed.

The disadvantage for lenders of dealing with a TBV rather than a company such as the FCo is that all the FCo's assets (including, perhaps, even its other projects) will not be made available either to support the particular project being financed or to repay the lenders if the project runs into trouble. However, even if lenders do deal directly with a company such as the FCo, the documentation is likely to involve a certain amount of protection for the other assets. In addition, the existence of negative pledges imposed on the borrower by other creditors may prevent the lenders from exerting much influence. (A negative pledge is a covenant whereby a borrower and/or guarantor will agree not to create, or allow the creation of, encumbrances on its assets.)

Prospective lenders may be subject to restrictions that forbid them to finance the project in the way the sponsors and their financial advisers may have anticipated. Examples of such restrictions are:

banks may have their own policies regarding customer, country, and business exposure;

involvement beyond the basic banker-client relationship may give rise to liabilities that banks are not prepared to accept, such as the risk of environmental damage;

banks in some countries may be subject to regulatory restrictions when participating in facilities involving specific country risk;

some banks are subject to restrictions on doing business other than banking and cannot undertake commercial activity or maintain significant equity holdings in commercial enterprises; and

some jurisdictions may restrict the ability of foreign banks to acquire security interests.

5. PROJECT FINANCE STRUCTURES

Although every instance of project finance has its own special features, the basic structure is, in essence, either (1) a limited or nonrecourse loan repayable out of project cash flows or (2) the purchase of an interest in the project output (sales proceeds) in consideration for the payment, up front, of a capital sum, as either a *forward purchase* or a *production payment*. A forward purchase is a financing structure whereby one party purchases agreed quantities of future production and/or cash proceeds from the project company sufficient to produce a return to the purchaser of the purchase price plus an amount equivalent to interest. A production payment is a financing structure whereby one party purchases a share in the minerals, hydrocarbons, or other production of the project company in return for periodic production payments by the project company during the production phase of the project.

In both cases (1) and (2), "hell or high water" provisions on the part of the suppliers, purchasers, or users connected with the project may operate effectively to ensure that the lenders recover their capital and make a commercial return. In appropriate cases, the basic structures can be adapted to accommodate other financing structures, such as:

export credits, in which case the basic financing structure can be adapted to accommodate the requirements of the relevant agency;

lease financing, which may be an attractive way of financing project costs, particularly in those countries where leasing permits the benefit of tax allowances for capital expenditure on the project to be front-loaded; and

issues of securities in cases where it is possible to provide finance at a lower all-inclusive cost through the issue of securities backed by a commercial bank or other guarantees.

We will now examine project finance structures related to the project phase, cofinancing between commercial banks and multilateral institutions such as the World Bank, production payments, forward purchases, finance leases, and build-operate-transfer (BOT) arrangements.

The Project Phase

The loan agreement normally recognizes two distinct phases in the project, namely, the construction, or development, phase and the operation phase. The construction phase is the period of highest risk for lenders. Such risk may be mitigated with guarantees that are legally binding on the project sponsors and/or by acquiring a security in the construction contract and related performance bonds. A performance bond is a guarantee given by a bank in favor of the project company on behalf of a contractor or supplier of a specified percentage of the value of the relevant contract, for instance, a construction contract or supply agreement. The completion of construction marks the beginning of the operation phase, when cash flows are anticipated and the debt begins to be serviced and/or amortized. During the first phase, the loan is disbursed and debt service may be postponed, either by rolling forward the interest pending the generation of cash flows in the operation phase or by allowing further drawdowns to finance interest payments prior to the operation phase.

In the operation phase, the lenders will take further security over the sales proceeds or other revenues generated by the project. The anticipated level of output and receivables normally stipulates the rate of debt service and repayment. That is, a "dedicated percentage" of net cash flows will go to the lenders automatically. The loan terms often provide for this percentage to be increased in the event that output and/or demand for the product are lower than anticipated. In the operation phase, net cash flows are normally calculated on an after-tax basis. In fact, if lenders have made financing available on a pretax basis, they will be lending more than the net returns justify. Figure 1.2 presents the loan structure of a typical project during the construction and operation phases. The thinner arrows indicate items that may or may not exist.

Cofinancing between Commercial Banks and the World Bank

With cofinancing, loans are syndicated in a relatively conventional manner. That is, the government will give top guarantees to the World Bank and second-priority commitments to the commercial banks. The World Bank normally does not require security for its own account; however, it does impose a strict negative pledge on the borrower, which may be the government or a state entity, and will usually wish to share the benefit of any security taken by the commercial banks. If such security is granted, the coordination provisions of the documentation usually permit enforcement by the banks only with the approval of the World Bank. The commercial banks are normally required to acknowledge that they have entered into the transaction by exercising their own credit judgments and without reliance on the decisions taken by the World Bank. Figure 1.3 gives a simple example of the financing structure.

Cofinancing between Commercial Banks and the IFC

The International Finance Corporation (IFC) lends to the private sector and seeks no government support. The borrowers are locally incorporated enterprises, but these may have 100 percent foreign participation if local laws permit this. IFC-financed projects typically benefit the host country's economy by increasing its hard currency–earning capacity. Figure 1.4 presents an IFC cofinancing structure involving a mining company that establishes a local subsidiary (LCo) to exploit

Figure 1.2
Project Phases

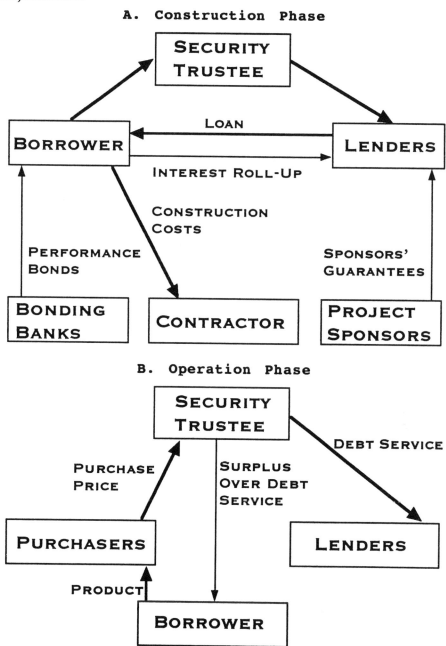

A. Construction Phase

SECURITY TRUSTEE

BORROWER

LENDERS

LOAN

INTEREST ROLL-UP

CONSTRUCTION COSTS

PERFORMANCE BONDS

SPONSORS' GUARANTEES

BONDING BANKS

CONTRACTOR

PROJECT SPONSORS

B. Operation Phase

SECURITY TRUSTEE

DEBT SERVICE

PURCHASE PRICE

SURPLUS OVER DEBT SERVICE

PURCHASERS

LENDERS

PRODUCT

BORROWER

Figure 1.3
World Bank Cofinancing

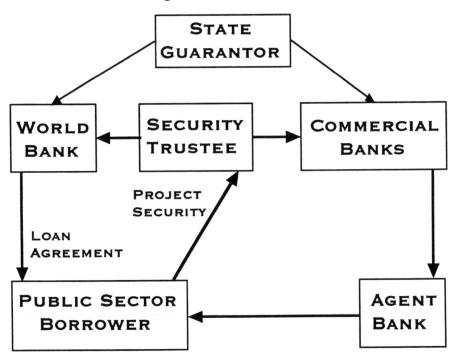

mineral deposits in a developing country. The financing structure consists of the following steps:

1. The LCo obtains a government license and enters into project agreements (construction contracts and transportation and supply agreements). It also signs an off-take agreement with its parent, the mining company (MCo).
2. The IFC enters into an investment agreement with the LCo, which amounts to $200,000 U.S., and makes separate deposit agreements with commercial banks for 80 percent of the total loan.
3. The structure involves no direct contractual relationship between the banks and the borrower. Under the documentation, the IFC retains control of covenant performance, possible acceleration, and payments.

It should be noted that there is no agent bank involved as would be in cofinancing between commercial banks and the World Bank or in a conventional syndicated loan agreement.

Figure 1.4
IFC Cofinancing

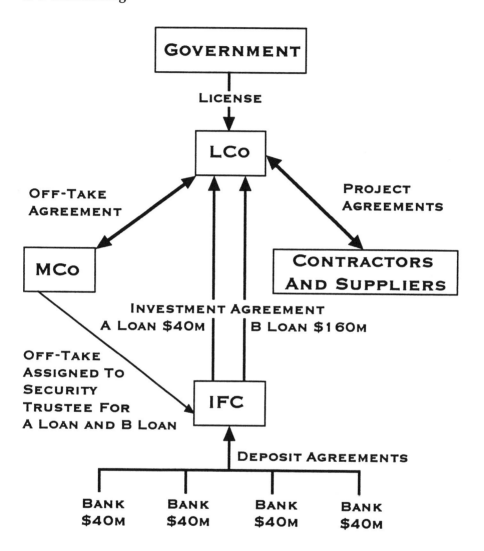

Production Payments

Project finance through production payments normally involves U.S. gas, oil, and minerals project financing. It achieves no or limited recourse financing with complete security over the production and sales proceeds and involves the creation of a special-purpose vehicle (SPV) to purchase an interest in the gas, oil, or minerals from the project company. The use of an SPV may help to isolate potential liabilities, such as environmental risks, arising from ownership of the reserves. Typically, the production payment schedule is arranged so that:

the project's production is the exclusive source of debt service;

the period over which the debt will be repaid is shorter than the expected economically viable productive life of the project; and

the lender is not responsible for financing the project's operating expenses.

The debt service profile is established on the basis of the net present value of future production proceeds. The lender may be entitled to all, or an agreed fraction, of the project's production until the debt is repaid. The structure usually calls for the project company to repurchase the product delivered to the lenders or to sell it on their behalf so as to realize cash. The costs of financing include premiums for risk insurance taken out by the lenders to protect against any liabilities arising out of their nominal ownership of the product. Figure 1.5 gives an example of a production payment structure designed to develop a U.S. oil field. It shows that banks lend the SPV the purchase price of the agreed interest in oil production from Oilco, which agrees to make production payments, to be met from the sale of oil. Oilco uses its funds to pay the development costs while the banks take a security in the SPV's interest purchased and sales contracts.

Forward Purchase

The forward purchase structure shares many of the features of the production payment structure. The lenders may establish an SPV to purchase agreed quantities of future production and/or the cash proceeds. The project company's obligation to deliver the product or proceeds is formulated to match the agreed amortization profile and service the debt. The lenders take out insurance coverage against risks attributable to their ownership of the product.

Figure 1.5
Production Payment Structure

A. Development Phase

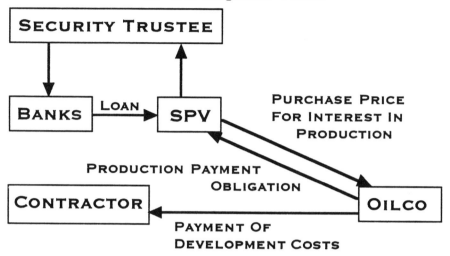

B. Operation Phase

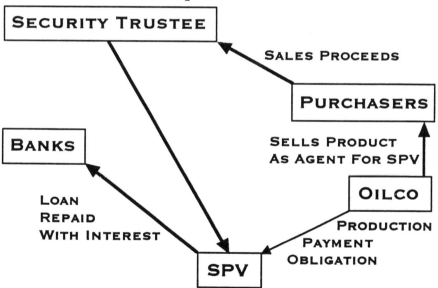

Finance Leases

The use of a leasing structure is particularly common in aircraft and ship financing, although it is also increasingly being used for the financing of plant and machinery. Project sponsors consider leasing because of the opportunities it provides for benefits from the tax treatment, uncertain security laws should the ownership of assets remain with the lenders, and cases where the project company requires the use of specific assets only for a particular phase of construction or development. Generally, banks seek to restrict their guarantees to cover only rental payments and financial liabilities that can be specified. They are particularly reluctant to cover environmental liabilities that may arise during a long lease period.

Figure 1.6 presents the contract and lease stages together with the construction, operation, and lease termination phases of a structure of finance lease. It shows that a typical structure includes the following:

1. Identification of the plant and machinery that the project sponsors wish to acquire and incorporation of an SPV project company (PCo). The PCo or one of the sponsors may enter into a contract for the purchase and construction of the assets and subsequent novation (the substitution of a new obligation or contract for an old one by the mutual agreement of all parties concerned) of the purchase contract; alternatively, the contract will not be entered into until the finance leasing company has committed itself to the transaction.
2. The finance leasing company leases the plant and machinery to PCo. The construction contract is supervised by PCo or one of the project sponsors on behalf of the lessor under a supervisory agreement.
3. During the construction period, rentals are limited to an amount equivalent to interest on the acquisition and construction costs and are guaranteed by one or more banks and/or the project sponsors since lessors, in general, are not prepared to accept project risk.
4. The banks acquire security over the project assets and construction contract from the lessor. During the construction phase, the banks may well require guarantees from one or more project sponsors to address the PCo's indemnity obligations (an indemnity is an undertaking to protect a party against the consequences of particular circumstances, in particular, for any financial loss).
5. During the operation phase, the lease provides for rentals to be reviewed to cover principal plus interest over the balance of the primary lease period. The sponsors' guarantees may be removed, leaving the banks with project risk, which is secured by assignments (transfers) of the sales contracts and receivables as well as charges over the leased assets.

Figure 1.6
Structure of a Finance Lease

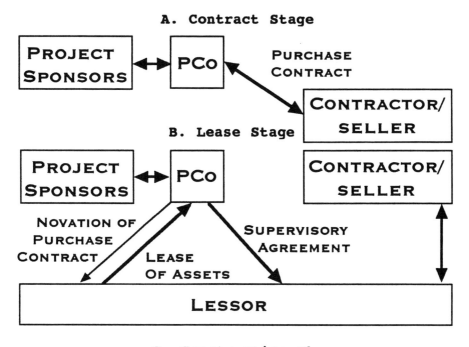

A. Contract Stage

PROJECT SPONSORS ◄► PCO

PURCHASE CONTRACT

CONTRACTOR/ SELLER

B. Lease Stage

PROJECT SPONSORS ◄► PCO

CONTRACTOR/ SELLER

NOVATION OF PURCHASE CONTRACT

LEASE OF ASSETS

SUPERVISORY AGREEMENT

LESSOR

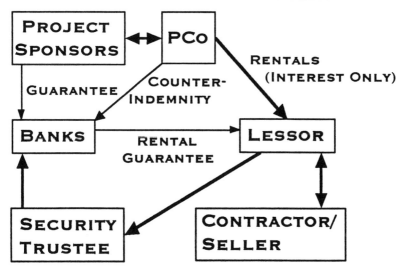

C. Construction Phase

PROJECT SPONSORS ◄► PCO

RENTALS (INTEREST ONLY)

GUARANTEE

COUNTER-INDEMNITY

BANKS

RENTAL GUARANTEE

LESSOR

SECURITY TRUSTEE

CONTRACTOR/ SELLER

Figure 1.6
Continued

D. Operation Phase

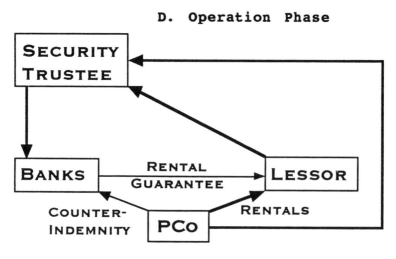

E. Final Phase--Termination of Lease

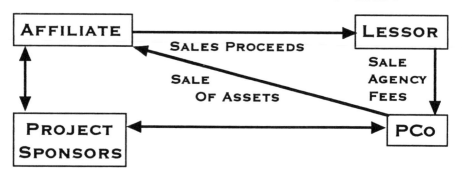

6. Often, at the end of the primary lease period, when the lessor's costs have been paid off, the lease may continue for secondary or tertiary periods of substantial length at minimal rental fees.

The lease does not contain a purchase option exercisable by the PCo since this would make the transaction a hire-purchase and eliminate the tax benefits related to the structure. The lease could provide that the PCo acts as sole agent to sell the assets at the end of the term at a price acceptable to the lessor; naturally, the PCo would receive sales agency fees. It may well happen that the purchaser is connected to one or more of the project sponsors.

Build-Operate-Transfer (BOT)

A BOT structure is a way of turning over to the private sector, for a given period of time, the development and initial operation of what would otherwise be a public sector project. Thus, an essential element of a BOT structure is the return transfer of the operational project to the relevant state authority. Governments are interested in the BOT approach because it (1) minimizes the impact on their capital budgets, (2) introduces new technology, and (3) introduces increased efficiency from the private sector. A BOT structure normally involves a concession agreement between a government or government agency and a vehicle company created by the sponsors to carry out the construction and operation of the project.

If liabilities undertaken by the project vehicle are substantial and the vehicle was incorporated to obtain the concession, the sponsors may be required to provide support for the performance, whether by entering into the concession agreement or by providing independent commitments. In addition, the sponsors may wish to ensure that the government party accepts that in certain circumstances it may need to provide continuing support. For instance, connecting infrastructure may be needed to maximize the anticipated benefits from the project. Sponsors may also ask for adequate compensation in the event that the government subsequently acts inconsistently with its expressed intentions and to the detriment of the project. Conversely, the government party may wish to ensure that the concession company (1) observes relevant safety and environmental protection standards, (2) provides an adequate service, (3) levies reasonable charges on the consumers or users, and (4) carries out proper maintenance and repairs. The government party could achieve these objectives by specific regulatory enactments or by maintaining a "golden" (sufficiently large) share in the concession company. BOT projects differ from most other projects since the host government plays a greater role and often has little direct contact with the lenders.

Figure 1.7 presents a BOT structure, including the concession, construction, finance, and operation phases. It shows that a typical structure consists of the following:

1. The sponsors incorporate an SPV to undertake the concession agreement; shareholders enter into letters of comfort with the government agency (GA). A letter of comfort (sometimes called a letter of support) describes the understandings that have been reached. It may also contain a statement to the effect that, historically, the parent has supported its subsidiaries in their financial difficulties. Sometimes the letter contains more than just statements of present intentions,

Figure 1.7
BOT Structure

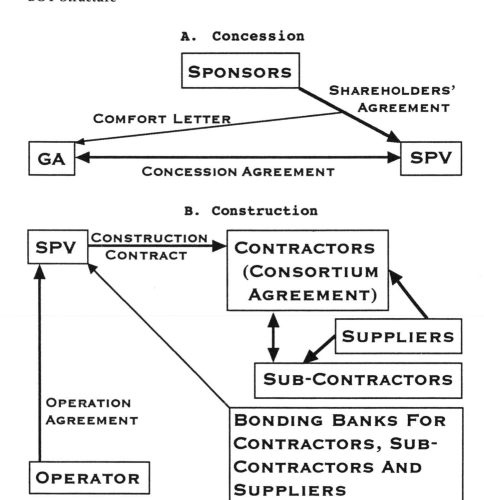

Figure 1.7
Continued

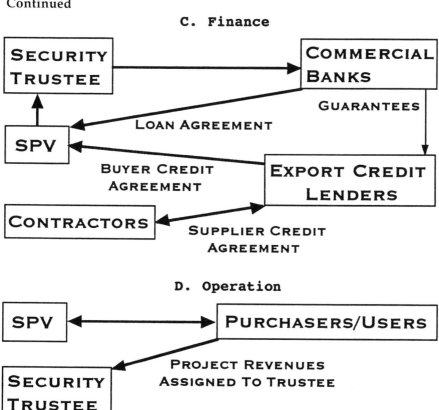

C. Finance

SECURITY TRUSTEE → COMMERCIAL BANKS

GUARANTEES

LOAN AGREEMENT

SPV

BUYER CREDIT AGREEMENT

EXPORT CREDIT LENDERS

CONTRACTORS

SUPPLIER CREDIT AGREEMENT

D. Operation

SPV ⟷ PURCHASERS/USERS

PROJECT REVENUES ASSIGNED TO TRUSTEE

SECURITY TRUSTEE

as, for instance, when it states the guarantees on which the lenders intend to rely in the event of problems. There is no such thing as a standard letter of comfort.

2. The SPV enters into a construction contract, takes bonds and assigns the bonds of the subcontractors and suppliers, and enters into an operation agreement.

3. The SPV enters into loan agreements with commercial banks and buyer credit agreements with export credit lenders; the commercial banks will guarantee the export credit loans and acquire security in the project. The security includes the assignment of revenues, bonds, insurance policies, and concession and project agreements. Export credits are credit or guarantee instruments made available to exporters to promote the manufacture of goods or the provision of services for export.

4. The SPV assigns to the security trustee revenues such as proceeds (under sales contracts) or toll fees (for a road, bridge, or tunnel).

SUGGESTIONS FOR FURTHER READING

Alston, J. P. *The Social Dimensions of International Business: An Annotated Bibliography*. Westport, CT: Quorum Books, 1992.

Beenhakker, H. L., and J. G. Sirdeshpande. "Planning Procedures for a Process Industry." *AIIE Transactions*, 6, no. 2 (June 1974): 126–34.

Chukwumerije, O. *Choice of Law in International Commercial Arbitration*. Westport, CT: Quorum Books, 1994.

Friedland, J. H. *The Law and Structure of the International Financial System*. Westport, CT: Quorum Books, 1994.

Gutterman, A. S. *The Legal Considerations in Business Financing: A Guide for Corporate Management*. Westport, CT: Quorum Books, 1994.

Hoffman, W. M., J. Brown Kamm, R. E. Frederick, and E. S. Petry. *Emerging Global Business Ethics*. Westport, CT: Quorum Books, 1993.

Horton, M. J. *Import and Customs Law Handbook*. Westport, CT: Quorum Books, 1992.

James, H. S., and M. Weidenbaum. *When Businesses Cross International Borders*. Westport, CT: Quorum Books, 1993.

CHAPTER 2

Interventionist Government Policies

Stupidity consists in wanting to reach conclusions. We are a thread,
and we want to know the whole cloth.

—Gustave Flaubert

Interventionist policies in various nations often give rise to distortions
in the national economy that result in slow economic growth. Sources
of distortions discussed in this chapter include overvalued exchange
rates, subsidies, administrated prices, and entry and capacity controls.
Different interventions are reviewed separately to highlight their specific effects, although in practice they generally work in combination
and often reinforce each other in the same direction. Instead of reliance
on these interventionist measures, economic theory and the available
evidence indicate that marketing and transport can be made more
efficient by relying on markets to determine supply, demand, and
prices. The rationale for this contention is that private industry operates
primarily in contestable markets.

The core of contestability theory is that contestable markets yield
efficient production and prices that preclude excess profits in the long
run. When an industry is characterized by both significant sunk costs
(costs which can no longer be retrieved) and scale economies, one
producer can obtain the position of a natural monopolist, in which case
there may be a need for price regulation in order to prevent overly high
monopoly prices. To determine the administered price, the concept of
a stand-alone cost (SAC) is introduced.

One widespread form of interventionist government policies has been overvalued exchange rates, which undermine exports, harm agricultural production, stimulate imports while breeding protection against them, discourage the maintenance of trucking fleets, and promote rent-seeking economies. As a result, they often precipitate a debt crisis. To believe that overvalued exchange rates curb inflation is a misconception and disregards the existence of black markets. Overvalued currencies often result in excess import demand, requiring foreign exchange to be rationed quantitatively. To prevent import agents from making excessive profits, foreign exchange quotas are normally accompanied by price controls. However, the low official prices on imported goods give rise to black markets and a dual pricing structure, whereby only some imports are sold at officially controlled prices.

Subsidies are another widespread form of government intervention. They often result in inefficient operations due to vague public accountability, poor financial management, and lack of incentives to be efficient due to the provision of compensating resources for loss-making activities.

While price regulation may be required in markets with a natural monopoly, these markets are the exception. Administrated prices in the agricultural marketing of food crops and export and import crops are normally pan-territorial and pan-temporal. Pan-territorial prices have shifted the pattern of production and consumption and led to an increased demand for transport. Pan-temporal prices have resulted in a peaked marketing season. Transport costs have been inflated due to the need for a greater total capacity to meet the highly increased demand.

Entry controls are used to screen private operators who want to enter a market, while capacity controls aim at controlling the supply of each type of operator, and thus total supply. These controls have worked to protect, for instance, inefficient millers, marketing agents, and transport operators, and to reduce their incentives to adopt innovative approaches.

Capacity restrictions in the transport industry are either individual/firm-oriented or market-oriented. Under the former type, individuals or firms have to obtain a permit to procure a vehicle. Market-oriented licensing systems are designed to control the expansion of total capacity, either in the entire road transport industry or in separate markets.

The principal reason why there is little discussion in the literature of the effects of interventions in one sector on another or of the macroeconomic framework on individual sectors is that decision makers and professionals tend to concentrate on their specific area of competence. With the movement toward the globalization of markets, it is important to be aware of interventionist policies since they can affect a project's outcome. In other words, one can reduce project risks by analyzing the impact of such policies.

1. CONTESTABILITY THEORY AND ECONOMIC EFFICIENCY

The economic policies of developing countries would be expected to encourage the efficient allocation of resources. The thrust of national policies would therefore aim to exploit the country's comparative advantages by promoting exports for which prices on the world market exceed the local cost of production and by stimulating the production of commodities for domestic consumption, at less cost than the imports. International trade at world market prices would, in other words, be expected to serve as a vehicle for economic growth. In response to competition from within the country as well as from abroad, such economic policies would also be expected to permit the exploitation of economies of scale and generate technological improvement as further spurs to economic growth.

Many studies have shown that government interventions to control demand, supply, and prices have fostered inefficiencies and had undesirable side effects (Friedlaender and Spady 1981). A system whereby demand, supply, and prices are determined by market forces is a better means to promote efficiency. The basis for this contention is that marketing agents and road haulers operate in contestable markets. The core of contestability theory is that contestable markets are the best source of efficient production and prices that will serve to preclude excess profits in the long run. Contestability is a wider concept than competition; in fact, a competitive market is merely one type of contestable market. The main requirement for a market to be contestable is that entry into and exit from it are not impeded or, in practical terms, are fairly easy. There is, therefore, no need for an industry to be made up of a large number of firms, as is required for a market to be perfectly competitive. According to contestability theory, even markets served by one or a few firms can be compatible with economic efficiency provided that entry into and exit from the market are (1) possible at relatively low costs, (2) not hampered by limited access to capital, and (3) not hindered by lack of information about alternative technologies. The threat of potential competitors will suffice to prevent one or several firms from exploiting a potential monopoly situation in the market. Thus, the threat of competition should stimulate cost-effective production and prices equal, or close, to marginal costs.

Contestability theory is particularly relevant to the marketing of agricultural commodities in developing countries. The reason is that many market segments are thin in rural areas, with little room for more than one or a few marketing agents. However, in general, entry into agricultural marketing is easy. The main factors of production, not considering processing, are labor, vehicles, and some working capital. These factors should be easy to mobilize provided the markets for them operate reasonably well. Thus, given that information is available about market conditions in thin markets, potential competition should act as a spur to cost-effectiveness and the promotion of cost-related prices.

Similarly, entry into road transport can be expected to be easy, even in thin markets. In fact, with the possible exception of barge transportation, trucking should perhaps be the most contestable of the economy's industries. Casual observations in many countries reveal that road transport is an industry where firm size is not determinative, as small firms can compete successfully with large ones. In fact, one reason why the regulation of road transport has often been advocated so forcefully by established members of the trucking industry—as well as by the railways—is that competition is tough.

With growing insight into the deficiencies of regulatory regimes, several countries, including the United Kingdom, the United States, and Sweden, started to deregulate road transport in the late 1970s and early 1980s. The experience to date shows no evidence of the negative effects that advocates of regulation normally cite. As a whole, bankruptcies have not been abnormally high and there has been no significant move toward concentration of the industry due to predatory pricing on the part of large carriers. Prices, which have tended to increase in thin markets and decrease in thick (large) markets, have become more closely related to costs. Deregulation seems also to have acted as a spur toward quicker technical development, and toward lower prices and/or improved customer services.

Another argument against regulations is that their implementation requires the development and maintenance of costly and inefficient bureaucracies, which also offer extensive opportunities for favoritism and graft. For example, the many roadblocks for traffic inspection are the first evidence visitors to many African countries encounter. Roadblocks are used to check compliance with various kinds of regulations, including transport and agricultural-marketing regulations. They cause considerable costs in administration and also lower the productivity of road transport.

The One-Stage versus the Gradualist Approach

The issue of undesirable government intervention raises the question of whether reforms should be introduced in entirety or according to a more gradualist route. The former approach may increase transition costs relative to the gradualist approach, and several reforms at once may be politically unacceptable in view of expected public uproar. Naturally, however, the gradualist approach delays the benefits expected from reform. The following types of transitional questions should be raised in order to decide on the proper approach:

1. If a gradualist approach is undertaken, should there be uniform or discriminating treatment of subsectors during the transition period?
2. If uniform, what are the choices among alternative uniform processes?
3. If nonuniform, what should be the nature of the discrimination between activities?

It is important to identify transitions that are sustainable even if this involves a reform package that is less than perfect. The following types of questions should be asked to examine sustainability: Who are the winners and losers from the policy reform? How long will it take for the winners to feel the gains and for the losers to feel the losses? What is the role of other compensatory policies in minimizing losses?

Warranted Government Intervention

This discussion is not intended to advocate mindless deregulation. However, an all-pervasive, laissez-faire position on the spread of regulation is certainly not desirable. We will now consider examples of warranted government intervention.

One implication of contestability theory for marketing and road transport is that government policies are most effective if directed toward enhancing competitive conditions. The aim of such policies is to ease entry into markets by reducing entry barriers and making the market more transparent—to ensure that information about market prices and other conditions is easily available. Information about market prices can be conveyed via radio or newspapers, or it can be posted in marketplaces. Transparency can also be improved by setting aside separate areas in towns and villages to serve as wholesale markets for agricultural products or places where transport brokers can operate as intermediaries. In transport, competition can be enhanced by promoting the availability of a wide range of transport options. Thus, combined rail/road transport services are made more competitive if railway services can be sold by independent transport brokers. Finally, other forms of warranted government intervention to facilitate entry include the provision of extension services and training and the ensured availability of credit. (Additional examples are given in this chapter.) The principal aim should be to improve the supply and quality of transport and marketing services so that they can respond flexibly to demand at minimum cost.

While contestable markets may be widespread through agricultural marketing and transport (at least potentially), there are also markets that lack this feature, especially where there are significant economic barriers to entry and exit. The most important constraint on unimpeded entry and exit is the presence of considerable sunk costs. Sunk costs arise when a factor of production proves difficult to transfer into another market. When an industry is characterized by both sunk costs and scale economies, one producer can obtain the position of a natural monopolist. An example in the transport sector pertains to railways. In marketing, processing is sometimes characterized by scale economies, which favor production by only one or a few firms, with large sunk costs. For natural monopolies there is a need for price regulations in order to prevent overly high monopoly prices in either the transport or the marketing and processing of products.

To determine the administered price, the concept of stand-alone cost (SAC) is useful. SAC is used to compute the price a competitor in the marketplace would need to charge in serving a captive operator, or a group of operators, who benefit from sharing joint and common costs. For instance, a railway rate level calculated by the SAC methodology represents the theoretical maximum rate that a railroad could levy on shippers without a substantial diversion of traffic to potentially competing road-transport services. It is, in other words, a simulated competitive price. The competing service could be a shipper providing services or a third party assumed to be ready to compete with the railroad for traffic. In either case, the SAC represents the minimum cost of an alternative to the service provided by the railroad.

Within the context of sunk costs as an entry barrier, it should be noted that the use of a few large mills with large sunk costs entails more transport than the use of many small mills and fosters capital-intensive transport means. With large mills, the grain needs to be moved longer distances for milling and distribution compared to the distance it must be carried from many smaller mills situated throughout the country. In addition, it appears that the costs of production of large mills are often equal to, or more than, those of artisanal mills. Consequently, policies promoting the construction of large mills for their large-scale economies should be carefully examined to determine their comparative cost advantage over small mills (if any), as well as their impact on the total transport cost of hauling the grains and distributing the processed products.

Within the context of contestable and free market economies, the normal practice is to rely primarily on international prices as determinants of domestic prices. However, international prices of certain commodities and products may not be fully reliable for this purpose if, for example, they are temporarily subsidized or commodities are dumped in the world market by major suppliers. Government intervention in the form of, for instance, subsidized export prices for certain products would be warranted if other countries—or major suppliers—subsidize or resort to dumping practices and thereby temporarily distort the world prices of these products. In this situation, governments are well advised to use the internationally subsidized prices as determinants of domestic prices and to direct their limited resources in manufacturing or agricultural activities to where their comparative advantages can be exploited. International prices may also be influenced by the strength or weakness of world currencies due to, for example, sizable movements of international capital flows into or from these currencies. In addition, sizable swings in international capital flows may affect a country's exchange rate. These factors need to be taken into account when formulating tariff and domestic price policies. Adequate capabilities to monitor and assess the impact of these factors should be put in place to formulate compensatory policies whenever necessary.

To reduce the risks related to foreign investments it clearly is advisable to examine the extent to which unwarranted and warranted government intervention exist in the country under consideration. In addition, we should find out what, if anything, the government intends to do about the problem. Moreover, if the government does intend to eliminate unwarranted intervention, will it follow the one-stage or the gradualist approach?

2. OVERVALUED EXCHANGE RATES

Many developing countries have pursued, or are pursuing, policies resulting in overvalued exchange rates. A currency is overvalued when the price of foreign exchange is lower than it would be under free trade equilibrium. Overvaluation requires either that import duties be imposed on some or all imports or that imports be rationed by allocating foreign exchange according to import quotas. Although both measures are often used simultaneously, developing countries have tended to rely more on quantitative restrictions.

The two main arguments advanced to support the maintenance of overvalued exchange rates are closely interlinked. One is the belief that the foreign demand for traditional exports of developing countries is income inelastic and that the growth in demand is sluggish. Consequently, the other argument has been that the best way of achieving economic growth is to promote industrial development through substituting domestic manufactured goods for imported ones. Foreign exchange control regimes have thus aimed at promoting primarily the industrial sectors of developing countries. The substitution has been promoted by imposing import duties or quantitative import restrictions on goods to be substituted, while duties have been low or nonexistent on the inputs required by the emergent industries. Another commonly used tool has been the provision of credit to emergent industries at relatively low or subsidized interest rates. Another argument sometimes advanced to support the maintenance of overvalued exchange rates is that they curb inflation. There is, however, sufficient evidence that in the long run, this is not the case (Pfefferman 1985).

In retrospect, protectionist policies have proved to be ineffective and their economic costs have been substantial. One reason is that an overvalued exchange rate prevents a country from exploiting its comparative advantage as determined by world market prices. Protected industries often have monopolistic positions and operate in an environment that lacks incentives to operate efficiently, to innovate, or to modernize in order to stay in tune with global progress. In addition, the small size of the domestic market often prevents such industries from exploiting economies of scale. The economic costs of these industrial policies have resulted in lower economic growth.

Experience shows that the demand for exports of developing countries is not as inelastic as claimed (Riedel 1983). Several empirical studies also show that countries that have pursued export-promoting policies have been more successful in achieving economic growth than those that have not. However, several developing countries have been reluctant to devalue their currencies in order to reduce or eliminate overvaluation for fear that eliminating overvaluation will give rise to inflation and undermine the financial viability of many companies. In the short run, an adjustment of the exchange rate may well have such consequences, but in the long run, overvaluation means that many imports and potential exports consumed locally are being provided at artificially low prices, below the real cost to the country (Krueger 1982).

Effects on Demand for Transport

Protectionist policies harm agricultural and industrial development in developing countries. For instance, overvalued currencies reduce the incentives to produce crops for exports as relative prices favor production for the domestic market. Moreover, protectionist policies often promote imports of products through liberal foreign exchange quotas or low or nonexistent import duties. Overvalued currencies may thus result, not only in a shift in production away from products earning foreign exchange, but as a whole in reduced activity, including production for domestic consumption. They tend to aggravate the foreign exchange position, requiring, eventually, that imports be reduced and domestic food production be stimulated by increasing domestic producer prices.

Currency reform to reduce or eliminate overvaluation can be expected to affect the pattern of agricultural production substantially, and the consequent impact on the transport system can be complex. Not only will quantities, in terms of volumes and distances, be affected, there will also be changes in the composition and direction of transport flows. If the reform has its desired development impact, it will also lead to a higher rate of growth in transport demand. An important implication for the planning of new transport facilities when major reforms of the foreign exchange regime are being considered or implemented is that past and present traffic flows may be poor indicators of future demand. A much broader approach to demand forecasting is required to take into account the expected impact of currency and other reforms on the growth and pattern of agricultural production and consumption.

One example of the effects of an overvalued exchange rate is its effect on the marketing of maize in Tanzania, where the unofficial exchange rate for the shilling (TSh) varied between five and ten times the official rate during the first half of the 1980s. Producer prices for maize were low because they were set by the government on a par with import prices; maize was not subject to any import duty. This policy has hampered Tanzania's goals to become self-sufficient in food crops and promote the production of export crops. Whereas in the 1960s, the country was able to export maize (its most important food crop), the overvalued currency later reduced producer prices to such an extent that maize began to be imported. In 1984–1985, about 150,000 tons of maize grain were imported to supplement the 75,000 tons bought locally by the country's official marketing board, the National Milling Corporation (NMC).

Valued at the official exchange rate, in 1984–1985 the per-ton cost of maize grain in Tanzania, including marketing and transport costs up to the wholesale level, was, on average, TSh 2,000 per ton lower for imported maize than for what was locally procured. The higher cost of local maize reflected the government's more recent policy to stimulate domestic production by increasing real producer prices. If the shilling had been less overvalued in 1984 and worth, say, one-third of the official value, then a ton of imports would have become about 1,000 TSh more expensive than the local product. In that event, it would have been possible to raise the producer prices so that the local farmers' net receipts, namely, after deduction for expenses for inputs such as fertilizers, would have increased by at least 25 percent. Such an increase might well be sufficient to encourage production to a level where imports would be reduced substantially or even eliminated altogether.

As to the transport of maize, a more balanced exchange rate in Tanzania might result in:

1. the elimination of, or at least a reduction in, the unloading of maize in the ports;
2. an increase in domestic traffic by road and rail, as well as a change of the traffic flows, as imported maize consumed near the ports in the eastern part of the country would be replaced by local maize mainly grown in the western portion; and
3. a greater variation in traffic flows during the year since imports would be replaced by local production sold by the farmers during a very short period during the year (due to pan-temporal prices); however, the change would have been insignificant as imports had been arriving intermittently rather than evenly (due to the shortage of foreign exchange).

Effects on Supply of Transport

Overvalued currencies and quantitative import restrictions on, for example, vehicles and spare parts may have significant repercussions on the efficiency and cost of road transport. To prevent import agents from making excessive profits, foreign exchange quotas are normally accompanied by price controls. The low official prices on imported goods give rise to black markets and a dual-pricing structure whereby some imports are sold at the officially controlled prices and some at unofficial prices. As unofficial prices are often much higher, the competitive conditions in transport tend to become distorted.

The allocation of import quotas gives rise to other problems as well. Import quotas require the government to determine how much foreign exchange should be allocated to each sector of the economy as well as to each type of import item or category. Due to lack of reliable data in many developing countries, it is virtually certain that the quota system will result in unbalanced allocations so that, for instance, far too much may be allocated to new vehicles compared to spare parts for existing trucks. Some quantity rationing systems are even more restrictive in that the authorities may decide in detail on, for example, which truck owner should receive what and how much. Experience shows that such detailed allocation systems all too often mean that resources are allocated to operations that are not necessarily the most efficient ones. The effects of overvaluation on the performance of the transport industry are highlighted in the following example, drawn from my own observations in Tanzania.

In 1985 the Tanzanian government controlled the domestic prices of vehicles and spare parts, in the same way as for other goods, by regulating the margins between import, wholesale, and retail prices (Whitworth 1982). The officially low prices resulted in excess demand for trucks, spare parts, tires, and sometimes fuel, forcing the government to ration the numbers of imports. The allocation of trucks is handled through a two-tier system. The type and quantity of trucks are determined by the State Motor Corporation under the Ministry of Trade and Industry. The corporation recommends national and regional distributions of trucks for approval by the prime minister's office. At the regional level, the trucks are allocated by a Regional Motor Vehicle Allocation Committee to crop authorities, parastatal transport companies, village cooperatives, and private truck owners. There are no set rules or principles for allocation at either the national or regional levels; moreover, decisions are confidential and cannot be appealed. The priorities of regional authorities are that vehicles should be primarily distributed to experienced and reliable operators in order to ensure the reliable transport of crops. Truckers claimed that a disproportionate number of the new vehicles were allocated to the transport wings of parastatal crop authorities and trucking companies. Data for 1984 and 1985 show that two-thirds of total vehicle imports went to the public sector, whereas its share in the trucking fleet was 23 percent and the private sector had an acute need for new vehicles and spare parts. Vehicle imports did not include trucks provided as donations, which normally were also allocated to the public sector.

The quantitative allocation system operated by the Tanzanian government has not been successful, as evidenced by a flourishing black market for tires, fuel, and spare parts. Since Tanzania is not isolated from the neighboring economies, the unofficial prices tend to be influenced by what the inputs could fetch in Kenya, Burundi, and Zambia at the unofficial exchange rate. The black market prices of tires and spare parts in 1984 were about five times the official prices, reflecting the difference between the unofficial and official rates of exchange between Kenyan and Tanzanian shillings.

Although transport rates were not officially fixed in Tanzania, the fact is that the rates were determined by parastatal marketing boards as a result of their dominance in the market. In 1984, a typical long distance rate was about TSh 2.5/ton-kilometer (t-km). The operating cost for a 25-ton truck-trailer combination was estimated at TSh 2.0/t-km, provided inputs were bought at official prices. If inputs were bought at unofficial prices, the cost was about TSh 3.0/t-km. Rates in interregional traffic were thus insufficient to sustain an operator who had to rely heavily on inputs at unofficial prices, whereas truckers with access to inputs at official prices probably found long distance traffic to be quite lucrative.

This dual-pricing structure has led to a shortage of transport capacity, which has been recognized by the government as a major constraint on development. The problem was not caused by a real shortage of trucks, but by the fact that the rates were unremunerative. The early scrapping of vehicles aggravated this artificial shortage. Consequently, overvalued currencies foster production processes that are more capital intensive than warranted from economic efficiency considerations, on account of the fact that capital becomes too cheap in relation to labor. In road transport, overvaluation reveals itself in a heavy demand for new vehicles. Truck owners typically wanted to replace their vehicles after only two to three years, if possible. Although road conditions in Tanzania were poor and vehicle maintenance costs rose quickly after a few years of operation, the relatively low price of new trucks reduced the desired replacement time considerably below what was economically justified. A further impetus to early replacement was that spare parts often had to be obtained in the unofficial market at high cost.

Overvalued currencies combined with quantitative allocations of imports thus have multiple effects on the economic cost of transport, and hence on the cost of marketing. Marketing and transport costs are inflated due to the fact that: (1) resources are allocated to less efficient truckers in cases where parastatals have a senior claim; (2) transport becomes too capital intensive; (3) unbalanced allocations are made between different types of inputs; and (4) a shortage of capacity to undertake transport may arise when rates do not cover the costs of inputs purchased at unofficial prices. In addition, the allocation system requires a considerable bureaucracy. As these problems stem from the use of import quotas, it can be argued that it would be more efficient to use import duties exclusively to ration foreign exchange, and then for all imported goods and not just inputs to road transport. While import duties would have no effect on overvaluation as such, they would: (1) eliminate the black market; (2) lessen the risk of supplies going to inefficient operators; (3) eliminate most of the costs associated with the allocation system; and (4) ensure a better balance in the supply of different types of inputs. Import duties would also alter the price relations among inputs, thereby fostering less capital-intensive techniques in road transport. The danger of imposing import duties is, however, that it may result in an absence of neutral incentives across and within sectors. Since import duties would have to be used for all imported goods, it would be better to devalue the overvalued currency, which would be less cumbersome and costly in terms of administrative costs; it would also make exports more competitive in the world market and optimize the country's comparative economic advantages in world trade.

When considering an investment in a country with an overvalued exchange rate, it is crucial to be aware of the possible consequences. First, if the investment is intended to produce for export, the exported product will not be very competitive in the world market; however, this situation will change if the government of the country corrects the exchange rate, which, sooner or later, most governments do accomplish. Second, if the investment is intended to produce goods for domestic consumption, it may be difficult to compete with imports as long as the exchange rate is overvalued. Third, overvalued exchange rates make the price of imports of materials needed for the production process in which we wish to invest artificially low.

3. SUBSIDIES

Agricultural marketing in developing countries is frequently affected by the subsidization of food consumption as well as transport. We will, therefore, consider subsidies that relate primarily to the agricultural and transport sectors, although subsidies are received by other sectors as well. It should not be difficult, however, to extend this discussion to other sectors (for instance, the industrial sector). Subsidies can be extended directly by covering part of the costs of parastatal companies in either marketing or transport. Subsidies may also be extended by making inputs available at prices below cost. Another policy practice favoring food consumption as well as road transport is to make certain imports subject to no, or low, import duties while other imports pay heavy duties; this difference in import duties may be viewed as another form of subsidy. Finally, another form of subsidy is the provision of access to credit at low or negative real interest rates. Subsidized food affects the demand for transport, while subsidized transport affects the cost of transport services, and thereby the demand for agricultural products.

Food Subsidies

The justification for food subsidies is closely linked to the reasons for maintaining overvalued exchange rates. The strategy pursued by a number of developing countries to attain economic growth emphasizes the substitution of locally manufactured products for imported ones. Consequently, resources must be shifted out of agriculture into manufacturing. Low food prices have been one of the means to achieve such a transition by providing incentives to people to become laborers in the industrial plants, which are usually located in or near urban areas.

Subsidized food prices have a detrimental effect on agricultural production and economic development since they distort relative prices in several different ways. First, for local food, subsidized consumer prices must be accompanied by higher producer prices or subsidized input prices in order to maintain a balance between supply and demand. This induces farmers to produce for the local market rather than for export. Second, subsidized food imports reduce the market for local production, an outcome that can also result from newly acquired tastes on the part of the urban population for imported food products that are not available domestically. Third, subsidies have to be financed, and the required taxes have further repercussions on efficiency and agricultural production.

In developing countries, an important source of revenues to finance government expenditures, including subsidies, is to levy taxes on international trade, including agricultural exports. The policy's popularity can be explained by the fact that the cost of collection is generally low and control relatively easy. However, export taxes on agriculture may give rise to hidden costs in that they tax a sector in which the country may have comparative advantages and which may be an important earner of foreign exchange. The reason is that since world market prices can generally be viewed as fixed, the incidence of the tax falls entirely on the producer and distributor. As a consequence, the production of exports is reduced. These hidden costs may be far higher than the cost savings related to administrative ease in taxing exports.

The impact of subsidies and taxes on the economy of developing countries can be seen from their share in government budgets. In total, revenues from export and import taxes make up about 15 to 30 percent of government revenues in low- and middle-income economies that import oil. In these countries, about 15 to 25 percent of total government expenditures is accounted for by subsidies and transfers, of which a large part goes for food subsidies.

Predicting the consequences of removing a subsidy requires information about its incidence—about who actually benefits from it. In the case of subsidized food prices for consumers, due to the prevalence of overlapping policies there may be several beneficiaries, so that only part—if any—of the benefits may actually accrue to consumers. First, part or all of the subsidy may be absorbed by producers, as higher producer prices may have to be paid to induce farmers to produce more.

Second, part of the subsidies may be absorbed by inefficient marketing agents. This is due to the fact that subsidized food is often channeled through parastatal marketing boards, which normally are legal monopolies. Third, part or all of the subsidy may be absorbed by transport in cases where, for instance, pan-territorial prices favor producers in distant regions.

The presence of several interventions in agricultural marketing makes it exceedingly difficult to predict the specific effects on the demand for transport in the event that food subsidies should be removed. For example, the elimination of subsidies may obviate the need for a monopolistic marketing board, whose inefficiencies may have absorbed all or most of the entire subsidy. These inefficiencies may have been due partly to weak incentives to be cost conscious and partly to the fact that the required subsidies were not being provided on a timely basis. As a consequence, consumer prices may, after the abolishment of monopolistic marketing boards and subsidies, turn out to be lower rather than higher (as might be expected if only the removal of subsidies were considered). Incidentally, the elimination of a marketing board generally alters the pattern and cost of related transport.

Another problem with subsidized prices is that they may lead to excess demand over supply, precipitating a black market, and hence a dual-pricing system. In this situation it is difficult to predict the effects on the demand for transport should the decision be made to remove the subsidies and eliminate the black market. This is partly due to the fact that there are normally few data available on the flow of illegally marketed food crops.

An example of subsidization pertains to the subsidies provided for the consumption of imported white rice in the Ivory Coast, which have had a more direct impact on the total demand for transport. In the Ivory Coast, the Caisse de Perequation des Prix des Produits de Grande Consommation (CPPGS) handles all imported rice, while wholesaling and retailing are done by private, licensed agents. CPPGS sets consumer and producer prices and supervises the marketing of both imported and locally produced rice. During the 1970s and early 1980s, the government gradually increased import duties to offset the increasing overvaluation of the local franc (CFA), but imports of white rice were exempt from duty. The relative low price of imported rice stimulated total consumption, as evidenced by the increase in imports from next to nothing in the mid-1970s, to 363,000 tons in 1982. In addition, as official producer prices for rice were influenced by world market prices, the country's low import prices led to a fall in producer prices from CFA 152.20 per kilogram (kg) in 1974 (in 1982 prices) to CFA 50.00 per kg in 1982. This decline did not, however, affect local production materially, as most of it was distributed at much higher free market prices through unofficial channels. Unofficial rice prices were much higher than the official ones because local rice was preferred by consumers and therefore could fetch a premium. The low import prices led to an overall increase in consumption, and hence in the demand for transport.

The marketing of imported rice in the Ivory Coast has had further repercussions on the demand for transport as subsidies were extended, not only through low import prices, but also through the subsidization of transport costs, as follows. The wholesale price was fixed by a margin over the import price to cover the wholesalers' handling costs, including transport. However, this margin is the same throughout the country and insufficient to cover long-distance transport. CPPGS therefore agreed to pay for transport of rice in excess of 100 km, including the first 100 km, while it expected wholesalers within a radius of 100 km of its two distribution centers to cover all transport costs up to 100 km from their price margin. This system provided no incentive for wholesalers located between 50 and 100 km from CPPGS distribution centers to buy from CPPGS. Instead, these wholesalers bought their rice from wholesalers located at a distance of over 100 km from the distribution centers, so that on average, rice was transported over a circuitous route of about 125 km rather than the direct route of 75 km.

Subsidies for Road Transport

Subsidies in road transport may be general, in that they may benefit all transporters. One example is the provision of credit at low, or even negative, real rates of interest; for instance, in the early 1980s, credit was available for the purchase of trucks in Tanzania at 8.5 to 11 percent rates of interest, while the inflation amounted to about 20 to 30 percent. Subsidies may also be earmarked for certain organizations, such as parastatal trucking companies and transport wings of parastatal crop authorities, which play important roles in the road transport sector. These operators sometimes receive inputs free of duties, as well as trucks, spare parts, and technical assistance at concessional prices, or even at no cost. One argument advanced for earmarked subsidies is that the payment of duties or taxes by parastatal trucking operations is viewed as an unnecessary transfer between different government accounts. Another argument is that the subsidies are supposed to induce the companies to undertake work that private operators are not willing to do.

Subsidies and exemptions from import duties work to make the transport industry more capital intensive than warranted from an economic point of view since low prices induce operators to buy new equipment. Consequently, although financial costs and rates may become lower, the economic costs of transport are higher than they would be without the subsidy. Subsidies directed to only one segment of the industry distort competitive conditions. They may result in higher economic costs, and even in higher rates in cases where subsidies benefit less-efficient operators who would not survive in the absence of subsidies. Vague public accountability, poor financial management, and the lack of incentives to be efficient are often the reasons why these subsidies result in inefficient operations. Transport subsidies may therefore be counterproductive and increase the economic cost of marketing agricultural products.

Subsidies for road transport often emanate from donor-financed projects in cases where donors fail to consider the impact of their projects on the overall performance of the road transport industry. One example is the trucking fleet operated by the international Relief and Rehabilitation Commission in Ethiopia in the early 1980s. Most of the trucks, parts, and shop facilities were provided free of charge to the commission, while substantial technical assistance was made available by donors. The assistance was justified by the drought in Ethiopia and the need to provide transport from the ports to areas in need. In 1985, the private sector remained competitive but its share of the market was shrinking as a result of import restrictions limiting their access to essential supplies, while public sector operations were able to expand thanks to the acquisition of relief trucks. It should also be noted that subsidies to organizations with limited experience in the transport industry do often result in a less-than-optimal use of resources.

Subsidized transport rates are sometimes used as an instrument of regional development policy. In other words, subsidized rates to and within depressed areas are intended to stimulate economic development in these regions. The success of such a strategy is not guaranteed since these rates may retard a depressed region's development by reducing its natural economic protection against competition from more advanced regions in the country. In addition, practice has shown that such rates can result in secondary distortions. For instance, competitive relations among road and rail transport may be affected. For these reasons, in depressed areas policy instruments such as temporary tax privileges and/or subsidies for investment or employment are preferred to subsidized transport rates, since they are less likely to result in secondary distortions.

Scheduled carriers in developing as well as developed countries are often assisted by restrictions in competition from unscheduled services in the same market. By creating monopolistic market conditions, government authorities enable the scheduled carriers to earn profits on some routes, which are often used to cross-subsidize nonprofitable but desirable services on other routes. Cross-subsidization causes secondary distortions by raising the price of transport services on the profitable routes above the most efficient level. In addition, the creation of monopolistic conditions must be supplemented with some control over prices and operations to ensure that the monopolistic position is not abused. The outright granting of public subsidies is preferred to cross-subsidization since it does not require the creation of monopoly positions. Public subsidies also give rise to smaller economic distortions since the burden of the corresponding general taxes is more widely spread.

If a government insists on employing subsidized, scheduled carriers, services can often be made more cost-effective by inviting bids for routes with given frequency of services, to be published in national and local newspapers. The invitation may state a monthly amount of subsidy to be paid to the award winner or lowest bidder. Alternatively, the bid may be the amount of subsidy the local government would have to pay the operator at a set transport rate. Awards for franchise operations should be given for periods of three to five years to make the operations attractive to the bidder and to enable the government to assess the performance of the licensee.

In developing countries, scheduled transport services often serve the transport market for semifinished and finished goods rather than agricultural products. The use of scheduled passenger services (buses) in developing countries is widespread. Insofar as farmers often transport their produce in buses, government intervention in the provision of these services may affect the efficiency of product marketing.

Warranted Subsidies

The previous discussion may have given the impression that subsidies should never be considered. However, in some situations, such as the introduction of new techniques in agricultural production or the development of a new industry in a poor region such as the northeast of Brazil, a subsidy may be justified on the basis of the presence of an "infant" industry. Furthermore, subsidies may be warranted for equity reasons, such as to combat malnutrition or to extend primary health care or education. However, while there may be valid reasons for the subsidy, caution must be exercised when a proposed subsidy is considered. The following basic questions should be addressed when analyzing a subsidy program:

1. What are the objectives of the subsidy?

2. What is the estimated effectiveness of the subsidy in achieving its objectives?
3. What is the appropriate duration of the subsidy?
4. How affordable is the subsidy?
5. Is the subsidy appropriate to the government's institutional and administrative capabilities and its need to maintain policy credibility?
6. Can the subsidy be made understandable to both the decision makers and beneficiaries?

All subsidy programs should be reviewed periodically (about every five years) to determine whether the subsidies reach the intended beneficiaries or others and whether the program is cost-effective, since over time the pool of beneficiaries tends to expand beyond the target group. The need for a subsidy may have declined or disappeared altogether, it may have become too heavy a burden on the budget in relation to alternative expenditures, or it may have caused unexpected, costly distortions in the economy. Therefore, there may be a need to revise, retarget, and reorganize a subsidy program—or to eliminate it altogether. The cautious investor who contemplates an investment in a country where subsidies prevail is well advised to analyze how these subsidies will affect the investment during its predicted life, including the impact should some or all of these subsidies be eliminated.

4. ADMINISTERED PRICES

A common feature in both agriculture and road transport is that prices are controlled by the government. In agriculture, both consumer and producer prices of staple food crops are often fixed, as well as producer prices of export crops. Occasionally, controls of producer prices are limited to the setting of minimum prices. Price reviews normally take place once a year. To administer the system of fixed prices, governments have often resorted to parastatal marketing boards. These boards have the exclusive right to trade in specified agricultural products and often also in the marketing of inputs such as fertilizers. Parastatal marketing boards may opt to perform part of their duties through cooperatives and licensed agents.

The control of prices or rates in road transport is more varied and less pervasive than in agriculture. Besides fixed tariffs, which do not permit deviation in any direction, price controls may consist of bracket, or fork, tariffs which allow prices to vary within a prescribed margin. Rate regulation can also be in the form of either a ceiling or a floor to free market prices.

Agricultural Prices

Administered agricultural prices are normally pan-territorial and pan-temporal—they are the same throughout the country and do not vary during a given period of time (usually one year). Different prices may be fixed for different-quality grades and varieties. There are also administered prices, which may vary within the country to reflect the cost of transporting the product from a surplus region to a region of deficit. This system tends to minimize transport costs through its influence on the location of production. However, it increases the volume of transport and the economic cost of marketing the crops.

Several arguments are advanced to justify administered price systems:

1. A major reason is the need to eliminate or reduce the uncertainty for consumers and producers caused by fluctuating prices. Due to the risk aversion of farmers, fluctuating prices are a disincentive to production, and therefore lead to higher prices in the long run.
2. Income distribution may be another reason. Producer prices are fixed at a high level in order to improve farmers' incomes or encourage production in certain areas; however, low consumer prices to assist urban populations are more common. A related reason may be the belief that it is "fair" that every producer should be paid or that every consumer should pay the same price for the same product.
3. Price control may also be initiated to avoid monopolistic elements in the production/marketing cycle. For instance, cotton seed must be separated from the fiber by ginning before the cotton can be marketed. The most economical way of ginning is to do so near the farm, but typically there is no room for more than one gin in a given area. As the cost of an existing gin is largely sunk, the ginning market is not easily contestable. In other words, the gin represents a natural monopoly. Price control may be necessary in such a situation to prevent the owner of the gin from reaping monopoly profits.

While price regulation may be required in markets with a natural monopoly, these markets are the exception. Most markets can be expected to be contestable, and many are even characterized by constant returns to scale. Hence, the argument against price controls in the form of fixed prices and against price differentials to certain areas is that they give rise to distortions, either because they lead to a market disequilibrium, or because they make the cost of transport and marketing unnecessarily high. Using price controls as an instrument of income distribution is generally ineffective, partly because the price of an agricultural commodity is only a part of a household's real income and partly because price controls can benefit both rich and poor people; their impact may, therefore, extend beyond the intended target population.

An alternative solution often recommended to overcome, or at least reduce, the uncertainty of fluctuating prices in the absence of insurance markets is to establish a parastatal marketing board as a buyer and seller of last resort with set floor and ceiling prices. The marketing board then essentially plays the same role as a central bank in a system of exchange rates, which are fixed within given bounds. The marketing board enters the market by selling from its own stock when consumer prices start to rise above the ceiling and by buying when producer prices start to fall below the floor price. The floor and ceiling prices in such a pricing system will vary with location as well as with changes in world market prices, and will therefore approximate a price regime conducive to the efficient use of resources, including transport. Marketing systems for food crops that operate partially according to these principles have been shown to be more cost-effective than the system of fixed prices in a number of countries (for instance, India).

As pan-territorial prices do not penalize producers and consumers in faraway locations, they cause farmers in distant locations to produce more and consumers in deficit regions to consume more than justified from an economic efficiency point of view. They may, therefore, divert the attention of producers and consumers alike from other commodities with market potential. Pan-territorial prices may be regarded as a readily available instrument to assist remote areas, but they leave unanswered the question of whether the production of the relevant commodities is in accordance with the comparative potential advantage of these regions, which, if it is to be realized, may require different supports from government. Pan-territorial prices, therefore, result in high marketing and transport costs. A further consequence of pan-territorial prices is that transport investments to reduce transport costs have little or no impact on farmers' incomes, and therefore on development; any expected increase in transport demand from reduced transport costs usually does not materialize. In a competitive system with prices set by market forces, reduced transport costs will be translated into higher producer prices being paid to farmers, which will result in an increase in production, and subsequently in the demand for transport.

In southern Ghana, much of the land can be used to grow food or cocoa. The government pays the farmers a fixed price for cocoa, yet in 1982 farmers in many places dug up their cocoa farms or failed to replace old and poor-yielding trees in order to grow food in response to relatively higher food prices, although on the international market the price of cocoa was nine times the price of maize. The shift in production produced a corresponding increase in transport distances and costs. Naturally, it can be argued that it would have been better to concentrate on growing more cocoa and less food and, if necessary, to import extra food with the extra export earnings from cocoa. In light of the modern approach to agricultural development, which calls for extensive extraindustry support, it is interesting to note that cocoa growing developed in Ghana in the nineteenth century, without government supplies of inputs, capital, extension advice, seeds, or insecticides. The main ingredients for success were a profitable market, suitable land, local entrepreneurship, capital, labor, and a source of cocoa seedlings.

Pan-territorial agricultural prices primarily affect transport costs by lengthening the transport distances to be covered, while pan-temporal prices, on the other hand, inflate the cost per ton-kilometer, that is, the supply side of transport. Pan-temporal prices induce the producers to sell their product as soon as it is harvested, since they have no incentive for maintaining their own stock in anticipation of better prices later in the year. Similarly, when the price is low consumers have no incentive to buy and to maintain their own stock piles; instead, they buy as needed. As a result, prices fixed over the year concentrate the marketing operations in a very short season and force the marketing agents to take on the entire storage function. This inflates, not only storage costs, but also the cost of transport as a rise in demand for transport services increases the size of the required vehicle fleet and reduces the likelihood of obtaining back-hauls. Both these effects decrease truck utilization and push up transport rates.

Transport Rates

Maximum and minimum rates are based on different types of arguments. Maximum rates are used: (1) to limit profits where shortages of trucking services would drive up free market rates; (2) as an anti-inflationary instrument; and (3) as a means to stimulate the development of remote areas. Minimum rates have been defended on the grounds that they protect the less knowledgeable trucker from quoting too low a price or that they will prevent underpricing by aggressive firms attempting to increase their market share.

Rate ceilings are not effective to solve the problems associated with a shortage of capacity in either the short or long run. If anything, they can make things worse. Long-run shortages of capacity in the industry and excessive profits are evidence of entry and capacity controls (discussed in the following section). Rate control in the presence of long-run shortages is likely to give rise to a black market and create inefficiencies in the performance of the industry, thereby creating higher economic costs in transport and marketing. Moreover, it fails to remedy the real cause of the problem, namely, the capacity shortage. The only effective way of improving market performance and reducing profits is to reduce barriers to entry and allow competition.

Temporary shortages tend to occur in countries where major crops are harvested and sold within a short time and, especially, where the harvesting seasons of two or three major crops overlap. While short-term capacity problems cause free market rates to show high volatility, this does not normally signify that excessive profits are being made. The high prices in effect during peak seasons are necessary in order to make effective use of the available fleet and ensure its intensive use during the harvest season. An alternative policy for solving the capacity problem often pursued by developing countries is to increase the size of the fleet. This policy is more costly than stimulating better use of existing trucks by paying higher rates. Indeed, the variability of transport rates over a year demonstrates that the pricing system is functioning and also provides signals to marketing agents that they should examine whether transport and distribution costs could be reduced by constructing additional storage near farms.

Maximum rates are ineffective as a means to control inflation as transport is not a price leader. If rates are capped, inflation will make them unremunerative, thereby causing shortages and bankruptcies and stifling the development of the industry; alternately, they may be ignored. Maximum rates are also ineffective as an instrument of regional development as they may work to retard the development of a depressed region, since its natural economic protection against competition from more advanced regions in the country would be reduced. Maximum rates may also reduce the supply of services below justified economic requirements, thereby reducing the incentive for production.

The validity of both mentioned arguments advanced for minimum rates is doubtful. Experience in developing countries shows that truckers are generally well informed about costs and prices. They are also well aware of the fact that road transport is normally very competitive and that attempts to enlarge market shares by lowering their rates below cost will prove self-defeating. The practice of setting minimum rates may have negative effects if the floor is set above the free market rate. This will attract additional operators into the sector, causing capacity utilization to fall and the economic cost of transport to rise. It may also lead to an expansion of own-account fleets, which cannot be subjected to minimum prices since the operators are only involved in the movement of goods that they themselves own or produce.

Fixed rates are normally expressed as the fee to be paid per ton-kilometer. They may vary as a function of distance and commodity transported, and sometimes also with the size of the truck, with lower rates being paid for the larger trucks. Frequently, fixed rates do not fully account for back-hauls or allow for differences in the costs of transport on bitumen, gravel, and dirt roads. Neither do they allow for variations over the year. The inflexibility of fixed transport rates hampers development. For example, the absence of rebates for back-hauls provides no incentive for marketing agents to coordinate maize and fertilizer flows. Fixed rates also mean that investments to reduce transport costs will have no development impact, since any cost savings will be pocketed by the truckers rather than translated into higher producer, or lower consumer, prices.

In short, maximum, minimum, and fixed rates are impractical. The demand for transport services is highly variable over time and place, and therefore, any rate system would have to be rather complex to avoid economic inefficiencies and distortions. If a government decides to control transport rates, fork tariffs are more efficient than fixed rates, especially if adequate information about the recommended rate brackets covering such factors as distance, road conditions, and nature of goods to be transported is publicized in the media. Naturally, such a program requires monitoring, since road conditions change over time. The system would reduce the distortions in the supply and demand for transport associated with fixed rates, and thereby improve the marketing and production of agricultural products.

In order to reduce risks related to a planned investment in a country with administered prices, investors should be thoroughly familiar with them and acquire information about how long the government of this country intends to keep the system. The subsequent elimination of these prices could affect the potential profits of such an investment significantly.

5. ENTRY AND CAPACITY CONTROLS

Entry controls screen private operators who want to enter a market, while capacity controls regulate the supply of individual operators, and thus total supply. Entry and capacity controls are found both in agricultural marketing and in road transport. The "need" for the controls in agriculture stems largely from other agricultural policies such as administered prices. Their effects on the demand for transport are, in general, dominated and masked by the effects of these other policies. This section therefore focuses on the controls in the road transport sector alone.

Entry Controls

Entry into the transport industry is often restricted in developing countries. These restrictions may be qualitative or quantitative in nature. Qualitative entry restrictions establish certain minimum standards of personal qualifications of the operator and are primarily designed to prevent unsuccessful ventures, which would not be in the public interest. Qualitative restrictions may consist of moral qualifications such as the absence of a criminal record, professional qualifications such as sufficient knowledge of the transport industry, and/or financial qualifications such as adequate involvement of the carrier's own capital. Decisions on moral qualifications seem inappropriate for a regulatory agency, since they are the concern of the judicial system. It is doubtful whether financial restrictions are effective since the licensee can withdraw his capital from the road transport business as soon as a license has been obtained. The case for some types of professional qualifications may, however, be argued. For example, there may be a need for an adequate track record in road safety and for some ability to maintain books and prepare financial statements for tax purposes. It is important that such qualifications are very clearly specified so that they are not subject to discretionary interpretation by the regulatory agencies. It is also important that extension services be provided so that newcomers can easily overcome entry hurdles in the form of professional qualifications.

Quantitative entry restrictions usually assign operating rights for specific routes, regions, commodity classes, and so forth. They do not usually regulate the number of vehicles to be used by a licensed carrier. It is therefore a misconception that quantitative entry restrictions prevent overinvestment, which is the argument often advanced by their advocates. Quantitative restrictions prevent:

1. efficient, complementary operation on routes or in regions for which a firm or individual's license is not valid;
2. capacity utilization on the back-haul for commodities other than those for which the carrier is licensed; and/or
3. temporary excess capacity in one submarket from being utilized in other submarkets and optimum utilization of the existing fleet during peak demand periods.

As a consequence, quantitative restrictions tend to result in overcapacity, thereby driving up the costs of transport and marketing.

The importance of easy entry into the trucking industry queries the validity of regulations that separate operators of own-account trucks from those doing business for hire. Own-account trucks are typically not authorized to carry freight for others, which reduces their utilization. Especially in developing countries, where agriculture is dominant, it is important to be able to mobilize capacity from all segments of the industry to meet peak demand, particularly since own-account trucks are owned not only by large companies but also by small businesses, such as wholesalers and retailers. These trucks can be mobilized during peak demand and thereby facilitate the evacuation of crops and reduce potential losses. For example, to draw in these trucks during the peak season, Zambia issues temporary licenses valid for about three months. Mobilization of the own- account trucks also enhances competition and the overall utilization rate of the fleet.

The supply of transport services may also be influenced by collusion among truck operators, as, for instance, prevailed in Yemen. Following the sharp increase in oil prices in 1973, many Yemenis became migrant workers in the Gulf States, especially in neighboring Saudi Arabia, and their remittances spurred high economic growth in their country. Quite a number of returning migrant workers then used their earnings to enter into the trucking industry. In line with tight-knit tribal and village traditions, the truckers organized themselves in groups, primarily to distribute the traffic among themselves. Since entry into the group was free for kinship members, many more truckers than needed found it attractive to join. That there was an excessive number of trucks was evidenced by the very slow turnover. In the early 1980s, truckers frequently had to wait several days, and at times even more than a week, before their turn came up for a new haul. This arrangement has tended to keep transport and marketing costs high, since the truckers were able to maintain tariffs higher than those that would have prevailed under free competition.

Restricted competition, as prevailed in Yemen, is very costly, particularly in trucking, where it results in low load factors and poor vehicle utilization. It also encourages parastatal and private companies to establish their own vehicle fleets, which further aggravates efficient vehicle utilization and raises operating costs. The cost in terms of the excessive size of the vehicle fleets can be high. In the case of Yemen it is believed that the country could have managed with less than half, and perhaps even a quarter, of the available fleet.

The practice of truckers restricting competition by collusion cannot be combated by resort to legislation alone. Antitrust and similar types of legislation are very difficult to implement effectively in many developing countries. An approach that might be more effective would be to assess the feasibility of those types of measures that loosen economic entry barriers and either reduce the cost of entry into the market or enhance its transparency. For instance, one approach would be to promote brokerage activities, which could be done by designating areas in towns and cities near main market places as truck stops. Freight forwarders and brokers of transport services would operate at these stops, and the establishment there of gas stations, repair shops, and other service facilities would also be encouraged. To get the truck stops established might require the government or municipality to allocate the land and set up simple terminal facilities.

Another approach to strengthen competition in the transport market is to promote the availability of many different means of transport in addition to trucks. Particularly in rural areas, transport can often be undertaken by simpler forms of transport, including carts and bicycles. If such simple transport aids are available in rural areas, the small farmers could limit their exposure to restrictive transport and marketing practices by themselves bringing the produce to the marketplaces, where competition is stronger. Simple transport aids can play a significant role in agricultural marketing in remote areas, and their absence is a characteristic of many countries displaying poor agricultural performance (Beenhakker et al. 1987).

Capacity Controls

The purpose of capacity regulations is to ensure that the right capacity is available in the market or in specific submarkets. However, capacity licensing generally also serves the function of controlling the entry of emergent truckers. One argument advanced for the imposition of capacity controls is that without them, competition will lead to excess capacity and result in low utilization, low profitability, and a drain on foreign exchange. Another reason for capacity licensing has been the protection of railways, which has been the primary motive for licensing schemes of many countries. Resorting to such regulations may result in a high level of vehicle utilization but with poor levels of service. It also tends to drive up the cost of transport and marketing and may contribute to a short supply of services during peak demand.

Capacity restrictions are either individual/firm-oriented or market-oriented. A mixture of these two systems sometimes exists, for instance, in cases where, in a firm-oriented system, the issuing of new licenses is suspended during a dip in demand. In the former system, individuals or firms have to obtain a permit to procure a vehicle. Some countries have an extreme form of capacity restriction whereby individuals and privately owned industries and commercial firms do not have free choice in deciding on the load capacity of a truck they wish to buy. For a farmer, this capacity is instead sometimes determined by the amount of irrigated and nonirrigated land and/or the number of herd animals owned. For businesspersons and industrial/commercial firms, the capacity is determined by the annual amount of tax paid in the year prior to the purchase of the vehicle. Naturally, such arbitrary measures are costly and are not recommended.

If a government decides on a restrictive policy (which is generally not a wise policy), carriers should be granted a license for additional capacity based on a demonstration that the investment can earn a return at least equal to the standard imposed by the licensing authority. Although an individual/firm-oriented capacity restriction is preferable to market-oriented restrictions and quantitative entry restrictions, it is still not recommended since government authorities are normally not in a better position to judge a firm's future prospects than the individual carrier. The use of capacity restrictions to protect state-owned and parastatal transport companies has almost universally resulted in inefficient operations of these companies and consequent heavy subsidies. The realization of other objectives of individual/firm-oriented restrictions, such as the prevention of a drain on foreign exchange, can better be achieved by taxation. Vehicle sales taxes normally avoid the discretionary administrative power inherent in the evaluation of prospective returns under capacity restrictions.

Market-oriented licensing systems are designed to control the expansion of total capacity, either in the entire road transport industry or in separate markets. They require a rationing scheme to distribute capacity among individual applicants, who always demand more capacity than what is to be licensed. Market-oriented licensing systems, which are found in several developing countries, may be subdivided into quota and proof-of-need systems. In practice, quota systems are the outcome of conflicting political pressures from different interest groups. Available capacity tends to be interpreted in terms of tons, regardless of differences in services. Sometimes, available capacity involves the number of vehicles, which may produce a bias in favor of large vehicles and consequent inefficiencies. Given the fact that most developing countries lack adequate statistical data on demand and available capacity and that allocation often depends on deliberate policy and/or unknown user preferences, it is of no surprise that quotas tend to be based on political pressures rather than economic considerations. They usually involve the established carriers' right to object against a new license being granted on the basis that they already provide the needed services or plan to do so. Quota systems may result in a bias against new dynamic firms wishing to use new marketing, production, and/or management systems. They may also lead to favoritism, graft, and corruption. In short, they prevent a rational distribution of available resources. If a country wishes to maintain a quota system, the public auction of licenses, as practiced in Lebanon in the 1970s, seems to be a more efficient and equitable method, although it, too, tends to increase the cost of transport.

Proof-of-need systems involve separate decisions on individual applications. The total number of licenses is not established explicitly as in the quota systems. Moreover, individual decisions are made during public inquiries, in which all interested parties have the right to be represented. In Zambia, for instance, public inquiries are held twice a year. The applicant has to demonstrate that there is a market for the proposed services and that the existing facilities are insufficient to satisfy demand. Competing carriers are given an opportunity to discredit the applicant's claims, while the country's parastatal trucking company officially has the right to veto all applications.

On the surface, individual/firm-oriented systems appear similar to proof-of-need systems. The difference is, however, that in the latter, the licensing authorities consider what competitors are already supplying together with existing capacity that could be used to supply the proposed services. The public inquiry is often cumbersome and costly to both the individual applicant and the licensing authority.

Advocates of entry and capacity controls often argue that their removal would cause the transport industry to become more unstable, resulting in less reliable and/or more expensive transport services. The available evidence of the performance of road transport in countries that have abandoned entry and capacity controls (e.g., the United Kingdom and the United States) shows that it has not given rise to any significant negative effects such as bankruptcies of transport firms, although some firms may have opted for mergers. In essence, there is ample evidence showing that trucking regulations tend to drive up the cost of transport and marketing and, at worst, may contribute to a shortage of trucks to meet peak demand and thereby cause agricultural losses and a lack of timely inputs.

In short, entry and capacity controls may result in (1) a bias against new, dynamic firms wishing to use new marketing or management systems, and (2) favoritism and corruption. Potential investors in countries using such controls are well advised to familiarize themselves with them before making a final decision on investment.

SUGGESTIONS FOR FURTHER READING

Beenhakker, H. L., S. Carapetis, L. Crowther, and S. Hertel. *Rural Transport Services: A Guide to Their Planning and Design.* London: Intermediate Technology Publications, 1987.

Friedlaender, A. F., and R. H. Spady. *Freight Transport and Regulation: Equity, Efficiency and Competition in the Rail and Trucking Industries.* Cambridge, MA: MIT Press, 1981.

Krueger, A. O. "Analyzing Disequilibrium Exchange-Rate Systems in Developing Countries." *World Development,* 10, no. 12 (December 1982): 1059–68.

Pfefferman, C. "Overvalued Exchange Rates and Development." *Finance and Development,* 22, no. 1 (March 1985): 17–19.

Riedel, J. "Trade as the Engine of Economic Growth in Developing Countries: A Reappraisal." Staff Working Paper No. 555, World Bank, Washington, D.C., 1983.

Whitworth, A. "Price Control Techniques in Poor Countries: The Tanzanian Case." *World Development,* 10, no. 6 (June 1982): 475–88.

CHAPTER 3

Quantitative Treatment of Risk

> Evil is uncertain in the same degree as good, and for the reason that we ought not to hope too securely, we ought not to fear with too much dejection.
>
> —Brian Johnson

This chapter examines sources of risk and uncertainty and discusses procedures to measure risk through the determination of, for instance, a standard deviation or coefficient of variation. The probability that the net present value of a proposed investment will be equal to or less than zero is discussed. Naturally, it is important to know this probability because if it is too high, the investment should be rejected.

Next, the chapter explores how the concepts of game theory can be applied to determining strategies that maximize an investor's minimum possible gain and reduce risk. Game theory refers to the philosophy and solution techniques for those decisions under uncertainty that involve conflict or competition between two or more decision makers. It is not clear why this powerful optimization technique has been largely neglected by investment analysts.

This chapter also introduces two of the most commonly used indices for project acceptance, namely, net present value and internal rate of return. Rules for the acceptance or rejection of an independent project and the selection of a project from a set of mutually exclusive projects are presented. These rules do not explicitly consider uncertainty and risk. However, readers will learn how these rules can be used in combination with a project's expected monetary value and standard deviation.

Finally, we will examine a policy for dealing with risk. It is important to avoid a situation where one type of project is favored over another without consideration of the general risk policy.

1. RISK, UNCERTAINTY, AND CERTAINTY

Investment decisions deal with future outcomes. We may view the future as taking four basic forms:

1. Unknown: the future is seen as a blank about which we are unwilling or unable to make any useful statement. Decisions made under such conditions may be called heroic rather than rational decisions.
2. Uncertain: a variety of future outcomes are possible, but we are unable to make any statement about the probability of occurrence of any particular outcome.
3. Probabilistic: the inability to predict exactly what is going to happen in the future is recognized. However, we are able to say that several possible outcomes may occur with stated probability.
4. Certain: the outcome of an investment is known. For example, the decision to purchase a U.S. government bond is one in which it is reasonable to assume complete information about the future outcome.

It is impossible to analyze the unknown form of the future or the heroic decisions it elicits. We will, therefore, limit our discussion to the last three forms of the future. Accordingly, we may classify investment decisions as decisions made either under uncertainty, risk, or assumed certainty.

A decision for which the analyst elects to consider several possible futures, the probabilities of which cannot be stated, is a decision under uncertainty. An investment decision for which the analyst elects to consider several possible futures, the probabilities of which can be stated, is a decision under risk. For some investment decisions it is practical to assume that there is no uncertainty connected with the analysis of the decision. These decisions are decisions under assumed certainty or deterministic decisions.

Sources of risk and/or uncertainty include the following:

1. Insufficient numbers of similar investments: generally, the number of investments of a particular type considered by an organization is relatively small. This means that there will be insufficient opportunity for the effect of unfavorable outcomes to be canceled by favorable outcomes.

2. Bias in the data and its assessment: for example, it is not uncommon to find that individuals involved in conducting cost-benefit analysis appear eager to raise estimates of benefits but not of costs.
3. Changing external economic environment: estimates of future conditions are often based on past results, whereas changing economic conditions invalidate past experience.
4. Misinterpretation of data: a high danger of data misinterpretation exists if the relationship among parameters influencing the investment decision is not clear.
5. Errors of analysis: these errors can occur in the analysis of the investment decision as well as in the analysis of the technical operating characteristics of a project.
6. Managerial talent availability and emphasis: generally, management talent is a limited resource within an organization. Thus, there is a risk that insufficient management talent will be applied to the implementation of investment projects.
7. Salvageability of investment: in judging risk, it is important to consider the relative recoverability of investment commitments in cases where a project, for performance considerations or otherwise, is to be liquidated. The salvage value expressed as a percentage of the original price of special purpose equipment is likely to be less than that of general purpose equipment.
8. Obsolescence: the problem of predicting obsolescence is complex since technological change and progress may occur more rapidly than anticipated.

It should be noted that these definitions of investment decisions as being made under risk or uncertainty are not universally accepted in the literature of managerial economics. *Uncertainty* sometimes refers to investments whose outcomes are uncertain, while the term *risk* is used for the consequential effect of possible uncertain outcomes. Consequently, risk exists if the future outcome of an investment is uncertain. We will not use these definitions.

Risk may be dealt with by introducing a risk premium or risk loading on the interest rate. Strictly speaking, we should, according to our definitions of uncertainty and risk, talk in terms of an uncertainty or risk premium (or loading), depending on whether probabilities related to various possible future outcomes are used in order to arrive at the value of the risk premium. In practice, this value is usually based on previous experience, intuition, or even a random guess. Thus, the terms *uncertainty premium* and *uncertainty loading* may be more appropriate.

Risk or uncertainty loading on the interest rate results in a decrease in the net present value (NPV) of a project with no negative terms in its cash flow. Extreme caution is called for if some negative terms exist in the cash flow, since the loading on these terms counteraffects the loading on positive terms of the cash flow. The following simple example illustrates that in such a case, the NPV can increase rather than decrease.

Consider a cash flow consisting of +$50 at the end of the first year, +$100 at the end of the second year, –$160 at the end of the third year, and +$30 at the end of the fourth year. NPVs of this cash flow with interest rates of 10 and 15 percent are as follows:

$$10 \text{ percent: } 0.9091(\$50) + 0.8264(\$100) - 0.7513(\$160) + 0.6830(\$30)$$
$$= \$28.39$$

$$15 \text{ percent: } 0.8696(\$50) + 0.7561(\$100) - 0.6575(\$160) + 0.5718(\$30)$$
$$= \$31.05$$

A lower NPV reduces the chances of acceptance for a project when competing with other projects. It is clear that this is what we want for projects with uncertainty and/or risk involved. It is noted that the method of loading on the interest rate fails to be effective if a project has so short a life that discounting cannot take effect.

Relatively simple methods to deal with uncertainty other than uncertainty loading on the interest rate are sensitivity analysis and the allowance of contingencies. The principle of sensitivity analysis consists of an examination of the impact of variations in the values of the input variables of a decision process on the final decision. For instance, we may make various contingency assumptions with respect to the main variables or the ones that most profoundly affect the analysis. Naturally, if the proceeds of an investment project are not affected much by the variations in the value assumed by a given variable, there is no need to incur the cost of developing an accurate estimate of that variable. A range of assumptions—including, at least, an optimistic and a conservative extreme—may be assumed for each variable that is expected to have a major effect on the costs and benefits of the investment project. In some situations, the investment decision will be the same under both optimistic and pessimistic assumptions. In other cases, one investment will be preferred under one (realistic) set of assumptions, and another on the basis of a different set of (equally realistic) assumptions. In these circumstances, experienced judgment, with an awareness of the importance of the various assumptions, must be exercised.

A traditional engineering method of handling uncertainties has been to allow for *contingencies*—adverse events or conditions that are expected to occur with sufficient probability to require explicit provision for their costs. If escalation clauses are included in contracts for equipment or construction, the contingency allowances will include payments that can be anticipated in addition to bid prices due to the effect of such clauses. Contingencies may be classified as either physical or price contingencies.

It is clear that physical contingencies will vary with the nature and size of a project. The investment analyst is well advised to seek engineering assistance to determine the nature of the physical contingency allowances, which may relate to difficult access to the project site, the degree to which field work has been completed, geophysically difficult areas, design work quality, contract supervision, degree of precision with which quantity estimates have been prepared, unusually adverse weather conditions, or unforeseen technical difficulties.

We should consider the justification of incurring additional costs for the refinement of designs, improvement of supervision, or further site investigations in cases where the physical contingencies are relatively large. Physical contingencies should be expressed as a percentage of the base costs rather than of the costs including price contingencies.

Price contingencies are allowances for cost increases arising from expected increases in prices after the date specified for the prices used in the same estimation of the base costs of a project. Price contingencies may be due to domestic or foreign inflation, the extent to which a large project may increase the cost of local resources, or possible delays in the project's implementation time.

Note that the adjustment for price risk related to inflation should only be made in appraisals if inflation is expected to result in changes in the relative prices. Thus, price contingency allowances should not be made if general inflation is expected to affect all prices proportionally. General inflation is really a change in the value of the monetary unit in which costs are measured; it does not result in changes in commodity values in relation to each other. Higher prices due to general inflation should not be considered when determining price contingency allowances (or interest rates), since potential investments are always analyzed in terms of costs expressed in constant prices.

2. EXPECTED VALUE AND STANDARD DEVIATION

The expected value of a random variable is the sum of its values multiplied by their associated probabilities. Suppose X is a random variable that assumes the values $a_1, a_2, ..., a_N$ with probabilities $p_1, p_2, ..., p_N$, then:

$$E(X) = \sum_{i=1}^{N} a_i p_i$$

where $E(X)$ is the expected value of X. The standard deviation is a measure of the relative dispersion of a probability distribution about its expected value. The standard deviation of X is defined as the square root of its variance:

$$\sigma_x = \sqrt{V(X)}$$

where:

σ_x = standard deviation of X
$V(X)$ = variance of X

The variance of X is given by:

$$V(X) = \sum_{i=1}^{N} [a_i - E(X)]^2 p_i$$

Let us first consider an investment decision under risk that involves the evaluation of a project in which the probability distributions of net receipts for various future periods are independent of one another. In other words, the outcome in period t does not depend on what happened in period $t-1$. The service life of the project is deterministic. The expected value of the probability distribution of net present value for the project is:

$$E(P) = -C + \sum_{t=0}^{n} \bar{B}_t / (1 + i)^t \tag{1}$$

where:

$E(P)$ = expected net present value (in dollars)
C = initial capital outlay required at time 0 (in dollars)
n = service life in years
t = time in years
i = interest rate

$\bar{B}_t$ = expected value of net receipts in year t (in dollars)

The standard deviation of possible net receipts for year t, σ_t, is computed by:

$$\sigma_t = \sqrt{\sum_{j=1}^{m}\left(B_{j,t} - \bar{B}_t\right)^2 p_{j,t}} \tag{2}$$

where:

$\bar{B}_t$ = as previously defined
j = index denoting a possible net receipt
m = number of possible net receipts considered
$B_{j,t}$ = the jth possible net receipt for year t (in dollars)
$p_{j,t}$ = probability of occurrence of $B_{j,t}$

Given the assumption of mutual independence of net receipts for various future years, the standard deviation of the probability distribution of net present values is:

$$\sigma = \sqrt{\sum_{t=0}^{n} \sigma_t^2 /(1 + i)^{2 \cdot t}} \tag{3}$$

where the symbols are as previously defined.

Let us elucidate these symbols and formulas with the following example. Suppose a project costing $10,000 at time 0 is expected to generate the net receipts shown in Table 3.1 during its service life of three years. The table clearly shows the concept of risk. That is, we do not estimate deterministic values of net receipts in years 1, 2, and 3, but rather indicate five probabilistic values for the net receipts in each year. Notice that the sum of the probabilities in each year amounts to 1 (for instance, in year 1 we have: $0.10 + 0.25 + 0.30 + 0.25 + 0.10 = 1$).

Table 3.1
Expected Net Receipts for the Example Problem

Year 1		Year 2		Year 3	
Probability	Net Receipt	Probability	Net Receipt	Probability	Net Receipt
0.10	$4,000	0.15	$3,000	0.10	$2,000
0.25	5,000	0.20	4,000	0.20	3,000
0.30	6,000	0.30	5,000	0.40	4,000
0.25	7,000	0.20	6,000	0.20	5,000
0.10	8,000	0.15	7,000	0.10	6,000

Assuming an interest rate of 10 percent, the expected values of net receipts during years 1, 2, and 3 are:

$\bar{B}_1 = 0.10(4,000) + 0.25(5,000) + 0.30(6,000) + 0.25(7,000) + 0.10(8,000) =$
$$\$6,000$$
$\bar{B}_2 = 0.15(3,000) + 0.20(4,000) + 0.30(5,000) + 0.20(6,000) + 0.15(7,000) =$
$$\$5,000$$
$\bar{B}_3 = 0.10(2,000) + 0.20(3,000) + 0.40(4,000) + 0.20(5,000) + 0.10(6,000) =$
$$\$4,000$$

We now use equation (1) to calculate the expected value of net present value for the project:

$$E(P) = -10,000 + 6,000/(1.10) + 5,000/(1.10)^2 + 4,000/(1.10)^3 = \$2,592$$

Next, we use equation (2) to compute the standard deviation of the possible net receipts for year 1:

$$\sigma_1 = [0.10(4,000 - 6,000)^2 + 0.25(5,000 - 6,000)^2 + 0.30(6,000 - 6,000)^2$$
$$+ 0.25(7,000 - 6,000)^2 + 0.10(8,000 - 6,000)^2]^{1/2} = \$1,140$$

The standard deviations of the possible net receipts for years 2 and 3 are also computed with equation (2); they amount to $\sigma_2 = \$1,183$ and $\sigma_3 = \$1,095$, respectively. Using equation (3), under the assumption of mutual independence of net receipts over time, the standard deviation about the expected value is as follows:

$$\sigma = \sqrt{(1,140)^2/(1.10)^2 + (1,183)^2/(1.10)^4 + (1,095)^2/(1.10)^6} = \$1,718$$

Obtaining the value of $1,718 is a way for management to express the risk associated with the project costing $10,000 and with the net receipts of Table 3.1. The higher the value of the standard deviation, σ, the more risk is involved.

The standard deviation of the probability distribution of possible net present values may also be used to obtain additional information for the evaluation of risk of a proposed investment project. This information consists of determining the probability of a project providing a NPV of less or more than a specified amount. Assuming that the probability distribution of possible NPVs is approximately normal, we are able to determine this probability by using the table in Appendix 1, which presents probabilities of a value of Z being greater than the values tabulated in the margins.

The Z value is defined as follows:

$$Z = [P - E(P)]/\sigma \qquad (4)$$

where:

P = the net present value considered for the use of Appendix 1;
$E(P)$ and σ are as defined in equations (1) and (3), respectively.

To illustrate the use of equation (4) and Appendix 1, let us determine the probability that the net present value of the previous example will be equal to or less than zero. Thus, in equation (4) we enter $P = 0$, $E(P)$ = \$2,592, and σ = \$1,718, and find:

$$Z = [0 - 2,592]/1,718 = -1.509$$

Looking in Appendix 1, we find that there is a 0.0559 probability that the NPV of our project will be zero or less. Notice that the numerals *1.5* and *09* of $Z = -1.509$ are read from the left and upper margins of Appendix 1, respectively. This example illustrates that Appendix 1 can also be used for finding the probability that Z values are smaller than the values tabulated in the margins if the Z value is negative.

However, we can only use the Z table of Appendix 1 if we are willing to assume that the probability distribution of possible NPVs is approximately normal. In view of the central limit theorem of mathematical statistics, there is a good chance that this approximation is reasonable. The theorem informs us that when summing random variables having distributions other than normal, the distribution of this sum still approaches a normal distribution under certain conditions. The required conditions are not very stringent. Although the most common version of the central limit theorem requires that the random variables be independent and identically distributed, various other versions also exist in which one or both assumptions can be replaced by much weaker conditions. With reference to equation (1), we notice that each $\bar{B}_t$ value represents the sum of the random variables referred to in the theorem.

Chebyshev's inequality theorem rather than Appendix 1 may be used to make reasonably strong probability statements if the normal distribution assumption cannot be made. A discussion of this theorem requires an advanced knowledge of mathematical statistics and is, therefore, not presented here. Readers with such a knowledge will most likely be able to use Chebyshev's inequality theorem, since the approach is similar to the one using Appendix 1.

We have made an assumption of mutual independence of net receipts from one year to another in our use of expected values and standard deviations for the evaluation of risky investments. Frequently, however, the net receipt in one future period depends upon the net receipts in previous periods. For instance, if an investment project turns bad in the early years, the probability is high that net receipts in later years also will be lower than originally expected. The consequence over time of the autocorrelation of annual net receipts (whereby one or more net receipts in one or more future periods depend on the net receipts in one or more previous periods) is that the standard deviation of the probability distribution of possible net present values is larger than it would be under the assumption of mutual independence of net receipts. The greater the degree of correlation, the greater the dispersion of the probability distribution. Thus, equation (3) cannot be used. The expected value of net present value (see equation (1)), however, is the same, regardless of any correlation over time. The examination of autocorrelated cash flows requires a knowledge of applied statistics, which is beyond the scope of this book.

Heretofore, we have used the standard deviation as a measure of risk. However, the coefficient of variation, CV (defined as $\sigma/\hat{k}$, where $\hat{k}$ = the expected rate of return) is a better measure of risk in situations where investments with substantially different expected returns are being compared. The CV indicates the risk per unit of return. Figure 3.1, which shows two projects, X and Y, with different expected rates of return, illustrates a situation where the CV is necessary. The expected rates of return, standard deviations, and CVs for projects X and Y are as follows:

Project X: $k = 10$, $\sigma = 5\%$, $CV = 5/10 = 0.5$
Project Y: $\hat{k} = 50$, $\sigma = 15\%$, $CV = 15/50 = 0.3$

Is project Y riskier than project X because its σ is larger than that of project X? It is not, because the CV of project X is larger than the CV of project Y. In other words, project X has more risk per unit of return than project Y, in spite of the fact that Y's standard deviation is larger. According to the CV measure, project X is riskier. Figure 3.1 clearly shows that the chances of a very low return are higher for X than for Y because Y's expected return is much higher than that of X.

3. GAME THEORY

Game theory refers to the philosophy and solution techniques for decisions under uncertainty that involve conflict or competition between two or more decision makers. Game theory has been successfully

Figure 3.1
Comparison of Probability Distributions and Rates of Return for Projects X and Y

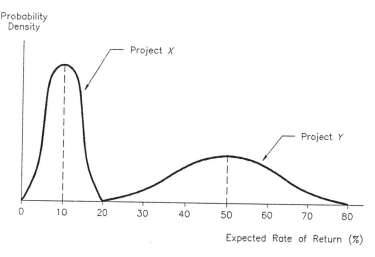

applied to a number of business problems and warfare policies. Although it has been neglected by investment analysts, there is no reason why this powerful optimization technique cannot be used in the context of risk management.

A complete theoretical treatment of game theory is beyond the scope of the present text, which, instead of delving into theories, presents rules and examples pertaining to capital investment problems.

The following four-step procedure is recommended for solving game theory investment problems.

1. develop the game matrix;
2. check for dominance;
3. solve the game by finding the strategy or strategies that maximize the investor's minimum possible gain; and
4. find the value of the game.

Consider a competitive situation with an investor (or an organization that examines alternative strategies for certain investments) and an opponent. In many investment situations, the opponent cannot be identified by name. In general, the opponent may be thought of as all other investors in the competitive environment. Actually, the name of an investor's adversary is unimportant, but to provide an identity, the competitor is called the investor's opponent. We may also think of the investor's opponent as a state of the world. The investments that an

organization makes are likely to create a conflict situation. Consequently, the returns may be less than the investor's expectation. This
results in a situation with two competitors—the investor and the
investor's opponent.

The first step, comprising the development of the game matrix, is
performed by examining the possible outcomes of one or more investments under all conditions. In two-competitor games, the rows of the
game matrix contain the outcomes (usually interpreted as gains) for one
competitor and the columns show the outcomes (usually interpreted as
losses) for the other competitor. As an example, consider Table 3.2,
which shows that the investor has four alternative strategies (X_1, X_2, X_3,
and X_4), while three alternative future conditions (Y_1, Y_2, and Y_3) are
identified for the opponent. The entries in the matrix cells represent the
gains related to specific strategies of the investor and specified alternative outcomes; they can be in any unit—for example, thousands of
dollars.

The alternatives X_1 through X_4 may, for instance, relate to different
sizes of proposed factory buildings needed to supply a certain market
size. The alternative future conditions (Y_1, Y_2, and Y_3) could relate to
alternative actions on the part of competitors that will affect the product
demand that the new factory is intended to satisfy.

Consider another interpretation of X_1 through X_4 and Y_1 through Y_3.
Suppose we evaluate alternative investments to produce bathing suits
(X_1), raincoats (X_2), umbrellas (X_3), or sunglasses (X_4). Thus, Y_1, Y_2, and
Y_3 may relate to three different forecasts concerning rainy days. The
principles of game theory apply only to situations where each alternative action does not affect the outcome of another action.

Note that the matrix of Table 3.2 assumes that the sum of the payoffs
for any choice of alternatives is zero. That is, when one competitor
gains, the other one loses by the same amount, and vice versa. Such a

Table 3.2
Example Two-Competitor Game Problem

| Alternatives | Investor's Opponent | | |
	Y_1	Y_2	Y_3
X_1	4	2	1
X_2	3	2	4
X_3	2	1	4
X_4	3	1	-1

(Investor)

game is called a zero-sum game. Most of the development of game theory to date has concerned this type of game. Some work on nonzero-sum games has been done and more is in progress, but the subject is beyond our scope. Most two-competitor conflict situations may be treated as if they were zero-sum games. However, a situation in which nominally equal payoffs differ in utility to the two competitors cannot be handled as a zero-sum game. This may be the case when a competitor can be identified.

The second step for game theory investment problems is to check for dominance. That is, the investor should check for any strategy (or strategies) that clearly would always be less desirable than some other strategy (or strategies). The same check should be done concerning the investor's opponent. The investor should also check for any alternative (or alternatives) that would clearly be less desirable than some other alternative (or alternatives) from the opponent's viewpoint. If any such strategy or alternative is found, it should be eliminated from consideration. For example, in Table 3.2, strategy X_4 is always less desirable than strategy X_1. That is, regardless of the possible future conditions that may affect the investor's investments, he or she will always rationally prefer strategy X_1 to strategy X_4. Similarly, strategy Y_1 is always less desirable to the opponent than strategy Y_2. Once these dominated strategies (X_4 and Y_1) have been eliminated, the matrix of interest will change (see Table 3.3).

The assumption made in checking for dominance is that both the investor and the opponent are intelligent. That is, the investor should realize that a wise opponent would not select Y_1; likewise, the opponent should realize that a wise investor would not choose X_4.

When the investor's opponent relates to alternative weather forecasts—as in the example of alternative investments to produce bathing suits, raincoats, umbrellas, or sunglasses—it is impossible to think of the opponent as being intelligent. However, this should not tempt

Table 3.3
The Problem in Table 3.2 after Removal of the Dominated Strategies

	Alternatives	Investor's Opponent	
		Y_2	Y_3
Investor	X_1	2	1
	X_2	2	4
	X_3	1	4

the investment analyst to consider Y_1 just because it looks like the best future condition. That would be a gamble. One can never be certain whether condition Y_1 will prevail; if that were certain, there would be no need to use game theory. Game theory is most helpful in the realm of uncertainty in that it identifies the strategies that maximize the investor's minimum possible gain. Using these strategies secures a gain that cannot go below a certain value (the "value of the game"), regardless of how an adversary behaves or what future condition prevails. These strategies also minimize the opponent's maximum possible loss.

The third step in game-theory investment problems calls for a determination of the strategy or strategies that maximize the investor's minimum possible gain. This is done by first checking whether the game matrix has a saddle point, which occurs when the minimum and maximum payoffs of the two competitors are exactly equal. Thus, a saddle point exists if the maximum of the row minimums (the *maximin*) corresponds to the minimum of the column maximums (the *minimax*). Table 3.4 shows that the point at which strategies X_2 and Y_2 of Table 3.3 are followed is a saddle point. The saddle point defines a unique solution to a game theory investment problem. This means that the resulting value of the sample game is 2, as indicated in Table 3.4. The strategy to be followed by the investor is called a pure strategy, since the solution of the game indicates that the investor should decide on strategy X_2 rather than a combination of strategies X_1, X_2, and X_3. Similarly, Y_2 is called the opponent's pure strategy.

How are the solution to the game and the value of the game obtained if the game matrix does not have a saddle point? Consider the game matrix of Table 3.5, in which there is no dominance among the alternatives and no saddle point.

Table 3.4
Pure Strategy Solution to the Problem in Table 3.2

		Investor's Opponent		
Alternatives		Y_2	Y_3	Row Minimum
Investor	X_1	2	1	1
	X_2	2	4	2 (maximin)
	X_3	1	4	1
Column maximum		2 (minimax)	4	(saddle point)

Table 3.5
2 × 2 Game Matrix

		Investor's Opponent	
Alternatives		Y_1	Y_2
Investor	X_1	6	2
	X_2	3	4

The matrix of Table 3.5 does not indicate a pure strategy for the investor. In other words, the optimal strategy will be mixed. The problem is to find the extent to which strategies X_1 and X_2 should each be used. The following procedure applies to obtaining the investor's optimal mixed strategy for a 2 × 2 game matrix in which each opponent has two alternatives:

Step 1: obtain the absolute value of the difference in payoff for each row and add these values.

Step 2: form a fraction associated with each row by using the payoff difference as the numerator and the sum of the row differences as the denominator.

Step 3: interchange the row fractions obtained in step 2. This specifies the proportions in which the investor should use each of the strategies X_1 and X_2 (the optimal mixed strategy).

Table 3.6 shows the solution to the 2 × 2 game matrix of Table 3.5. The indicated solution from Table 3.6 is that the investor should use strategies X_1 and X_2 in proportions of one-fifth and four-fifths. This optimal

Table 3.6
Solution Steps to the Problem in Table 3.5

		Investor's Opponent				
Alternatives		Y_1	Y_2	Step 1	Step 2	Step 3
Investor	X_1	6	2	$|6-2| = 4$	4/5	1/5
	X_2	3	4	$|3-4| = 1$	1/5	4/5

$$\Sigma = 5$$

mixed strategy is presented by (1/5, 4/5). This means that if the alternative strategies refer to alternative investment projects, the best strategy calls for investing one-fifth of the available capital in project X_1 and
four-fifths in project X_2, or ratios close to these. Naturally, it may not be
feasible to undertake project X_1 with only one-fifth of the available
capital.

Many investment situations can be classified as repetitious. In these
cases, the best strategy solution specifies the proportions of time for
which the investor should randomly use each of the strategies X_1 and
X_2. Thus, the solution of Table 3.6 shows that the investor should use
alternative strategy X_1 one-fifth of the time and alternative strategy X_2
four-fifths of the time.

To determine the value of a 2 × 2 game matrix without a saddle point,
one merely sums the cross-products of the proportions in which the
investor should use each of the strategies and the related payoffs of
either the left or right columns. Thus, the value of the game of Table 3.5
is (1/5)(6) + (4/5)(3) = 3.6 or (1/5)(2) + (4/5)(4) = 3.6, where payoffs of
6 and 3 are obtained from the left column and payoffs of 2 and 4 from
the right column. The investor is secured of winning not less than the
value of the game, or 3.6, by adhering to the optimal mixed strategies,
regardless of what the opponent (the competitive environment) does.

It was noted that game theory assumes that the investor's opponent
acts intelligently. Thus, it is also assumed that the opponent adheres
to an optimal mixed strategy. This strategy is obtained by using a
three-step procedure similar to the one presented for obtaining the
investor's optimal mixed strategy for a 2 × 2 game matrix. The
difference is that the word *column* is substituted for the word *row* in
the procedure. The reader can see that the optimal mixed strategy for
the opponent of the matrix of Table 3.5 is (2/5, 3/5). If the investor's
opponent, through ignorance or error, fixes upon any strategy other
than the optimal one, the investor may take advantage of this to
improve the expected payoff. For example, if the opponent of Table
3.5 plays (4/5, 1/5), then the investor may play (1, 0) to result in an
expected game value of (4/5)(1)(6) + (4/5)(0)(3) + (1/5)(1)(2) +
(1/5)(0)(4) = 5.2, which is higher than the game value of 3.6. The
expected game value if one or two of the players do not stick to the
optimal strategies (e.g., the value of 5.2) is obtained by summing the
cross-products of proportions and payoffs for all strategy conditions.

Note, however, that the investor's opponent of Table 3.5 may also
fix on a nonoptimal strategy (1/5, 4/5). The resulting expected game
value if the investor plays (1, 0) is equal to (1/5)(1)(6) + (1/5)(0)(3) +
(4/5)(1)(2) + (4/5)(0)(4) = 2.8, which is lower than the game value of
3.6. Thus, the investor should have adhered to the optimal mixed

strategy. The value of the game, or $(1/5)(1/5)(6) + (1/5)(4/5)(3) + (4/5)(1/5)(2) + (4/5)(4/5)(4)$, would have remained at 3.6. This example shows that it is risky for the investor not to use the optimal mixed strategy out of a belief that the opponent cannot make wise decisions. The fact is that in the beginning of an investment game, the investor does not know in what direction from the optimal strategy the opponent may move.

This solution applies to a 2 × 2 game matrix. There are a variety of methods for solving games in which one competitor has two alternatives and the other competitor has n alternatives ($n > 2$). Perhaps the easiest way to solve such larger games is graphically. To illustrate, consider the game situation of Table 3.7 involving two alternative strategies for the investor and six alternative future conditions. The graphical solution consists of plotting the payoffs of each of the alternatives Y_1 through Y_6 on separate vertical axes and connecting the points related to each of these alternatives (see Figure 3.2). Next, darken the line segments that bound the figure from below; then find and mark with a dot the highest point on this double-weight boundary. The lines that intersect at the dot identify the alternative conditions the investor should consider. Thus, the sections of lines (1) and (2) in Figure 3.2 indicate that the investor should base the strategy on alternatives Y_1 and Y_2. Note that this single graph permits the investor to identify instantly the significant alternative among numerous choices. Now it can be seen that Y_3 through Y_6 are not part of the solution, so the game can be reduced to a 2 × 2 format and solved accordingly.

The graphical method for identifying the significant pair of the investor's strategies for n × 2 games in which the investor has n strategies is similar. Mark the line segments that bound the graph from above and dot the lowest point in this boundary; the lines that pass through the dot identify the investor's critical strategies.

Table 3.7
2 × n Game Matrix

		Investor's Opponent					
Alternatives		Y_1	Y_2	Y_3	Y_4	Y_5	Y_6
Investor	X_1	−6	−1	1	4	7	4
	X_2	7	−2	6	3	−2	−5

Figure 3.2
Graphical Solution to Problem in Table 3.7

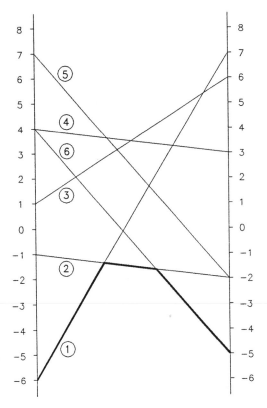

When a game matrix has more than two alternatives per player, one should check first for dominance and a saddle point (Table 3.2). If this fails to result in a solution, or at least in a matrix reduced to two alternatives for a minimum of one player, other special methods (such as linear programming) must be employed to obtain a solution. The present understanding of games involving more than two competitors is less complete than that for two-competitor games and lies beyond the scope of this text. The purpose of this section is to show how game theory can be used in investment decisions under uncertainty. Perhaps the most important aspect of the application of game theory is that it forces attention to an opponent's strategy as well as one's own.

The principles of game theory may also be applied to the treatment of uncertainties involved in determining capital costs. The investor's alternatives relate in this case to alternative approaches to determining capital costs, while the opponent's alternative strategy actions represent alternative states of the world.

4. TREATMENT OF RISK IN RULES FOR PROJECT ACCEPTANCE

The most commonly used indices for project acceptance are the net present value (NPV) and the internal rate of return (IRR). To define NPV and IRR, we introduce the following symbols:

j = index denoting a specific project j (j = 1 means project 1, j = 2 means project 2, etc.)

i = weighted average cost of capital (see Chapter 9)

$b_{t,j}$ = gross receipts, in dollars, procurable from project j at time t (note that $b_{t,j} \geq 0$)

$c_{t,j}$ = gross cost, in dollars, to be incurred by project j at time t (note that $c_{t,j} \geq 0$)

$B_{t,j}$ = $b_{t,j} - c_{t,j}$ = net receipt, in dollars, procurable from project j at time t (note that $B_{t,j}$ is unconstrained in sign)

n_j = expected life of project j

b_j = $\displaystyle\sum_{t=1}^{n_j} b_{t,j}/(1+i)^t$ = discounted gross receipts, in dollars, procurable from project j

c_j = $\displaystyle\sum_{t=1}^{n_j} c_{t,j}/(1+i)^t$ = discounted gross costs, in dollars, to be incurred by project j

Using these symbols, we now define:

$$Bj = b_j - c_j = \sum_{t=1}^{n_j} B_{t,j}/(1+i)^t$$

C_j = initial capital outlay, in dollars, required for project j at time 0 (note that $C_j > 0$)

Figure 3.3 presents graphically the net cash flow pattern for project j.

The NPV, which is sometimes referred to as present worth, is now defined as $B_j - C_j$. The IRR is defined as the rate of interest that equates the present values of capital outlays and their resultant cash flows. With

Figure 3.3
Net Cash Flow Pattern for Project *j*

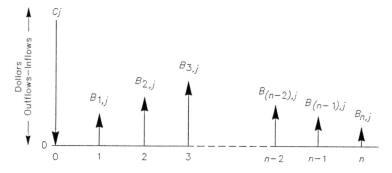

the aforementioned notation, the internal rate of return for project *j* is an interest rate R_j such that

$$\left[\sum_{t=1}^{n_j} B_{t,j}/(1+R_j)^t\right] - C_j = 0$$

(Those readers interested in other indices for project acceptance and their pitfalls are referred to Beenhakker 1996.) When we employ the NPV index, the rules for project acceptance are as follows:

Rule 1: a given independent project, *j'*, should be accepted if, and only if, NPV*j'* ≥ 0.

Rule 2: for a set, *J*, of mutually exclusive projects, a given project *j'* belonging to set *J* should be accepted if, and only if, NPV$_{j'}$ ≥ 0 and NPV$_{j'}$ ≥ NPV$_j$ for all other projects *j* belonging to set *J*.

Alternatively, if we use the internal rate of return, the rules are interpreted as follows:

Rule 1: a given independent project, *j'*, should be accepted if, and only if, $R_{j'}$ ≥ *i*.

Rule 2: for a set, *J*, of mutually exclusive projects, a given project *j'* belonging to set *J* should be accepted if, and only if, $R_{j'}$ ≥ *i* and $R_{j'}$ ≥ R_j for all other projects *j* belonging to set *J*.

Rule 1 applies to the examination of whether a proposed independent project should be accepted. The independent project is given a name, namely, *j'*.

Rule 2 applies to the selection of a project (called project j') from a set or group of mutually exclusive projects. A set or group of projects is mutually exclusive if the implementation of one project of this set makes the implementation of the other projects in the set impossible. This may be the case if the mutually exclusive projects have the same objective (a highway or railway track to connect two locations) or if resource constraints (money or manpower) limit the implementation to one project. Thus, in the case of rule 2 we are faced with the problem of selecting one project from a group of alternatives.

Rules 1 and 2 deal with deterministic investment decisions, since uncertainty and risk are not explicitly considered. It is clear, however, that any of the procedures to deal with uncertainty discussed in this chapter may be used in combination with these rules. For instance, uncertainty may be incorporated by uncertainty loading on the interest rate used to determine the NPV, as employed in rules 1 and 2. Alternatively, these rules can first be applied to optimistic values of estimated costs and benefits, and next to conservative values, if the approach of sensitivity analysis is followed. In other words, each possible outcome of an investment is treated as deterministic.

Let us now consider the treatment of risk in rules 1 and 2. We will consider the use of the NPV index in these rules. The traditional method of handling decisions under risk amounts to reducing the estimates of possible values of a project's prospective cash flow during each year to a single expected value, as given by equation (1). Next, the problem is analyzed as if this expected value were certain to occur. Naturally, this traditional method is rather crude, since standard deviations are ignored. Its attractiveness is that the economic desirability of an investment is expressed in a single measure.

It is clear that because of the use of this single measure, both rules 1 and 2 can be easily used in combination with expected monetary values. That is, we simply use these measures of a project's NPV.

The standard deviation (see equation (3)) and expected value (see equation (1)) are used in combination with rule 1 by adding a provision pertaining to the maximal allowable value of the standard deviation of the probability distribution of net present values of project j'. (No project with a standard deviation larger than x units should be accepted.) This maximal value depends entirely on management's assessment of risk. Large, diversified firms are generally less averse to risk than small firms, and are, therefore, willing to accept higher values of the standard deviation.

The principle of dominance is used if rule 2 is applied to the selection of one project from two mutually exclusive projects in combination with the concepts of standard deviation and expected value. The principle of dominance states that if the investor is faced with the problem of choosing between two projects with equal expected net present values, the one with the smaller risk will be chosen. Similarly, when choosing between projects with equal risks but unequal net present values, the investor will select the project with the largest expected net present value. This project is said to dominate the other. In a more formal way, the principle of dominance is stated as follows: in making a decision between two projects, $[E(P), \sigma]$ and $[E'(P), \sigma']$, if either $E(P) < E'(P)$ and $\sigma \geq \sigma'$, or $E(P) \leq E'(P)$ and $\sigma > \sigma'$, the investor will select the second project, $[E'(P), \sigma']$. Repetitive application of this principle to a pairwise examination of projects is suggested if rule 2 is to be applied to the selection of one project from more than two mutually exclusive projects.

It is clear that the principle of dominance may not always result in a selection. For instance, what will the investor decide if $E(P) > E'(P)$ and $\sigma > \sigma'$? In this case we replace rule 2 by the following algorithm (step-by-step procedure). This algorithm may be applied to the selection of one project from two or more mutually exclusive projects.

Algorithm

Step 1: calculate the expected value and standard deviation of the net present value for each project considered. The expected value and standard deviation of the net present value of a project i are called $E(P)_i$ and σ_i, respectively.

Step 2: check for dominance by using the principle of dominance and eliminate the projects that are dominated by one or more others. The remaining set of projects is called the efficient set, which should be used in steps 3 through 7.

Step 3: for the two projects with the largest positive $E(P)$, calculate the expected difference $E(P)_d$ and the standard deviation of the difference, σ_d, as follows:

$$E(P)_d = E(P_i) - E(P_j)$$

and:

$$\sigma_d = \sqrt{\sigma_i^2 + \sigma_j^2}$$

Step 4: with the information obtained in step 3, determine the probability of reversal, which is defined as the probability that of two projects, the one with the greater $E(P)$ will turn out to be less successful than the other. Thus, the probability of reversal is the probability that the difference in net present values of projects i and j, or $(P_i - P_j)$, is smaller than zero.

Step 5: select the preferable of the two projects considered in step 4 based on management's preferences with respect to expected net present values and probabilities of reversal.

Step 6: repeat steps 3, 4, and 5 to compare the project selected in step 5 with the project having the next largest $E(P)$. Select the preferable of these two projects.

Step 7: repeat steps 3 through 6 as long as alternative projects exist and it seems that, based on the considerations of step 5, the project having the next smallest $E(P)$ may be sufficiently competitive to the current most desirable project. The final selection is the project that has the most positive $E(P)$ and has not been judged to be less desirable than some other project due to a consideration of the probability of reversal.

To illustrate the use of this algorithm, consider the four mutually exclusive projects with $E(P)$ and σ values as given in Table 3.8. It is assumed that the net present value for each project is normally distributed so that the distribution of differences between any two of the projects is normal.

Step 2 of the algorithm calls for elimination of project D. Step 3 calls for the following comparison of projects A and B:

$$E(P)_d = \$3,000 - \$2,500 = \$500$$
$$\sigma_d = \sqrt{625,000,000 + 144,000,000} = \$27,730$$

Step 4 calls for the calculation of the probability of reversal. Appendix 1 can be used since the distribution of the differences is normal. The Z value is:

$$[0 - E(P)_d]/\sigma_d = -500/27,730 = -0.018$$

Table 3.8
E(P) and σ Values for the Example Problem

Project	E(P)	σ	σ²
A	+$3,000	25,000	625,000,000
B	+ 2,500	12,000	144,000,000
C	+ 200	1,000	1,000,000
D	+ 100	8,000	64,000,000

Appendix 1 indicates that the probability of reversal is 0.49. Carrying out step 5, management decides that this probability of reversal is too high a risk to take. Therefore, project B is selected. Next, step 6 calls for the following comparison of project B with project C.

$$E(P)_d = \$2,500 - \$200 = \$2,300$$

$$\sigma_d = \sqrt{144,000,000 + 1,000,000} = \$12,020$$

The associated probability of reversal is now 0.42. Carrying out step 5, management decides that this probability of reversal is small enough to take the risk. Consequently, the final selection is project B. Note that the application of rule 2 without considering the information about standard deviations would result in the selection of project A.

It should be noted that the concepts of standard deviation and expected value may also be employed in combination with the use of the internal rate of return in rules 1 and 2. The internal rate of return, R, under considerations of risk may be computed with equation (1) by substituting 0 and R for $E(P)$ and i, respectively. Equation (2) remains the same, while i in equation (3) is replaced by R.

5. POLICY TOWARD RISK

The prerequisite to allowing for risks in investment decisions is for any organization, be it private or public, to establish its own policy toward risk. The amount of risk an organization is prepared to take to secure an actual or apparent monetary return is a general question of values, and there are no logical criteria by which the choice can be made. The policy a company may have in this respect will largely be determined by the preferences of its stockholders, the amount of risk the company is already exposed to, and its reputation. Thus, a company may opt for a policy of taking greater risks or one of conservatism, demanding a high return for risk. The choice is one of value judgments, in which the financial manager may have no special competence once the issues have been clearly stated and understood. It is essential, however, that the issues are clearly understood by those making the judgment. Often, a policy of conservatism is inconsistent within its own assumptions in that by rejecting some forms of risk investment, a company merely exposes itself to risks of a different type. This occurs frequently where a company refuses to undertake risky investments in research, new methods, or products, while failing to recognize that its policy exposes it to even greater risks of loss through the successful investments of this type that its rivals may undertake. In a competitive industry, the maximum safety generally lies in the intelligent balancing of risks.

Once an organization has decided on its general policy of risk, it must be clearly understood at all levels where investments are under consideration. Thus, it is generally advisable to establish requirements for specific rates of return for different types of investments. For instance, a company may establish that it is prepared to invest in relatively risk-free projects if these offer a return on total capital in excess of, say, 8 percent after tax. Projects in this category include those involving revenues or saving expenditures that are largely determined by contractual obligations such as lease decisions, and cost-saving investments that are relatively immune from the risks involved in the sale of the final product. These acceptable return figures are not merely helpful with regard to relatively risk-free investments but also serve as useful benchmarks for more risky investments. The aim of this strategy is to try to ensure that all projects are afforded equal consideration once due allowance for the differential risks involved has been made. It avoids a situation where one type of project is favored over another without considering the general policy of risk. It is not suggested that this is an easy or exact task, but hopefully, this explanation of uncertainty and risk demonstrates that it is worth attempting.

SUGGESTIONS FOR FURTHER READING

Beenhakker, H. L. *Investment Decision Making in the Private and Public Sectors.* Westport, CT: Quorum Books, 1996.

Bussey, L. E., and G. T. Stevens. "Formulating Correlated Cash Flow Streams." *Engineering Economist*, 18, no. 1 (Fall 1972): 1–30.

Hillier, F. S. *The Evaluation of Risky Interrelated Investments.* Amsterdam: North Holland Publishing Co., 1969.

Luce, R. D., and H. Raiffa. *Games and Decisions: Introduction and Critical Survey.* New York: John Wiley and Sons, 1958.

Reisman, A., and A. K. Rao. "Stochastic Cash Flow Formulae under Conditions of Inflation." *Engineering Economist*, 18, no. 1 (Fall 1972): 49–71.

CHAPTER 4

Hedging Risk

If you do not hope, you will not find what is beyond your hopes.
—St. Clement of Alexandria

This chapter, as well as Chapters 5 and 6, address the question of what a firm can do to reduce the risk posed by either a project or the firm as a whole. The approach is different from the one followed in Chapter 3, where we analyzed the risk of a project before deciding to accept or reject it, and where a firm treated a project's risk as unchangeable. Hedging, the approach introduced in this chapter, is based on the use of derivative securities.

A derivative security is a security whose value depends on the values of other, more basic, underlying variables. Expressed in a simple manner, a derivative product is a contract. Basically, there are two types of derivatives: the over-the-counter (OTC) derivatives, which are contracts between two parties, and those involved in organized and centralized trading or exchanges. The most important among the first group are forward contracts and swaps; futures contracts and options are actively traded on different exchanges. Swaps and options are dealt with in Chapters 5 and 6, respectively. During the late 1980s and early 1990s, the growth of derivatives has been explosive. In terms of the dollar value of outstanding (existing) positions in derivative securities, the market for exchange-traded instruments grew from $583 billion in 1986 to over $8,000 billion in 1995. The OTC market is similar in size to the exchange markets.

In derivative securities we frequently compare two or more pecuniary values at different points in time. Consequently, we must use interest factors for either discrete compounding (Appendix 2) or con-

tinuous compounding (Appendix 3). This chapter primarily uses continuous compounding. When writing about derivative securities we
cannot exclude the use of mathematics. Great care has been taken in the
level of mathematical sophistication since if the level is too high, it is
likely to be inaccessible to many practitioners, while if too low, some
important issues will inevitably be treated in a superficial way. Nones-
sential mathematical material has, therefore, been eliminated.

People dealing with derivative securities have developed their own
vocabulary. For instance, to "long" an asset means to buy an asset for a
specified price at a specified future date. To "short" an asset means to
sell it on the same date for the same price. Don't let this special language
discourage you in your attempts to understand derivative securities.
Their underlying logic is straightforward.

Derivative securities can be used to hedge or speculate. Since this
book deals with risk management, we will only consider hedging,
which involves safeguarding oneself from loss on a risk by making
compensatory arrangements on the other side. Thus, the economic
functions of derivative securities are (1) as risk management tools, and
(2) for price discovery for parties who are involved in the derivative
markets and also those who are not. These functions will become clear
after an introduction to the various types of derivative securities. The
possibilities of designing new and interesting derivative securities seem
to be limitless. For instance, ski slope operators could issue bonds on
which the payoff depends on the total annual snowfall at a certain
resort.

1. FORWARD AND FUTURES CONTRACTS

A forward contract is a private contract or agreement to buy or sell
an asset at a fixed price (called the delivery price) at a specific date in
the future. The party who will buy the asset takes the long position,
while the one who will sell takes the short position. The delivery price
is set at a forward rate, F, such that the value of the forward contract is
initially (before it is carried out) zero. Consider, for example, a U.S.
exporter who will receive 1 million deutsche marks (DM) six months
from now upon delivery of the merchandise to a German customer.
Since the exporter is in the business to produce a product, he or she is
not willing to incur a loss (or a profit) due to changes in the exchange
rate between the U.S. dollar and the German mark. The exporter wishes
to hedge, or eliminate, the risk of foreign exchange losses and therefore
contacts a bank today and signs an agreement stipulating that upon
receipt of the DM 1 million in Germany, the bank will give him or her
a specific amount of dollars in the United States in exchange for the

German marks. Rather than paying a commission to the bank, banks normally give their exchange rates as ask quotes and bid quotes depending on whether one wishes to obtain dollars for foreign currency or the other way around. They receive their compensation by setting ask quotes larger than bid quotes. There is no need to put up funds when signing such an agreement. When the exporter receives the deutsche marks, he or she delivers them to the bank in return for the agreed amount of U.S. dollars. In other words, the German marks are sold forward. Another example would be a farmer who sells a given number of bushels of wheat forward when planting the wheat to avoid the risk of not knowing how much he or she will get per bushel at harvest time.

Futures contracts are similar to forward contracts; the difference is that they are standardized. That is, the size of the contract is standardized (for instance, in the previous example the bank may only agree to the exchange of German marks for U.S. dollars in specified multiples of marks), the expiration date is fixed (generally, March 15, June 15, September 15, or December 15), and the credit risk is standardized. By a standardized credit risk we mean that each of the two parties of the futures contract are exposed, not to each other's risk of default, but rather to the risk of a clearinghouse. A clearinghouse is an adjunct of the exchange and acts as an intermediary in future transactions by guaranteeing the performance of the parties to each transaction. The clearinghouse will have a number of members, all of which will have offices close to the clearinghouse. Brokers who are themselves not clearinghouse members must channel their business through a member. Unlike forward contracts, futures contracts are normally traded on an exchange such as the Chicago Board of Trade (CBOT) and the Chicago Mercantile Exchange (CME). As the two parties to the contract may not necessarily know each other, the exchange provides the clearinghouse mechanism to guarantee that the contract will be honored. Futures contracts are fungible since they are standardized; this means that they can be sold or liquidated before the expiration date, which is not possible with forward contracts. It is estimated that about 90 percent of the futures contracts in the U.S. are sold before expiration.

Futures contracts call for:

1. the investor to deposit funds (referred to as the initial margin) in what is called the margin account at the time the contract is first entered into (the initial margin is like a performance bond in the construction industry);
2. the broker to adjust the margin account at the end of each trading day, which is known as marking to market the account;

3. the broker to give the investor a "margin" call if the investor's equity, as determined by the initial margin and the market value of the contract, falls below the maintenance level; and

4. the investor to pay an amount to reestablish the initial margin.

The following example elucidates this procedure. Suppose an investor contacts his or her broker on June 1 to buy three December (same-year) gold futures contracts and that the current futures price is $355 per ounce. Since the contract size is standardized in 100 ounces, the investor has contracted to buy a total of 300 ounces at this price. The broker requires the investor to deposit an initial margin equal to $2000 per contract, or $6,000 in total, on June 1; this initial margin is determined by the broker. The broker also requires the investor to maintain a maintenance level of $4,000.

Now suppose that at the end of the day on June 1, June 2, and June 3, the futures prices for gold are $360, $350, and $338 per ounce, respectively. Thus, at the end of each of these days, the margin account has to be adjusted to reflect the investor's gain or loss. By the end of June 1, the investor's equity increases to $6,000 plus the investor's gain of 300 × $5, or $7,500, which means that he or she can withdraw $1,500 from the margin account. By the end of June 2, the investor's equity drops to $6,000 minus a loss of 300 × $5, or $4,500, which is still above the maintenance level of $4,000. However, by the end of June 3, the equity drops to $6,000 minus a loss of 300 × $17, or $900, which is below the maintenance level. The broker gives the investor a margin call with a request to deposit $6,000 minus $900 or $5,100 in the margin account. If the investor is unable to receive the call or unable to deposit the $5,100, the broker will liquidate the long position in order to minimize the risk to the clearinghouse. This process is repeated at the end of each day until the futures contract is executed on its expiration date to ensure that there will always be enough funds available to cover losses. It is noted that the investor normally receives interest on the amount deposited in the margin account.

2. VALUATION OF FORWARD CONTRACTS

To carry out this evaluation, we introduce the following notation:

T = time when forward contract matures (in years)

t = current time (in years)

S = price of asset underlying the forward contract at time t

S_T = price of asset underlying the forward contract at time T (this price is unknown at the current time, t)

K = delivery price in the forward contract
f = value of a long forward contract at time t
F = forward price at time t
r = risk-free rate of interest per annum at time t, with continuous compounding, for an investment maturing at time t

By the term *risk-free rate* we mean the nominal risk-free rate, which includes an inflation premium equal to the average expected inflation rate over the life of a security. In general, we use the treasury bill (T-bill) rate to approximate the short-term risk-free rate, and the treasury bond (T-bond) rate to approximate the long-term risk-free rate. T-bills are short-term securities issued by the U.S. government with respective maturities of either 13, 26, or 52 weeks. T-bonds are long-term securities issued by the U.S. government with a fixed maturity of more than ten years. It is noted that the forward price, F, at any given time is the delivery price that would make the contract have a zero value. When a contract is initiated, the delivery price is normally set equal to the forward price so that $F = K$ and $f = 0$. As time passes, both f and F change.

In what follows we will assume that (1) the market participants can borrow money at the same risk-free rate of interest as they can lend money, (2) the market participants take advantage of arbitrage opportunities as they occur, (3) there are no transactions costs, and (4) all trading profits are subject to the same tax rate. An arbitrage opportunity is the profit that one could theoretically obtain in the securities market without any risk; naturally, such a situation does not exist.

We first consider the valuation of a forward contract that provides the holder with no income, such as non-dividend-paying stocks and discount bonds. Using the concept of continuous discounting, the relationships between F and S and between f, S, and K are given by equations (1) and (2):

$$F = S \cdot e^{r(T - t)} \tag{1}$$

$$f = S - K \cdot e^{-r(T - t)} \tag{2}$$

The dot in the equations is interpreted as "multiply." The following examples explain why these relationships must hold. Consider a forward contract on a nonpaying stock that matures in three months. Assume that the stock price is \$50, and the three-month risk-free rate of interest is 5 percent per annum. Thus, $T - t = 0.25$, $r = 0.05$, and $S = \$50$. Consequently:

$$F = \$50 \cdot e^{0.05 \times 0.25} = \$50.63$$

The amount of $50.63 represents the delivery price if a contract were negotiated today. If the actual forward price were greater than $50.63, an arbitrageur could borrow money, buy the stock, and short the forward contract for a net profit. If, on the other hand, the forward price were less than $50.63, an arbitrageur could short the stock, invest the proceeds, and take a long forward position. Either way, a net profit would be realized. Since we assumed that there are no arbitrage opportunities (which is correct in the real world), we conclude that equation (1) must hold.

Now consider a long six-month forward contract on a one-year discount bond when the delivery price is $975. The six-month risk-free rate of interest is 6 percent per annum, and the current bond price is $950. Thus, $T - t = 0.50$, $r = 0.06$, $K = \$975$, and $S = \$950$. We compute the value, f, of the long forward contract with equation (2):

$$f = \$950 - \$975 \cdot e^{-0.50 \times 0.06} = \$3.86$$

An arbitrage argument similar to the one given for the previous example leads us to conclude that equation (2) must hold.

In the example, the value of the long forward contract is $3.86. Similarly, the value of a short forward contract is –$3.86. This means that if someone had bought the long six-month forward contract on the one-year discount bond six months ago at $K = \$975$ and liquidated (sold) it today, the outcome would be a loss of $3.86. Naturally, this is a hypothetical situation since the definition of a forward contract refers to buying or selling at a fixed price, K, at a specific date in the future, T. Nonetheless, it serves to explain the meaning of the value of a long (or short) forward contract. It is also recalled that when a forward contract is initiated, the forward price equals the delivery price specified in the contract and is chosen so that the value of the contract at maturity is zero. In equation (2) we can verify that when $t = T$ the exponential factor, e, becomes 1, and since the value of S at $t = T$ is equal to K, the value of f is indeed zero.

Let us now consider a forward contract on a security that provides a predictable cash income to the holder such as a stock paying known dividends or a coupon-bearing bond. Following the arbitrage argument, we conclude that in this situation equations (1) and (2) become equations (3) and (4), respectively;

$$F = (S - I)e^{r(T - t)} \tag{3}$$

$$f = S - I - K \cdot e^{-r(T - t)} \tag{4}$$

where:

I = the present value (using the risk-free discount rate) of income to be received during the life of the forward contract

all other symbols are as previously defined

Consider, for example, a five-year bond with a price of $900. Assume that a forward contract on the bond with a delivery price of $910 has a maturity of 1 year. After 6 and 12 months, coupon payments of $50 are expected. The second coupon payment is due immediately prior to the delivery date in the forward contract. The risk-free rates of interest are 9 percent per annum for 6 months and 10 percent per annum for 1 year. Thus, $S = \$900$ and $K = \$910$, and consequently:

$$I = \$50 \cdot e^{-0.09 \times 0.50} + \$50 \cdot e^{-0.10} = \$93.04$$

and the value, f, of a long position in the forward contract is obtained by using equation (4):

$$f = \$900.00 - \$93.04 - \$910.00 \cdot e^{-0.10} = -\$16.41$$

The value of the short position is +$16.41.

3. VALUATION OF FUTURES CONTRACTS

In this section we will use the notation introduced in the previous section. In addition, we will also assume that (1) the market participants can borrow money at the same risk-free rate of interest as they can lend money, (2) the market participants take advantage of arbitrage opportunities as they occur, (3) there are no transactions costs, and (4) all trading profits are subject to the same tax rate.

Through an arbitrage argument, we can arrive at the following two relationships between prices of forward and futures contracts:

1. When the risk-free interest rate is constant and the same for all maturities, the forward price for a contract with a certain delivery date is the same as the futures price for a contract with the same delivery date.
2. When risk-free interest rates vary (as they do in the real world), forward and futures prices are no longer the same; if the price of the underlying asset is strongly positively correlated with interest rates, futures prices tend to be higher than forward prices; however, if the price of the underlying asset is strongly negatively correlated with interest rates, forward prices tend to be higher than futures prices.

The first relationship is intuitively obvious. The second has to do with the daily settlement procedure described in the above Section 1. That is, if the price of an underlying asset is strongly positively correlated with interest rates, and if this price increases, an investor who holds a long futures position will make an immediate gain. This gain will tend to be invested at a higher-than-average interest rate since increases in the price of the underlying asset tend to occur at the same time as increases in interest rates. Similarly, if the price of the underlying asset decreases, the investor will suffer an immediate loss, which will tend to be financed at a lower-than-average interest rate. An investor holding a forward contract is not affected in this way by interest rate fluctuations because the daily settlement procedure does not apply. A similar argument can be given to demonstrate that forward prices will tend to be higher than futures prices if the price of the underlying asset is strongly negatively correlated with interest rates.

However, the differences between forward and futures prices are sufficiently small to be ignored for contracts that last only a few months. It is, therefore, not unreasonable to assume that forward and futures prices are the same. We will make this assumption in this chapter and use the symbol F to represent both the forward price and the futures price of an asset. The valuation of futures contracts will be discussed for the following categories: (1) stock index futures, (2) foreign currency contracts, (3) commodities held for investment (e.g., gold or silver), (4) commodities held for consumption, and (5) interest rate futures.

Stock Index Futures

A stock index tracks the changes in the value of a hypothetical portfolio of stocks. The weight of a stock in the portfolio is equal to the proportion of the portfolio invested in the stock. The percentage increase in the value of a stock index over a small interval of time is usually defined so that it equals the percentage increase in the total value of the stocks comprising the portfolio at that time. A stock index is normally not adjusted for cash dividends. Thus, any cash dividends received on the portfolio are ignored when percentage changes in most indices are being calculated.

The most common stock indices are:

1. The Standard & Poor's 500 (S&P 500) Index, which trades on the Chicago Mercantile Exchange (CME) and is based on a portfolio of 500 different stocks;

2. The New York Stock Exchange (NYSE) Composite Index, which is based on a portfolio of all the stocks listed on the New York Stock Exchange;
3. The Major Market Index (MMI), which is based on a portfolio of 20 blue-chip stocks listed on the New York Stock Exchange; and
4. The Nikkei 225 Stock Average, which is based on a portfolio of 225 of the largest stocks trading on the Tokyo Stock Exchange.

The MMI is closely related to the widely quoted Dow Jones Industrial Average, which is also based on relatively few stocks.

Stock index futures can be used to hedge the risk in a well-diversified portfolio of stocks. As will be further explained in Section 3 of Chapter 8, the relationship between the return on a portfolio of stocks and the return on the market is described by a parameter, β (beta). When $\beta = 1.0$, the return on the portfolio tends to mirror the return on the market; when $\beta = 2.0$, the return on the portfolio tends to be twice as great as the return on the market; when $\beta = 0.5$, the return tends to be half as great; and so on. In other words, the market beta is a measure of the exposure to market movements. A hedge using index futures separates the market risk from the portfolio risk.

Suppose an investor holding a portfolio of stocks worth V wishes to hedge against changes, Δ (delta), in this value during a period of time $T - t$. The investor has expertise in these particular stocks and expects them to outperform the market, but there is also the risk of market movements. These can be hedged against using stock index futures because movements in the portfolio can be decomposed into a portion due to the market (subject to risk related to the market; this is sometimes referred to as systematic risk), and an idiosyncratic portion (subject to unsystematic risk). We define:

ΔV = change during time $T - t$ in the value of $1 if invested in the portfolio
ΔM = change during time $T - t$ in the value of $1 if invested in the market
ΔF = change during time $T - t$ in the value of $1 if invested in the market index
V = current value of the portfolio
M = current value of the market
F = current value of one futures contract
N = optimal number of contracts to short when hedging the portfolio

The value of one futures contract, F, is the futures price multiplied by the contract size. In the case of the S&P 500, one contract is 500 times the index. For example, if the futures price of the S&P 500 is $300, then the value of one contract is $300 × 500 = $150,000.

From the definition of β, it is approximately true that:

$$\Delta V = \alpha + \beta \cdot \Delta M$$

where α is a constant. A futures contract on the S&P 500 (defined as the market in our example) essentially behaves as follows:

$$\Delta F = \Delta M$$

We can, therefore, construct a new portfolio consisting of the original portfolio plus a short position in N futures contracts, whose value will fluctuate as:

$$V \cdot \Delta V - N \cdot F \cdot \Delta F = V \cdot \beta \cdot \Delta M - N \cdot F \cdot \Delta M = (V \cdot \beta - N \cdot F) \Delta M$$
$$= \text{exposure} \times \Delta M \qquad (5)$$

where the exposure is that due to the systematic risk (the risk related to market fluctuations). The portfolio will be immunized against systematic risk by setting the exposure, defined as $(V \cdot \beta - N \cdot F)$ equal to zero, or choosing:

$$N = \beta \cdot V/F \qquad (6)$$

As demonstrated in the following example, equation (6) can be used to determine the number of contracts to sell short.

A company wishes to hedge a $2,000,000 portfolio using S&P 500 futures. The futures price is $300, with a multiplier of 500. The portfolio's β is 1.5. The number of contracts to sell short is $N = 1.5(\$2,000,000)/(500 \times \$300) = 20$.

A stock index hedge, if effective, should result in the hedger's position growing at approximately the risk-free interest rate. However, if that is the hedger's goal, why go through the trouble of using futures contracts rather than simply sell the portfolio and invest the proceeds in treasury bills? One reason is that the hedger is planning to hold a portfolio for a long period of time and requires short-term protection in an uncertain market situation. The alternative strategy of selling the portfolio and buying it back later might involve unacceptably high transaction costs. Another possibility is that the hedger feels the stocks in the portfolio are undervalued and is uncertain about the market's performance as a whole; however, he or she is confident that the stocks in the portfolio will outperform the market. Using index futures as a hedge removes the risk caused by market moves and leaves the hedger exposed only to the performance of the portfolio relative to the market.

Beta coefficients for thousands of companies are calculated and published by Merrill Lynch, Value Line, and numerous other organizations. They are based on a stock's historical values. Most stocks have betas in the range of 0.50 to 1.50, and by definition, the average for all stocks is 1.00.

Foreign Currency Contracts

A foreign currency has the property that its owner can earn interest at the risk-free interest rate prevailing in that foreign country by, for instance, investing the currency in a foreign-denominated bond. We will use the following notation:

S = the current price in dollars of one unit of the foreign currency

K = the delivery price agreed to in the futures contract

r = the domestic, risk-free interest rate per annum with continuous compounding

R = foreign risk-free interest rate per annum, with continuous compounding

f = value of a long futures contract at time t

t = current time (years)

T = time when contract matures (years)

To compute the price of a contract on a foreign currency we compare one long futures contract plus an amount of cash equal to $K \cdot e^{-r(T-t)}$ with an amount $e^{-R(T-t)}$ of the foreign currency. These two situations can be considered as two portfolios. Both will become worth the same at time T. They must, therefore, also be equally valuable at time t. Consequently:

$$f + K \cdot e^{-r(T-t)} = S \cdot e^{-R(T-t)}$$

or

$$f = S \cdot e^{-R(T-t)} - K \cdot e^{-r(T-t)} \tag{7}$$

The futures price (or futures exchange rate), F, is the value of K that makes $f = 0$ in equation (7). Hence,

$$F = S \cdot e^{(r-R)(T-t)} \tag{8}$$

Equation (8) is the interest rate parity relationship, as used in the field of international finance.

The *Wall Street Journal* publishes futures prices for contracts trading on the major currencies in the International Money Market of the

Chicago Mercantile Exchange. The futures exchange rate is quoted as the value of the foreign currency in U.S. dollars; in case of the yen, the value of the foreign currency is in U.S. cents.

Equation (8) shows that when the foreign interest rate is greater than the domestic interest rate, F is always less than S; moreover, F decreases as the maturity of the contract, T, increases. The foreign currency sells at a discount. When the domestic interest rate is greater than the foreign interest rate, F is always greater than S; the foreign currency sells at a premium.

Commodities Held for Investment

A significant number of investors hold gold or silver solely for investment. These investments can be considered analogous to securities paying no income provided the storage costs are zero. In the notation introduced in the beginning of Section 2 of this chapter, S represents the current spot price of gold. (The spot price is the price fixed today on a sale that is made today.) Equation (1) shows that the futures price, F, is given by:

$$F = S \cdot e^{r(T-t)} \tag{9}$$

Storage costs can be considered as negative income. It follows from equation (3) that if storage costs are incurred, the value of F is given by:

$$F = (S + U)e^{r(T-t)} \tag{10}$$

where:

U = the present value of all storage costs incurred during the life of a futures contract

The value of F is given by equation (11) if the storage costs incurred at any time are proportional to the price of the commodity, in which case they can be considered a negative dividend yield:

$$F = S \cdot e^{(r+u)(T-t)} \tag{11}$$

where:

u = the storage costs per annum as a proportion of the spot price

Consider, for example, a one-year futures contract on gold and suppose that it costs $3.00 per ounce per year to store the gold, with the payment made at the end of each year. Assume that the spot price is $450.00 and the risk-free interest rate is 7 percent per year for all maturities. Hence, $r = 0.07$, $S = 450$, $T - t = 1$, and $U = \$3 \cdot e^{-0.07} = \$2.80$. With the help of equation (10) we compute the futures price, F, as follows:

$$F = (\$450.00 + \$2.80)e^{0.07} = \$485.63$$

Commodities Held for Consumption

Companies or other parties that keep a commodity in inventory do so because of its consumption value, not because of its value as an investment. They would, therefore, be reluctant to sell the commodity and buy futures contracts that they can not consume. Since from the investment point of view there is an insignificant benefit from holding the commodity, we conclude that in equations (10) and (11), the equals sign must be replaced by the sign indicating that F is smaller than the quantities on the righthand side of the equation.

When F is smaller than $S \cdot e^{(r+u)(T-t)}$ the remaining users of the commodity must feel that there is nonetheless a benefit from its ownership. The benefit may be the ability to keep a production process running smoothly or to profit from a temporary local shortage. This type of benefit is sometimes referred to as the convenience yield provided by the commodity. It reflects the market's expectations about the commodity's future availability. If users of a commodity have high inventories, there is little chance of shortages in the near future and the convenience yield tends to be low. On the other hand, low inventories tend to lead to high convenience yields. In terms of our notation, the convenience yield, y, is defined so that

$$F \cdot e^{y(T-t)} = (S + U)e^{r(T-t)} \tag{12}$$

where:

$$U = \text{the present value of the storage costs}$$

If the storage costs per unit are a constant proportion, u, of the spot price, equation (12) becomes:

$$F \cdot e^{y(T-t)} = S \cdot e^{(r+u)(T-t)}$$

or

$$F = S \cdot e^{(r+u-y)(T-t)} \tag{13}$$

It is clear that for investment commodities, the convenience yield is equal to zero, since otherwise there would be arbitrage opportunities.

Interest Rate Futures

An interest rate futures contract is a futures contract on an asset whose price is dependent solely on the level of interest rates. Treasury bond (T-bond) futures contracts traded on the Chicago Board of Trade (CBOT) are the most popular long-term interest rate futures. In these contracts, any government bond with more than 15 years to maturity on the first day of the delivery month and not callable within 15 years from that day can be delivered.

T-bond prices and futures prices are quoted in dollars and 32nds of a dollar. A T-bond normally has a face value of $100,000.00. Thus, a quote of 90-05 means that the price for a bond with a face value of $100,000.00 is $90,156.25, where $156.25 = 5(1/32)(1,000)$. The quoted price is not the same as the cash price paid by the purchaser because the accrued interest since the last coupon date is added to the quoted price in order to arrive at the cash price.

In the T-bond futures contract there is a provision for the party with the short position to choose to deliver any bond with a maturity over 15 years and not callable within 15 years. When a bond is delivered, a parameter known as its conversion factor defines the price received by the party with the short position. The quoted price applicable to the delivery is the product of the conversion factor and the quoted futures price. Taking accrued interest into account, the cash received by the party with the short position equals the product of the quoted futures price and the conversion factor for the delivered bond plus the accrued interest on the bond. Suppose, for instance, that the quoted futures price is 90-05, the conversion factor for the bond delivered is 1.5705, and the accrued interest on this bond at the time of delivery is $3.50 per $100.00 face value. The cash received by the party with the short position upon delivery of the bond is $(\$90,156.25 \times 1.5705) + \$3,500.00 = \$145,090.39$.

The conversion factor for a bond is equal to the value of the bond on the first day of the delivery month on the assumption that the interest rate for all maturities equals 8 percent per year (with semiannual compounding). In order to enable CBOT to produce comprehensive tables and assist with calcuation, the bond maturity and the times to the coupon payment dates are rounded down to the nearest 3 months. If, after rounding, the bond lasts for an exact number of half years, the first coupon is assumed to be paid in 6 months. If, after rounding, the bond does not last for an exact number of 6-month periods (i.e., there is an extra 3 months), the first coupon is assumed to be paid after 3 months and accrued interest is subtracted. The following example elucidates the procedure.

Let us calculate the conversion factor of a 14 percent coupon bond with 18 years, 4 months to maturity. To simplify the calculation, it is first carried out for each $100.00 face value of the bond. In view of the rounding procedure, the bond is assumed to have exactly 18 years, 3 months to maturity. Discounting all the payments back to a point in time 3 months from today gives a value of:

$$\sum_{n=0}^{36} 7/(1.04)^n + 100/(1.04)^{36} = 163.74$$

The interest rate for a 3-months period is 1.98 percent. Discounting back to the present gives the bond's value as $163.74/1.0198 = 160.56$, and after subtracting the accrued interest of 3.5, we get 157.06. Since the calculation was carried out for each $100.00 face value of the bond, we divide by 100 to arrive at a conversion factor of 1.5706. Note that the 1.04 in the denominator of the expression is based on half the 8 percent mentioned in the definition of the conversion factor and that the accrued interest of 3.5 is equal to $(3/12) \cdot (14)$.

At any time, there are about 30 bonds that can be delivered in the CBOT T-bond futures contract. These vary as far as coupon and maturity are concerned. The party with the short position can choose which of the available bonds is "cheapest" to deliver. For example, suppose a party with a short position has decided to deliver and is trying to choose between the three bonds with the quoted prices, conversion factors, and the current quoted futures price (93-08, or 93.25), as given in the second, third, and fourth columns of Table 4.1. To compute which of the three bonds is the cheapest to deliver, the party computes the cost of delivering each of the bonds. This is done by first multiplying the current quoted futures price by the conversion factor of each bond. Next, the party computes the cost of delivering each bond as the difference

Table 4.1
Example of Deliverable Bonds

Bond	Quoted Price	Conversion Factor	Quoted Futures Prices	Cost of Delivering
1	98.50	1.0380	93.25	1.71
2	142.50	1.5177	93.25	0.97
3	117.75	1.2515	93.25	1.05

between the quoted price and the result of the aforementioned multiplication. The results of these computations, as shown in the last column of Table 4.1, indicate that the cheapest-to-deliver bond is bond 2. Note that the figure of 1.71 in the last column of Table 4.1 is the result of 98.50 − (1.0380 × 93.25). The other amounts in the last column are obtained in a similar manner.

An important concept in the use of interest rate futures is duration. The duration of a bond is a measure of how long, on average, the bond-holder has to wait before receiving cash payments. A zero-coupon bond that matures in n years has a duration of n years; however, a coupon-bearing bond maturing in n years has a duration of less than n years since some of the cash payments will be received prior to year n. The duration, D, of a bond is defined as:

$$D = \left(\sum_{i=1}^{n} t_i \cdot c_i \cdot e^{-yt_i} \right) / B \tag{14}$$

where:

t_i = the time at which a bond provides the holder with a payment c_i; during the duration there can be one or more payments
y = yield of the bond, continuously compounding (years)
B = price of the bond

The relation between the price, B, and the yield, y, is given by equation (15):

$$B = \sum_{i=1}^{n} c_i \cdot e^{-yt_i} \tag{15}$$

Taking the first derivative with respect to y of B, or equation (15), and using equation (14), yields:

$$\frac{dB}{dy} = -B \cdot D$$

or

$$\frac{\Delta B}{B} = -D \cdot \Delta y \tag{16}$$

Equation (16) shows that the percentage change in a bond price equals its duration multiplied by the size of the parallel shift in the yield curve.

The duration of a bond portfolio is defined as a weighted average of the durations of the individual bonds in the portfolio, with the weights being proportional to the bond prices. As we will see in the next paragraphs, duration measures the exposure to movements in interest rates.

We will use the following notation:

F = contract price for the interest rate futures contract
V = value of the asset being hedged
D_F = duration of the asset underlying the futures contract
D_V = duration of the asset being hedged
ΔV = change in value of the asset being hedged
Δy = change in the yield
N = optimal number of contracts to short when hedging the asset (portfolio)

The movement in prices can be described as:

$$\Delta V / V = - D_V \cdot \Delta y \qquad (17)$$

For a futures contract:

$$\Delta F / F = -D_F \cdot \Delta y$$

Similar to the derivation of equation (6), we can construct a portfolio consisting of the original asset plus a short position in N futures contracts, whose value will fluctuate as:

$$\Delta V - N \cdot \Delta F = -D_V \cdot V \cdot \Delta y - N(-D_F \cdot F) \cdot \Delta y = (N \cdot D_F \cdot F - D_V \cdot V)\Delta y$$
$$= \text{exposure} \times \Delta y$$

The portfolio will be immunized against interest rate risks by setting the exposure equal to zero, or choosing:

$$N = V \cdot D_V / F \cdot D_F \qquad (18)$$

Equation (18) is the duration-based hedge ratio. It is sometimes also called the price-sensitivity ratio.

Strictly speaking, equation (17) is only valid if (1) only small-yield changes are considered, and (2) all interest rates change by the same amount. When large-yield changes are considered, a factor known as convexity is sometimes important. When managing portfolios of assets and liabilities, some financial institutions try to match both duration and convexity. The effect of the second requirement for equation (17) can be minimized by hedging a portfolio with primarily long-term bonds with futures contracts with primarily long-term bonds or, similarly, hedging a portfolio with primarily short-term bonds with futures contracts with primarily short-term bonds.

To enhance our understanding of equation (18), we consider the following example. Suppose a company wishes to hedge a $10,000,000 portfolio invested in U.S. government bonds using T-bond futures. The current futures price is 93-04, or 93.13, with a face value of $100,000. The duration of the cheapest-to-deliver bond in the T-bond contract is 9.1 years. The portfolio duration is 6.7 years. Thus, $V = \$10,000,000$, $F = \$93,130$, $D_F = 9.1$, and $D_V = 6.7$. The value of N is obtained with equation (18):

$$N = \$10,000,000(6.7)/\$93,130(9.1) = 79.06$$

Consequently, the number of contracts to sell short is 79.

Consider the following observations about this example:

1. The company will hedge the value of its portfolio if there is concern that interest rates will be highly volatile over, for instance, the next three months. For example, if this occurred in the beginning of August, the company would use a December T-bond futures contract to hedge the value of its portfolio.
2. If interest rates decrease, a loss will be made on the short position, but there will be a gain on the bond portfolio. If interest rates increase, a gain will be made on the short futures position and a loss will be made on the bond portfolio.
3. The duration of the bond portfolio, 6.7 years, is obtained by applying equation (14) to each bond of the portfolio and then taking the weighted average of the durations of the portfolio bonds.
4. The company determines the cheapest-to-deliver bond in a manner similar to the example pertaining to Table 4.1. The bond's duration is again determined with the help of equation (14).

SUGGESTIONS FOR FURTHER READING

Chicago Board of Trade. *Commodity Trading Manual*. Chicago: Chicago Board of Trade, 1989.

Cox, J. C., J. Ingersoll, and S. Ross. "The Relationship between Forward Prices and Futures Prices." *Journal of Financial Economics*, 9 (December 1981): 321–46.

Duffie, D. *Futures Markets*. Englewood Cliffs, NJ: Prentice-Hall, 1989.

Figlewski, S. "The Use of Financial Futures and Options by Life Insurance Companies." *Best's Review*, March 1989, 94–97.

Kolb, R. W. *Understanding Futures Markets*. Miami, FL: Kolb Publishing Company, 1994.

CHAPTER 5

More About Hedging

A stumble may prevent a fall.

—Thomas Fuller

As we have seen, hedging can be used to eliminate risks, whether price risks or cost risks. For instance, a farmer who is going to sell a crop at harvest time (i.e., at a particular time in the future) can hedge by taking a short futures position. In this case, the hedge serves to eliminate the risk related to future price fluctuations. Hedging to eliminate price risks is normally done for short-term price fluctuations—if it were done long term, the farmer would be likely to go out of business. An example of using hedging to eliminate cost risks is an airline that takes a long futures position for buying fuel. A futures hedge reduces risk by making the outcome more certain. It does not, however, necessarily improve the overall financial outcome. In fact, we can expect a futures hedge to make the outcome better about half the time—and worse for the other half.

In general, one cannot hedge against a quantity risk. For instance, in the previous example, the farmer normally does not hedge the risk that, due to bad weather, the total crop may be less than expected in average weather conditions. As a rule of thumb, he or she takes a short futures position on two-thirds of the expected production. Although normally not done, the farmer could take a put option on one-third of the expected production for which he or she does not take a short futures position, if going by the rule of thumb (see Chapter 6).

In this chapter we first analyze the potential problems related to hedging. Next, we introduce forward rate agreements (FRAs), which are used to hedge borrowing or lending requirements by exchanging fixed-rate payments for variable-rate payments. We then move on to a discussion of how companies may hedge interest rate risk by matching liabilities with assets. This ability to hedge is based on the concept of duration (Chapter 4). This discussion is followed by a detailed example of how hedging can be used to reduce risk when making an advance commitment to deliver $1 million of mortgages to an insurance company or to loan a total of $1 million to various homeowners. Finally, we introduce interest rate and currency swaps. A swap is defined as an agreement between two parties to exchange cash flows in the future according to a prearranged formula. In the example, the parties enter into a swap because one has a comparative advantage in floating-rate (or dollar) markets and the other one has a comparative advantage in fixed-rate (or pound sterling) markets.

1. PROBLEMS RELATED TO HEDGING

In practice, the use of futures contracts may work less than perfectly since (1) the hedge may require the futures contract to be closed out before its expiration date, (2) the asset whose price is to be hedged may not be exactly the same as the asset underlying the futures contract, and (3) the hedger may be uncertain as to the exact date when the asset will be bought or sold. Situation 1 arises because futures contracts are standardized (Chapter 4). An example of situation 2 is the airlines, which sometimes use New York Mercantile Exchange (NYMEX) heating oil futures contracts to hedge their exposure to the price of jet fuel since suitable jet fuel futures contracts are not available. Situation 3 may arise when a company has experienced recent labor troubles or strikes and therefore is uncertain about the delivery date of a product to be sold. Any of the problems in 1 through 3 give rise to what is called *basis risk*; the basis in a hedging situation is defined as the spot price of the asset to be hedged minus the futures price of the contract used. If the asset to be hedged and the asset underlying the futures contract are the same, the basis should be zero at the expiration of the futures contract. Prior to expiration, the basis may be positive or negative.

From the definition of the basis, it is clear that when the spot price increases by more than the futures price, the basis will also increase. This is called a strengthening of the basis. Alternatively, when the futures price increases by more than the spot price, the basis will decline, in a weakening of the basis.

We will use the following notation to analyze the nature of basis risk:

$$S_1 = \text{spot price at time } t_1$$

$$S_2 = \text{spot price at time } t_2$$
$$F_1 = \text{futures price at time } t_1$$
$$F_2 = \text{futures price at time } t_2$$
$$b_1 = \text{basis at time } t_1$$
$$b_2 = \text{basis at time } t_2$$

It is assumed that a hedge is put in place at time t_1 and closed at time t_2.

Consider, for example, a situation where the spot and futures prices at the time when the hedge is initiated are \$2.40 and \$2.10, respectively, and that at the time the hedge is closed out, they are \$1.90 and \$1.80, respectively. Thus, $S_1 = \$2.40$, $F_1 = \$2.10$, $S_2 = \$1.90$, and $F_2 = 1.80$. Consequently, $b_1 = S_1 - F_1 = \$.30$, and $b_2 = S_2 - F_2 = \$.10$. Assume that a hedger takes a short futures position at time t_1 on an asset that will be sold at time t_2. The price realized for the asset is S_2, and the profit on the futures position is $F_1 - F_2$. The effective price obtained for the asset with hedging is, therefore, $S_2 + F_1 - F_2 = F_1 + b_2$, or \$2.20 in our example. The problem is that, unlike the value of F_1, the value of b_2 at time t_1 is not known (if it were known, a perfect hedge, eliminating all uncertainty about the price obtained, would result). The hedging risk is the uncertainty associated with b_2. Consider now a company interested in buying an asset at time t_2 and initiating a long futures position at time t_1. The price paid for the asset is S_2, and the loss on the hedge is $F_1 - F_2$. The effective price paid with hedging is, therefore, $S_2 + F_1 - F_2 = F_1 + b_2$, or \$2.20 in our example. Here again, the value of F_1 is known at time t_1 and the term b_2 is the basis risk.

As discussed in Chapter 4, arbitrage arguments lead to a well-defined relationship between the futures price and the spot price of an investment asset such as foreign currencies, commodities for investment (e.g., gold or silver), and stock indices. The basis risk for these investments tends, therefore, to be fairly small. The basis risk for an investment asset arises mainly from uncertainty as to the level of the risk-free interest rate in the future. In the case of commodities such as copper, oil, or soya beans, imbalances between supply and demand as well as difficulties associated with storing the commodity can lead to large variations in the basis.

An important factor affecting basis risk is the choice of the delivery month, which is likely to be affected by several factors. It might be assumed that when the expiration date of the hedge corresponds to a delivery month, the contract with that delivery month will be chosen; however, in these circumstances a contract with a later delivery month is often chosen. This occurs because futures prices are, in some circumstances, quite erratic during the delivery month. In addition, a long hedger runs the risk of having to take delivery of the physical asset if he or she holds the contract during the delivery month. This can be expensive and inconvenient. In general, basis risk increases along with the time between the hedge expiration and the delivery month. To choose a delivery month as close as possible to, but still later than, the expiration of the hedge is therefore a good rule of thumb.

Consider, for example, a U.S. company that expects to receive 100 million yen at the end of July. Moreover, today (March 1), the company wishes to short yen futures contracts. Yen futures contracts on the International Monetary Exchange have delivery months of March, June, September, and December. One contract is for the delivery of 12.5 million yen. The company therefore shorts eight September yen futures contracts. When the yen are received at the end of July, the company closes out its position. Suppose that the futures price on March 1 is .7700 in cents per yen and that the spot and futures prices when the contract is closed out are .7100 and .7150, respectively. Thus, the basis is –.0050 when the contract is closed out. The effective price obtained (in cents per yen) is .7700 – .0050 = .7650. The company receives a total of 100 × .007650 million dollars, or $765,000.00.

The hedge ratio is defined as the ratio of the size of the position taken in futures contracts to the size of the exposure. Until this point we have assumed a hedge ratio of 1.0. We will now see that a hedge ratio of 1.0 is not necessarily optimal if the objective of the hedger is to minimize risk. To do so, we introduce the following notation:

$$\Delta S \ = \ \text{change in the spot price, } S, \text{ during a period of time}$$
equal to the life of the hedge

$$\Delta F \ = \ \text{change in the futures price, } F, \text{ during a period of time}$$
equal to the life of the hedge

$$\sigma_s \ = \ \text{standard deviation of } \Delta S$$

$$\sigma_F \ = \ \text{standard deviation of } \Delta F$$

$$\rho \ = \ \text{coefficient of correlation between } \Delta S \text{ and } \Delta F$$

$$h \ = \ \text{hedge ratio}$$

The change in the value of the hedger's position during the life of the hedge when the hedger longs the asset and shorts futures is $\Delta S - h \cdot \Delta F$; for a long hedge, it is $h \cdot \Delta F - \Delta S$. In either case, the variance, v, of the change in value of the hedged position is given by:

$$v = \sigma_s^2 + h^2 \cdot \sigma_F^2 - 2h \cdot \rho \, \sigma_s \cdot \sigma_F, \text{ so that } \frac{dv}{dh} = 2h \cdot \sigma_F^2 - 2\rho \cdot \sigma_s \cdot \sigma_F$$

Setting this value to zero and noting that the second derivative of v with respect to h is positive, we obtain the value of h that minimizes the variance:

$$h = \rho \cdot \sigma_s / \sigma_F$$

In other words, the optimal hedge ratio is the product of the coefficient of correlation between ΔS and ΔF and the ratio of the standard deviation of ΔS to the standard deviation of ΔF.

A high correlation coefficient means that the variance of the hedged position will be very small in relation to the original variance. If it is unity, the hedge is perfect, while if it is zero, the hedge is useless. When a company has a choice of futures contracts to hedge a particular exposure, it should take the contract that has the highest correlation with the spot price. Let us consider the following example to elucidate the use of the hedge ratio.

Suppose an airline wishes to hedge a future payment for 1 million gallons of jet fuel in three months using heating oil futures. One heating oil futures contract is on 45,000 gallons. The standard deviation of jet fuel is 0.034 over a 3-month period, that of heating oil futures is 0.042 over a 3-month period, and the correlation coefficient is 0.8. The hedge ratio is $h = (0.8)(0.034)/(0.042) = 0.65$. Since one futures bears on 45,000 gallons, the company should buy $0.65(1,000,000)/(45,000) = 14.4$ contracts, or (rounding to the nearest whole number) 14 contracts.

Another example of the use of the hedge ratio is the following. Suppose the standard deviation of monthly changes in the spot price of live cattle is 1.2 (cents per pound). The standard deviation of monthly changes in the futures price of live cattle for the closest contract is 1.4. The correlation between the futures price changes and the spot price changes is 0.7. It is now October 15. A beef producer is committed to purchasing 200,000 pounds of live cattle on November 15. The producer wants to use the December live cattle futures contracts to hedge risk. Each contract is for the delivery of 40,000 pounds of cattle. What strategy should the beef producer follow? The optimal hedge ratio is $(0.7)(1.2/1.4) = 0.6$. The required long position is $200,000 \times 0.6 = 120,000$ pounds of cattle, or 3 futures contracts.

The expiration date of the hedge is sometimes later than the delivery dates of all the futures contracts used. In this case, the hedger can roll the hedge forward. This involves closing out one futures contract and taking the same position in a futures contract with a later delivery date. Hedges can be rolled forward many times. If this is done, and if, for instance , there are five futures contracts with progressively later delivery dates, then there are five basis risks, or sources of uncertainty.

2. FORWARD RATE AGREEMENTS

Chapter 4 described forward agreements in the form of buying or selling assets. It is also possible to hedge borrowing or lending requirements with forward contracts, since the price of a bond moves inversely with interest rates. Specifically, a more direct form of hedging instrument known as a forward rate agreement (FRA) exists for hedging short term loan costs.

An FRA is an agreement to exchange a fixed-rate payment at a rate k for a London Inter-Bank Offered Rate of payment (LIBOR) on an underlying loan with principal P for the period T to $T + m$. At time T, the FRA's settlement is made in discounted form. The floating rate is normally the LIBOR, which is the rate of interest offered by banks on deposits from other banks in European currency markets (including Euro-dollars). Similar to the prime rate, which is often the reference rate of interest for floating rate loans in the United States, the LIBOR is frequently a reference rate of interest in international markets. A one-month LIBOR is the rate offered on one-month deposits, a three-month LIBOR is the rate offered on three-month deposits, and so on. The use of the LIBOR is based on a discount factor (DF), which is defined as the value at t of \$1 paid at T, or:

$$DF = 1/[1 + i(N/M)] \qquad (1)$$

where

$$N = \text{number of days between interest reset days}$$
$$M = \text{the money market day count convention (360 for LIBOR)}$$
$$i = \text{LIBOR}$$

The difference between paying fixed and receiving floating interest payments at time $T + m$ on a loan of P from time T to time $T + m$ is:

$$P\,(i_{m,T} - k)(N/M) \qquad (2)$$

where

$$i_{m,T} = \text{an } m\text{-month LIBOR at time } T$$
$$N = \text{the number of days between } T \text{ and } T + m \text{ (number of days between interest reset days)}$$
all other symbols are as previously defined

The settlement amount for an FRA is:

$$FRA_T = P(i_{m,T} - k)(N/M)/[1 + i_{m,T}(N/M)] \qquad (3)$$

Note that equation (3) is based on equations (1) and (2).

The payoff on an FRA involves the exchange of LIBOR payments and a fixed-rate payment. A long FRA involves receiving LIBOR and paying a fixed-rate interest, while a short FRA involves paying LIBOR and receiving a fixed-rate interest. No loan principal changes hands with an FRA; however, the interest payments are determined by the size of the notional underlying loan principal, P.

Let us consider the following example to enhance our understanding of FRAs. Suppose that on April 2 (the "dealing" date), a firm buys a 12-month FRA on a 3-month LIBOR. The principal is $6 million, and the rate is fixed at 7 percent. The contract takes effect two days later, on April 4 (the spot date). The contract position is long, indicating that the firm buys the FRA; it will receive LIBOR and pay a fixed rate. Thus, in the example, the notional underlying loan principal is $6 million, and the underlying interest rate index on which payments will be based is the 3-month $LIBOR where $LIBOR indicates the LIBOR applicable to the dollar. The contract has a maturity of 12 months, meaning that the settlement date, T, is 12 months after the spot date. The loan maturity date is 3 months (91 days) after T. The payoff on this FRA is positive if $LIBOR in 12 months after the spot date exceeds 7 percent. Suppose, for example, that the 3-month LIBOR will be 8 percent. With equation (3) we determine the payoff at time T as follows:

Payoff = $6,000,000(0.08 − 0.07)(91/360)DF = $14,866.37

DF in this equation is calculated according to equation (1) as equal to 0.9802.

If, on the other hand, interest rates fall to, for instance, 6 percent, a loss will be incurred on the long FRA. The settlement amount at time T is, in this case:

Payoff = $6,000,000(0.06 − 0.07)(91/360)DF = −$14,940.68

where:

$$DF = 0.9851$$

The following observations can be made:

1. By taking a long position in the FRA, the hedger/borrower guarantees a loan rate of exactly 7 percent on the $6 million loan require-

ment. Firms protect themselves against unexpected movements in
LIBOR rates by using FRAs.

2. The problem with the hedging strategy is that the borrowing cost is
stuck at 7 percent even should the rates fall to 6 percent. In this case,
the firm ends up at a disadvantage compared to competitors who did
not hedge. One solution to this problem is to hedge only a proportion, say 60 percent, of the loan principal.

3. For a firm that trades FRAs, hedging is of the utmost importance, as
after having sold an FRA, the firm is exposed to adverse changes in
the interest rates.

4. The example showed that if the LIBOR goes to 8 percent, a profit of
$14,866.37 will be made on the FRA. Therefore, the borrower needs
to borrow the sum of $6,000,000.00 – $14,866.37, or $5,985,133.63, in
order to obtain a total of $6 million. Interest at 8 percent on this loan
is $5,985,133.63(0.08)(91/360), or $121,032.70. The total repayment
amount at the end of the loan period is, therefore, $6,106,166.33, and
the effective rate of interest is (6,106,166.33 – 6,000,000.00)360/
(6,000,000.00)91, or 6.9 percent.

5. The 12-month forward on the 3-month LIBOR in our example is
referred to in the market as a 12×15 FRA. (Note that $15 = 12 + 3$.)

6. In the case of most currencies, settlement takes place on the same day
as the LIBOR is determined. Thus, $i_{m,T}$ of equation (2) is determined
at time T, and settlement also takes place on that date. However, in
the case of U.S. dollars there is a gap of two business days between
the day on which the LIBOR is determined (the fixing date) and the
settlement date. Thus, $i_{m,T}$ is actually established two business days
before T.

7. If the date when the notional loan starts falls on a Saturday or
Sunday, the next Monday is taken, according to the Modified Business Day convention.

8. The money-market day count convention, M, is 360 when dealing
with the LIBOR related to dollars (as in our example), deutsche
marks, or yen values; however, when dealing with pounds sterling,
M is equal to 365.

If a bank agrees to sell an FRA at a contract rate k, how should it fix
k? Assuming that market participants take advantage of arbitrage opportunities as they occur (see Chapter 4), k has to be fixed at a level that
makes the forward contract a fair, or zero-value, contract. The fixed rate,
k, that achieves this at time t (current time) is the time t forward LIBOR
for m maturity loans, for delivery at $t + T$, which we denote as $f_{m,T}$.
Because the actual derivation of the expression for $f_{m,T}$ is far beyond the
scope of this text, we simply present the formula itself:

$$f_{m,T} = [i_{T+m}(T + m - t) - i_T(T - t)]/[1 + i_T(T - t)/M]N \qquad (4)$$

where:

i_{T+m} = LIBOR for $T + m$ at time t
i_T = LIBOR for T at time t
M = the money-market day-count convention (360)
N = the number of days between T and $t + m$
all other symbols are as previously defined

Suppose, for example, that on May 15, the LIBOR for 6 months is 7.0525 percent and the LIBOR for 3 months is 6.8025 percent. What is the forward rate for a 3×6 month FRA? To elucidate the use of equation (4), we note that the relevant time periods and interest rates in our example are:

t	T	T + m
May 15	August 15	November 17

$\longleftarrow$ 92 days $\longrightarrow$ $\longleftarrow$ 94 days $\longrightarrow$
6.8025%

$\longleftarrow$ 186 days $\longrightarrow$
7.0525%

Thus, the number of days of the forward loan is 94 days from August 15 to November 17 since November 15 and 16 fall on a Saturday and Sunday. With the help of equation (4), we compute the forward rate as follows:

$$f_{m,T} = [7.0525\%(186) - 6.8025\%(92)]/[1 + 6.8025\%(92/360)]94$$
$$= 7.1725\%.$$

This forward rate can now be used to establish the value of the 3×6 month FRA with equation (5), which represents the value of an FRA at time t.

$$\text{Value of FRA}_t = P[(f_{m,T} - k)N/M]DF \qquad (5)$$

where all symbols are as defined above.

Suppose that P = \$6,000,000 and k = 6 percent. With the help of equation (1) we determine:

$$DF = 1/[1 + 7.0525\%(94/360)] = 0.98073.$$

Thus, the value of our FRA is:

$$\$6,000,000[(0.071725 - 0.06)(94/360)]0.98073 = \$18,015.19.$$

Interest rate future markets provide a highly liquid hedge vehicle for FRAs. Using a technique similar to the determination of the optional number of contracts to short when hedging a portfolio (Chapter 4), we determine the number, n, of futures contracts in the hedge portfolio as follows:

$$n = (P/p)(N/M)(360/90)DF \qquad (6)$$

where:

p = the principal value of each contract in the hedge portfolio
all other symbols are as previously defined

For our 3×6 month FRA, we established that $DF = 0.98073$, while P, N, and M were equal to \$6,000,000, 94, and 360, respectively. Considering a value p equal to \$600,000 gives:

$$n = (6,000,000/600,000)(94/360)(360/90)0.98073 = 10.243$$

We note that:

1. Equation (6) assumes that forward and futures prices are the same (Chapter 4).
2. The number of futures contracts, n, in the hedge portfolio is discounted by DF; this is known as tailing the hedge.
3. In our example of the 3×6 month FRA, we used the \$LIBOR. In the case of the £LIBOR, we would have obtained $DF = 1/[1+7.0525\% (94/365)] = 0.98099$ and $n = (6,000,000/600,000)(94/365)(360/90) 0.98099 = 10.106$.

3. MATCHING LIABILITIES WITH ASSETS

In Chapter 4 we discussed how firms can hedge risk by trading in futures. Firms that are subject to interest rate risk can hedge with interest rate futures. Firms can also hedge interest rate risk by matching liabilities with assets.

Many of the financial problems of U.S. savings and loans institutions (S&Ls) of the 1970s could have been avoided had they matched liabilities with assets. S&Ls have often invested large portions of their assets in mortgages, which have long durations. An asset's duration is the weighted average time of its cash flows. Much of the funds available for mortgages were financed by short-term credit, especially savings accounts, which typically have a small duration. An S&L in this situation faced a large interest rate risk because any increase in interest rates would significantly reduce the value of the mortgages. The equity of the S&L would be reduced since an interest rate rise would only reduce the value of liabilities slightly.

The matching of liabilities with assets is also important in other areas of finance. For instance, the manager of a pension fund with obligations to retirees analogous to interest payments on debt, and with assets of the fund invested in fixed-income securities, should choose pension assets so that their duration is matched with the duration of liabilities. In this way, changing interest rates will not affect the value of a pension fund. Another example pertains to insurance firms, which frequently invest in bonds whereby the duration is matched to the duration of future death benefits. Similarly, leasing companies often structure debt financing so that the duration of the debt matches the duration of the leases.

The concept of matching liabilities with assets is based on the market-value balance sheet, which is a useful tool in financial analysis. It has the same form as the balance sheet used by accountants. Thus, assets are placed on the left-hand side and liabilities and owners' equity on the right. In addition, the left- and right-hand sides must be equal. However, the difference in this balance sheet is in the numbers. Financiers value items in terms of the market value, whereas accountants value items in terms of historical cost (original purchase price less depreciation).

Let us consider the following simple example of market-value balance sheets. Company *ABC* anticipates a net cash flow of $10 million (M) per year in perpetuity. There are 10 million shares outstanding; consequently, there is an annual cash flow of $1 per share. The company will soon build a new plant for $5 million; the plant is expected to generate an additional net cash flow of $1 million per year in perpetuity. Assuming that Company *ABC*'s cost of capital is 10 percent, the project's net present value (NPV) is $-\$5M + \$1M/0.1 = \$5M$.

Table 5.1 presents market-value balance sheets of Company *ABC* for the following situations: (1) prior to announcement of the equity issue to construct the plant (part A); (2) on announcement of the equity issue to construct the plant (part B); (3) on issuance of stock but before construction of the plant commences (part C); and (4) on completion of the plant (part D). In part A, the value of the firm is $100M because the annual cash flows of $10M are capitalized at 10 percent. A share of stock

Table 5.1
Market-Value Balance Sheets of Company *ABC*

A. Prior to announcement of equity issue to construct plant.

Balance sheet (all equity)	
Old assets: $10M/0.1 = $100M	Equity: $100M
	(10 million shares of stock)

B. Upon announcement of equity issue to construct plant.

Balance sheet			
Old assets:	$100M	Equity:	$105M
NPV of plant:		(10 million shares of stock)	
−$5M + $1M/0.1 =	5M		
Total assets:	$105M		

C. Upon issuance of stock but before construction starts on plant.

Balance sheet			
Old assets:	$100M	Equity:	$110M
NPV of plant:	5M	(10,476,190 shares of stock)	
Proceeds from new issue of stock (currently invested in bank):	5M		
Total assets:	$110M		

D. Upon completion of plant.

Balance sheet			
Old assets	$100M	Equity:	$110M
NPV of plant:		(10,476,190 shares of stock)	
$1M/0.1 =	10M		
Total assets:	$110M		

sells for $10.00 (or $100M/10M) because there are 10 million shares outstanding.

Suppose that Company *ABC* announces it will raise $5M in equity in the near future in order to build a new plant. The stock price will rise to reflect the positive NPV of the plant. According to efficient capital markets, the increase occurs on the day of the announcement, not on the date of the commencement of construction of the plant or the date of the forthcoming stock offering. An efficient capital market is one in which stock prices fully reflect available information. Part B of Table 5.1 shows the balance sheet of Company *ABC* after the announcement. Note that the plant's NPV is included in the market-value balance sheet and that the number of outstanding shares remains at 10 million because the new shares have not yet been issued. The price per share now rises to $10.50 (or $105M/10M) to reflect the news about the plant.

Shortly after announcement of the equity issue, $5M of stock is floated. Since the stock is selling at $10.50 per share, 476,190 (or $5M/$10.50) shares of stock are issued. The funds are temporarily deposited in a bank before being used to construct the plant. Part C of Table 5.1 presents the market-value balance sheet at this point in time. Note that the number of shares outstanding is now 10,476,190 because 476,190 new shares were issued. Also note that the price per share remains $10.50 (or $110M/10,476,190). The price per share did not change since no new information became available, which is consistent with the operation of efficient capital markets.

Part D of Table 5.1 reflects a situation in which the $5M is given to a contractor to build the plant and the bank account has been emptied to pay the contractor. To keep the example simple, we assume that the plant is constructed instantaneously (to avoid problems in discounting). The building expenditures of $5M have already been paid and therefore do not represent a future cost. Consequently, they no longer reduce the value of the plant. The NPV of cash flows of $1M a year from the new plant are reflected as an asset worth $10M. Note that total assets do not change, but their composition does. In addition, the price per share remains $10.50, which is consistent with the operation of efficient capital markets.

Now that we have mastered the principles of market-value balance sheets, we move on to the concept of matching liabilities with assets. Consider the market-value balance sheet of Bank *XYZ*, as shown in Table 5.2. The bank has $1,500 million in assets and $1,300 million in liabilities. Consequently, its equity is the difference between the two (or $200 million). Table 5.2 shows both the market value and the duration of each individual item of Bank *XYZ*'s balance sheet. Note that overnight money and checking and savings accounts have a duration of zero since interest paid on these instruments adjusts immediately to changing interest rates in the market.

The managers of Bank *XYZ* believe that interest rates are likely to move quickly in the coming month but do not know in which direction. Hence, they are concerned about the bank's vulnerability to changing interest rates. To make the bank immune to the risk of changing interest rates, the following relationship must hold:

$$\text{(duration of assets)(market value of assets)} = \text{(duration of liabilities)(market value of liabilities)} \qquad (7)$$

Thus, we first establish the duration of assets and the duration of liabilities:

$$\text{Duration of assets} = 0(\$40M)/(\$1,500M) + 1/4(\$750M)/ (\$1,500M) + 1/2(\$375M)/(\$1,500M) + 2(\$85M)/(\$1,500M) + 15(\$250M)/(\$1,500M) = 2.86 \text{ years,}$$

$$\text{Duration of liabilities} = 0(\$550M)/(\$1,300M) + 1(\$450M)/ (\$1,300M) + 10(\$300M)/(\$1,300M) = 2.65 \text{ years.}$$

In these calculations we assumed that the duration of a group of items is a weighted average of the duration of the individual items (weighted

Table 5.2
Market-Value Balance Sheet of Bank *XYZ*

Assets	Market value	Duration
Overnight money	$ 40 M	0
Accounts receivable–backed loans	750M	3 months
Inventory loans	375M	6 months
Industrial loans	85M	24 months
Mortgages	250M	180 months
	$1,500M	
Liabilities and Owners' Equity		
Checking and savings accounts	$ 550M	0
Certificates of deposit	450M	12 months
Long-term financing	300M	120 months
Equity	200M	
	$1,500M	

by the market value of each item). This simplification significantly increases the concept's practicality.

In order not to violate equation (7), we must now either decrease the duration of the assets without changing the duration of the liabilities or increase the duration of the liabilities without changing the duration of the assets, as follows. Decrease the duration of assets to:

(duration of liabilities) (market value of liabilities/
market value of assets) = 2.65($1,300M/$1,500M) = 2.30

or increase the duration of liabilities to:

(duration of assets) (market value of assets/
market value of liabilities) = 2.86($1,500M/$1,300M) = 3.30.

In other words, to make the bank immune to the risk of changing interest rates, we can either decrease the duration of the assets from 2.86 years to 2.30 years and keep the duration of liabilities at 2.65 years or increase the duration of liabilities from 2.65 years to 3.30 years and keep the duration of the assets at 2.86 years. In the former case, we get (2.30)($1,500M) = (2.65)($1,300M)—the equality is approximate rather than exact due to rounding—and in the latter case, we have (2.86)($1,500M) = (3.30)($1,300M). Thus, in either case the relationship of equation (7) holds. A decrease in the duration of the assets may be achieved by replacing some of the mortgages of the balance sheet by inventory loans; an increase in the duration of liabilities may be realized by replacing certificate of deposits by long-term financing. If replacements cannot be obtained, the management of Bank XYZ could add short-term loans to assets or long-term financing to liabilities.

Finally, in this example it would be incorrect to simply match the duration of the assets (2.86 years) with that of the liabilities (2.65 years) because the assets total $1,500M while the liabilities total only $1,300M. That is, if, in another problem, the durations of the assets and the liabilities are approximately the same, we cannot conclude that the bank is immune to risk of changing interest rates because the relationship of equation (7) is not likely to hold.

4. HEDGING IN INTEREST RATE FUTURES WHEN ISSUING MORTGAGES

Suppose a mortgage banker, Mr. Smith, promises to deliver mortgage loans to a financial institution before he lines up borrowers. Specifically, on April 1 his firm agrees to turn over 10 percent coupon mortgages with a face value of $1 million (M) to Insurance Company *XYZ*. The 10 percent coupon represents the going interest rate on mortgages at the time. Company *XYZ* is buying the mortgages at par; that is, it will pay Mr. Smith $1M on June 1. As of April 1, Smith had not yet signed up any borrowers; over the next one and a half to two months, he will seek out individuals who want mortgages beginning June 1.

Mr. Smith realizes that changing interest rates will affect him. If interest rates fall before he signs up a borrower, the borrower will demand a premium on a 10 percent coupon loan. That is, the borrower will receive more than par on June 1. The alternative, of the mortgage remaining at par and the coupon rate below 10 percent, is not considered since the insurance company, *XYZ*, only wants to buy 10 percent mortgages. If the borrower receives more than par on June 1, Mr. Smith must make up the difference, since he receives par from the insurance company. However, if interest rates rise, a 10 percent coupon loan will be made at a discount. That is, the borrower will receive less than par on June 1. In this case, the difference will be pure profit to Mr. Smith, who will still receive par from the insurance company.

Mr. Smith does not want to take the risk of having to make up the difference should interest rates fall. He therefore offsets his advance commitment with a transaction in the futures markets. He buys ten June treasury bond futures contracts to reduce the risk since he would lose in the cash market when interest rates fall, in which case the value of his futures contracts would increase. The gain in the futures market offsets the loss in the cash market. Conversely, the value of his futures contracts will decrease when interest rates rise, offsetting his gain in the cash markets. The details of Mr. Smith's transaction are given in Table 5.3. The column on the left is labeled "Cash markets" because the deal in the mortgage is transacted from an exchange.

This hedge is called a long hedge because Mr. Smith offsets risk in the cash market by buying a futures contract. In Chapter 4 we read that individuals and companies institute long hedges when their goods are to be sold at a fixed price. In our example, Mr. Smith buys a futures contract to offset the price fluctuation of his goods, that is, his mortgages.

Let us now consider another mortgage broker, Ms. Jones, whose company faces problems similar to those facing Mr. Smith's company. However, she tackles problems through a strategy that is the opposite of Mr. Smith's. That is, on April 1 she made a commitment to loan a total of $1M to various homeowners on June 1. The loans are 20-year mortgages carrying a 10 percent coupon. Thus, the mortgages are made at par, and the homeowner is buying a forward contract on a mortgage (although he or she is not likely to use this term). Ms. Jones agrees on

Table 5.3
Illustration of Advance Commitment for Mr. Smith, Mortgage Banker

	Cash markets	Futures markets
April 1	Mr. Smith makes a forward contract (advance commitment) to deliver $1M of mortgages to Insurance Company XYZ, which will pay par to Mr. Smith for the loans on June 1. The borrowers will receive their funding from Mr. Smith on June 1. The mortgages are to be 10% coupon loans for 20 years.	Mr. Smith buys ten June Treasury bond futures contracts (10 x $100,000 = $1M).
May 15	Mr. Smith signs up borrowers to 10% coupon, 20-year mortgages. He promises that the borrowers will receive funds on June 1.	Mr. Smith sells all futures contracts.
If interest rates rise:	Mr. Smith issues mortgages to borrowers at a discount. Mr. Smith gains because he receives par from insurance company.	Futures contracts are sold at a price below purchase price, resulting in a loss. Mr. Smith's loss in futures market offsets gain in cash market.
If interest rates fall:	Loans to borrowers are issued at a premium. Mr. Smith loses because he receives only par from insurance company.	Futures contracts are sold at a price above purchase price, resulting in gain. Mr. Smith's gain in futures market offsets loss in cash market.

April 1 to give $1M to her borrowers on June 1 in exchange for principal and interest from them every month for the next 20 years.

Like most mortgage bankers, Ms. Jones does not intend to pay the $1M out of her own pocket. Instead, she intends to sell the mortgages to an insurance company, which will actually loan the funds and receive principal and interest over the next 20 years. On April 1 Ms. Jones does not yet have an insurance company in mind, but she plans to visit the mortgage departments of insurance companies over the next two months to sell the mortgages to one or more of them. She sets May 31 as a deadline for making the sale because the borrowers expect the funds on the following day.

On May 15, Ms. Jones finds Insurance Company *ABC* interested in buying the mortgages; however, *ABC* agrees to pay only $950,000 since interest rates have risen. Since Ms. Jones agreed to loan a full $1M to the borrowers, she must pay the additional $50,000 out of her own pocket. Ms. Jones was aware of this risk, and to hedge it, she wrote ten June treasury bond futures contracts on April 1. As with mortgages, treasury bond futures contracts fall in value when interest rates rise. Because Jones writes the contracts, she makes money if they fall in value. Consequently, with a rise in the interest rate, the loss in the mortgages is offet by the gain in the futures market.

Treasury bond futures contracts rise in value if interest rates fall. Because Ms. Jones wrote the contracts, she would suffer a loss when rates fall. However, she would make a profit on the mortgages should the interest rate decrease. Table 5.4 gives the details of Ms. Jones's transaction. The risk of changing interest rates ends in the cash market, when the loans are sold. Thus, this risk must be terminated in the futures market at that time. Ms. Jones therefore nets out her position in the futures contract as soon as the loan is sold to Insurance Company *ABC*. This strategy is called a short hedge since Ms. Jones sells futures contracts in order to reduce risk (see Table 5.4).

The following observations about hedging in interest rate futures are of interest:

1. In these examples, *ten* treasury bond futures contracts are written because the deliverable instrument on each contract is $100,000 of treasury bonds. The total is $1M, equal to the value of the mortgages.
2. Although risk is clearly reduced via an offsetting transaction in the futures market, it is not likely to be eliminated because mortgages and treasury bonds are not identical instruments. They are not identical since mortgages (a) may have different maturities than treasury bonds, (b) require that a portion of the principal be paid every month, whereas the principal is only paid at maturity with treasury bonds, (c) may be paid off early and therefore have a shorter expected maturity than treasury bonds, and (d) have default risk whereas treasury bonds do not.
3. Since mortgages and treasury bonds are not identical instruments, they are not identically affected by interest rates. If treasury bonds

Table 5.4
Illustration of Hedging Strategy for Ms. Jones, Mortgage Banker

	Cash markets	Futures markets
April 1	Ms. Jones makes forward contract to loan $1M at 10% for 20 years. The loans are to be funded on June 1.	Ms. Jones writes ten June Treasury bond futures contracts (10 × $100,000=$1M).
May 15	Loans are sold to Insurance Company *ABC*. Ms. Jones will receive sales price from *ABC* on the June 1 funding date.	Ms. Jones buys back all the futures contracts.
If interest rates rise:	Loans are sold at a price below $1M. Ms. Jones loses because she receives less than the $1M she must give to the borrowers.	Each futures contract is bought back at a price below the sales price, resulting in a profit. Ms. Jones' profit in futures market offsets loss in cash market.
If interest rates fall:	Loans are sold at a price above $1M. Ms. Jones gains because she receives more than the $1M she must give to borrowers.	Each futures contract is bought back at a price above the sales price, resulting in a loss. Ms. Jones' loss in futures market offsets gain in cash market.

are less volatile than mortgages, Ms. Jones may wish to write more than ten treasury bond futures contracts. In fact, we could determine an optional hedge ratio of futures contracts to mortgages in a manner similar to the example pertaining to an airline wishing to hedge a future payment for 1 million gallons of jet fuel using heating oil futures (Section 1 of this chapter).

4. Mortgage bankers like Ms. Jones and Mr. Smith are interested in selling mortgages since in this way they can get two fees. The first is an origination fee, which is paid to the mortgage banker by the insurance company on the date the loan is sold. This fee often amounts to 1 percent of the value of the loan (in the examples, 1 percent of $1M, or $10,000). The second fee pertains to the mortgage

banker acting as a collection agent for the insurance company. For this service, he or she will receive a small portion of the outstanding balance of the loan each month. For instance, if Mr. Smith (or Ms. Jones) is paid .04 percent of the loan each month, he or she will receive $400 in the first month. Naturally, Mr. Smith (or Ms. Jones) will receive less as the outstanding balance of the loan declines.

5. SWAPS

Swaps are private agreements between two companies to exchange cash flows in the future according to a prearranged formula. Swaps are extensions of forward contracts. The most commonly used swaps are interest rate and currency swaps. The International Bank for Reconstruction and Development (IBRD), also known as the World Bank, entered the first currency swap in 1981, when it attempted to raise the equivalent of $200 million in Swiss francs. By directly raising funds in Switzerland, its funding cost would have been 8.38 percent, but because the World Bank has its headquarters in Washington, D.C., it has a comparative advantage in U.S. markets. Consequently, it issued a dollar-denominated bond and then entered a currency swap agreement to pay francs and receive dollars. As a result, the dollar cost was transformed into a franc cost of 8.10 percent. This derivative contract lowered the annual funding cost by $560,000, a savings that was passed along to the borrowing countries. Since 1981, swaps have saved the World Bank over $900 million. It is, therefore, worth our time to examine how swaps work.

In an interest rate swap, one party, A, agrees to pay the other party, B, cash flows equal to interest at a predetermined floating rate on a notional principal for a number of years (normally 2 to 15). At the same time, party B agrees to pay party A cash flows equal to interest at a fixed rate on the same notional principal for the same period of time. The currencies of the two sets of interest cash flows are the same. The swap has the effect of transforming a fixed-rate loan into a floating-rate loan, or vice versa. The reason why two parties enter into a swap is that one has a comparative advantage in floating-rate markets and the other one has a comparative advantage in fixed-rate markets. Naturally, it makes sense for a party to go to the market where it has a comparative advantage when obtaining a loan. By doing this, however, the party ends up borrowing at a fixed rate when it wants floating rate or vice versa.

In many interest rate swaps, the floating rate is the London Inter-Bank Offered Rate (LIBOR), which is the rate of interest offered by banks on deposits from other banks in Euro-currency markets. Similar to the U.S. prime rate, which is often the reference rate of interest for floating-rate loans in the United States, LIBOR is frequently a reference rate of interest in international markets. To enhance our understanding of how LIBOR is used, consider a loan where the interest rate is specified as the three-month LIBOR plus .5 percent per year. The life of the loan is divided into three-month time periods. For each period, the interest rate is set at .5 percent per annum above the three-month LIBOR rate at the beginning of the period. Interest is paid at the end of the period.

The simplest way of explaining how a swap works is by giving an example. Suppose that two companies, A and B, both want to borrow $15 million for a period of ten years and have been offered the following rates:

	Fixed Rate	Floating Rate
Company A	10.00%	six-month LIBOR + .35%
Company B	11.25%	six-month LIBOR + 1.00%

Assume that A wants to borrow floating funds at a rate linked to the six-month LIBOR, and B wants to borrow at a fixed interest rate. The fixed and floating rates in the table show that B has a lower credit rating than A since it pays a higher interest rate in both markets. Company A appears to have a comparative advantage in fixed-rate markets, while company B appears to have a comparative advantage in floating-rate markets since the extra amount that B pays over the amount paid by A is less in this market than in the fixed-rate markets. The fact that the difference between the two fixed rates is greater than the difference between the two floating rates (B pays 1.25 percent more than A in fixed-rate markets and only .65 percent more than A in floating-rate markets) allows a profitable swap to be negotiated, as follows. Company A borrows fixed-rate funds at 10 percent per annum, and company B borrows floating-rate funds at the LIBOR plus 1 percent per annum. Next, the two firms enter into a swap to ensure that A ends up with floating rate funds and B with fixed rate funds.

Typically, a swap is carried out through the intermediary of a bank. To enhance our understanding of how a swap works, we first assume that A and B get in touch directly. The sort of swap that they might negotiate is as follows:

Company A agrees to pay company B interest at the six-month LIBOR on $15 million, and company B agrees to pay company A interest at a fixed rate of 9.95 percent per year on $15 million. Company A has three sets of interest-rate cash flows: (1) it pays 10.00 percent per annum to outside lenders, (2) it receives 9.95 percent per annum from B, and (3) it pays the LIBOR to B. Cash flows (1) and (2) cost A .05 percent per annum. Thus, the net effect of the three cash flows is that A pays the LIBOR plus .05 percent per annum, or .30 percent per annum less than it would pay if it went directly to the floating-rate markets. Company B also has three sets of cash flows: (1) it pays the LIBOR + 1.00 percent per annum to outside lenders, (2) it receives the LIBOR from A, and (3) it pays 9.95 percent per annum to A. The first two cash flows taken together cost B 1.00 percent per annum. Consequently, the net effect of the three cash flows is that B pays 10.95 percent per annum, or .30 percent per annum less than it would if it went directly to the fixed-rate markets.

From this discussion it is clear that the swap arrangement improves the position of both A and B by .30 percent or 30 basis points (a basis point is .01 percent) per annum. The total gain is, therefore, 60 basis points per annum. The total gain from an interest rate swap is always $x - y$ where x is the difference between the interest rates facing the two parties in fixed-rate markets and y is the difference between the interest rates facing the two parties in floating-rate markets. In our example, $x = 1.25$ percent and $y = .65$ percent.

Let us now consider the financial intermediary or the bank. Thus, the total gain of 60 basis points per annum has to be split three ways: among A, B, and the bank. A possible arrangement is as follows:

Now A has the following three sets of interest rate cash flows: (1) it pays 10 percent per year to outside lenders, (2) it receives 9.90 percent per year from the bank, and (3) it pays the LIBOR to the bank. The net effect of these three cash flows is that A pays the LIBOR plus .10 percent per annum, which is a .25 percent per annum improvement over the rate it could get by going directly to the floating-rate markets. The interest rate cash flows of B are: (1) it pays the LIBOR + 1.00 percent per year to outside lenders, (2) it receives the LIBOR from the bank, and (3) it pays 10.00 percent per year to the bank. The net effect of these three cash flows is that B pays 11.00 percent per year, a .25 percent per year improvement over the rate if it went directly to the fixed-rate markets. The bank's net gain is .10 percent per annum, since the fixed rate it receives is .10 percent higher than the fixed rate it pays, and the floating rate it receives is the same as the floating rate it pays. The total gain to all parties is again 60 basis points.

Let us now examine currency swaps. Such a swap involves exchanging principal and fixed-rate interest payments on a loan in one currency for the principal and fixed-rate interest payments on an approximately equivalent loan in another currency. As in the case of interest rate swaps, currency swaps are done to benefit from comparative advantage. Suppose that companies A and B are offered the following fixed interest rates in U.S. dollars and British pounds sterling:

	Dollars	Pounds Sterling
Company A	7.0%	11.0%
Company B	6.2%	10.6%

Company B is clearly more creditworthy than company A since it is offered a more favorable interest rate in both currencies. Company A wishes to borrow dollars, and company B, pounds sterling. Since A has a comparative advantage in the pound market (the difference between the pound rates is smaller than the difference in the dollar rates), it borrows in the pound rate. For B it is advantageous to borrow in the dollar market. The two firms then use a currency swap to transform A's loan into a dollar loan and B's loan into a pound loan.

There are many ways in which the swap can be arranged. One is as follows:

The swap's effect is to transform the sterling rate of 11.00 percent per year to a dollar rate of 6.85 percent per year for company A. Note that the advantage of the swap to A is 7.00 percent – 6.85 percent = .15 percent per annum, and to B is 10.60 percent – 10.45 percent = .15 percent per annum. The bank gains .65 percent per annum on its dollar cash flows and loses .55 percent per annum on its pound cash flows. Ignoring the difference between the two currencies (for the sake of simplification), the bank comes out ahead with .10 percent per annum. The total gain to all parties is .40 percent per annum, which is equal to the difference between the dollar rates minus the difference between the pound rates.

Assume, for instance, that the principal amounts are 15 million dollars and 10 million pounds. At the beginning of the swap in our example, *A* pays 10 million pounds and receives 15 million dollars. Each year during the life of the swap, *A* receives 11.00 percent of 10 million pounds and pays 6.85 percent of 15 million dollars. At the end of the swap's life, *A* pays a principal of 15 million dollars and receives a principal of 10 million pounds. In our example the bank is exposed to foreign exchange risk. Each year it makes a gain of .65 percent of 15 million dollars, or 97,500 dollars, and a loss of .55 percent of 10 million pounds or 55,000 pounds. The bank can avoid the foreign exchange risk by buying 55,000 pounds per annum in the forward market during each year of the swap's life. By doing so, the bank locks in a net gain in U.S. dollars.

SUGGESTIONS FOR FURTHER READING

Fabozzi, F. J. *Bond Markets, Analysis and Strategies*. Englewood Cliffs, NJ: Prentice-Hall, 1993.

International Swap Dealer's Association. *Code of Standard Working: Assumptions and Provisions for Swaps*. New York: International Swap Dealer's Association, 1986.

Johnson, L. L. "The Theory of Hedging and Speculation in Commodity Futures Markets." *Review of Economics Studies*, 27 (October 1960): 139–51.

Nikkhah, S. "How End Users Can Hedge Fuel Costs in Energy Markets." *Futures*, October 1987, 66–67.

Stulz, R. M. "Optimal Hedging Policies." *Journal of Financial and Quantitative Analysis*, 19 (June 1984): 127–40.

Teweles, R. J., and F. J. Jones. *The Futures Game*. New York: McGraw-Hill, 1987.

CHAPTER 6

Options

Temptation laughs at the fool who takes it seriously.
                                                —Chofetz Chaim

An option is a private contract between two parties whereby one holder has the right to either buy an underlying asset at a fixed price, K, by a certain date, T, or the right to sell the underlying asset at a fixed price, K, by a certain date, T. For instance, an option on a building might give the buyer the right to buy the building for $3 million on or anytime before the Saturday prior to the second Thursday in February 2002. Options are a unique type of financial contract since they give the buyer the right, but not the obligation, to do something. In other words, the buyer uses the option only if it is to his or her advantage; otherwise the option can be discarded.

The option with a right to buy is called a call option, and the option with a right to sell is called a put option. The price in the option is called the exercise or strike price; the date in the contract is referred to as the exercise or expiration date, or maturity. With the use of options, one can reduce the risk of price fluctuations; however, there is a price to be paid for this reduction in risk.

In options, the underlying assets include stocks, stock indices, foreign currencies, debt instruments, commodities, and futures contracts. American options can be exercised at any time up to the expiration date, while European options can only be exercised on the expiration date itself. It is noted that the terms *American* and *European* do not refer to the location of the option or the exchange; some options trading on North American exchanges are European and vice versa.

The value of a call option at expiration date, T, which is referred to as S_T, is not know prior to expiration. If S_T is greater than the exercise price, K, the call is said to be "in the money." If S_T is smaller than K, the call is "out of the money." The circumstances that establish the value of a put option are the opposite of those for a call option because a put option gives the holder the right to sell an asset. If the price, S_T, of the underlying asset at expiration is greater than the exercise price, K, it will not make sense to exercise the option. In other words, the put option is worthless if $S_T > K$; the put option is out of the money. However, if $S_T < K$ the put option is "in the money."

This chapter starts with a description of different types of publicly traded options. Next, the factors that determine their values are identified and analyzed. We then move on to a discussion of how options may be considered as a form of insurance against adverse movements in asset prices. This leads us to interest rate options and, more specifically, interest rate guarantees, caplets, and floorlets. Finally, the importance of looking for hidden options in project finance is discussed.

1. PUBLICLY TRADED OPTIONS

There are four basic positions possible, namely (1) a long position in a call option, (2) a long position in a put option, (3) a short position in a call option, and (4) a short position in a put option. Let us again denote the strike price by K and the final price of the underlying asset by S_T. Consequently, the payoff from a long position in a European call option, not including the initial cost of the option, is:

$$\max[S_T - K, 0] \tag{1}$$

Equation (1) reflects the fact that the option will be exercised if S_T is larger than K and will not be exercised if S_T is equal to or smaller than K. The payoff to the holder of a short position in the European call option is expressed in two forms:

$$-\max[S_T - K, 0] \text{ or}$$
$$\min[K - S_T, 0] \tag{2}$$

The payoff to the holder of a long position in a European put option is:

$$\max[K - S_T, 0] \tag{3}$$

Finally, the payoff from a short position in a European put option is expressed in two ways:

$$-\max[K - S_T, 0] \text{ or}$$
$$\min[S_T - K, 0] \tag{4}$$

To enhance our understanding of equations (1) through (4), we graph them in Figure 6.1. In each of the drawings in this figure, we have two lines, one that partly overlaps with the horizontal axis and corresponds to one of the first four equations (where we ignored the initial cost of the option) and one that starts at the vertical axis at $-p$ or $+p$, where p is the present value of the premium one has to pay when buying or selling an option. This premium reflects the amount of money one is willing to pay in order to hedge a risk.

2. VALUATION OF OPTIONS

Before determining the value of options when bought well before expiration, we establish their worth on the expiration date. Let us

Figure 6.1
Payoff from Forward Contracts

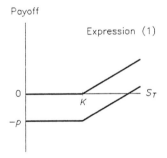

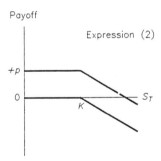

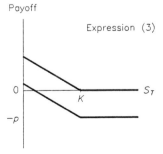

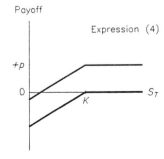

consider an American call option contract on common stock that is in the money prior to expiration. Assume that the stock price is $70 and the exercise price is $60. In this case, the option cannot sell below $10 since this would result in an arbitrage profit (a profit stemming from a transaction that has no risk or cost and cannot occur in normal, well-functioning markets). To see this, we note a simple strategy if the option sells at, for instance, $9 as follows:

Date	Transaction	
Today	(a) Buy call option	−$ 9
Today	(b) Exercise call (buy underlying stock at exercise price)	−$60
Today	(c) Sell stock at current market price	+$70
	Arbitrage profit	+ $1

The excess demand for this call option would quickly force its price up to at least ($70–$60) or $10.

In this example, the option price is likely to be above $10 since investors will rationally pay more than $10 in view of the possibility of the stock rising above $70 prior to expiration. However, the option to buy common stock cannot have a greater value than the common stock itself since it would not make sense to buy stock with a call option that could be purchased directly at a lower price.

From this discussion we conclude that the upper and lower boundaries of call option values are the price of the stock and the difference between this price and the exercise price, respectively. The factors that determine a call's value are expiration date, exercise price, stock price, interest rate, and the variability of the underlying asset.

Other things being equal, the value of an American call option must be at least as great as the value of another American call option with a shorter term to expiration. This must be so since the option with the larger term has the same rights as the one with the shorter term, while the former option has an additional period (the difference between two expiration terms) within which these rights can be exercised. It is noted that this relationship does not necessarily hold for European options. Consider, for example, two otherwise identical European call options, one expiring at the end of the June and the other at the end of September. Assume that a large dividend is paid early in July. If the first call is exercised at the end of June, its holder will receive the underlying stock, and if he or she does not sell the stock, he or she will receive the large dividend shortly thereafter. In contrast, the holder of the second call option will receive the stock through exercise after the dividend has been paid. The value of the second call could be less than the value of the first since the market knows that the holder of the second call will miss the dividend.

It is clear that if all other things are held constant, the higher the exercise price, the lower the value of a call option will be. No matter how high the exercise price, as long as there is some possibility of the price of the underlying asset exceeding the exercise price before the expiration date, the call option has a value. Consequently, the value of a call option cannot be negative.

It should be obvious that if all other things are equal, the higher the stock price, the more valuable the call option will be. In other words, the call price is positively related to the stock price. Although beyond the scope of the present text, it can be demonstrated that the change in the call price for a given change in the stock price is greater when the stock price is high than when it is low. Thus, the relationship is represented by a convex curve rather than a straight line.

The value of a call option is positively related to interest rates since buyers of calls do not pay the exercise price until they exercise the option (if they do so at all). The delayed payment is more valuable when interest rates are high and less valuable when they are low.

All other things being equal, the greater the variability of the underlying asset, the more valuable the call option will be. Suppose, for example, that just before the call expires, the stock price will be either $90 with a probability of .50 or $70 with a probability of .50. In this case, what will the value of a call option with an exercise price of $100 be? It is clear that it is worthless since no matter what happens to the stock, its price will always be below the exercise price. Suppose now that the stock price is more variable; that is, it has a half chance of being worth $110 and a half chance of being worth $50. In this case the call option has value because there is a 50 percent chance that the stock price will be $110, or $10 above the exercise price of $100. This example demonstrates that the fundamental distinction between holding an option on an underlying asset and holding the underlying asset. In the former case, the holder of a call option receives payoffs from the positive tail of the probability distribution, and therefore a rise in the variability in the underlying stock increases the market value of a call. However, a rise in the variability of the stock will decrease its market value if investors in the market are risk averse. Moreover, although we have spread the stock returns in the above example, the expected value of the stock remains the same:

$$(.50)(\$90) + (.50)(\$70) = \$80 = (.50)(\$110) + (.50)(\$50)$$

With a reasoning analogous to that of our discussion of the factors influencing a call's value, we conclude that:

1. the value of an American put with a distant expiration date is greater than an otherwise identical put with an earlier expiration date (this relationship is not necessarily true for a European put);
2. the value of a put with a high exercise price is greater than the value of an otherwise identical put with a low exercise price;
3. the put's value decreases as the stock price increases;
4. a high interest rate adversely affects the value of a put since the ability to sell a stock at a fixed exercise price sometime in the future is worthless if the present value of the exercise price is diminished by a high interest rate; and
5. the volatility of the underlying asset increases the value of a put (at expiration, a put that is far out of the money is worth zero, the same as a put only slightly out of the money; however, at expiration, a put that is far in the money is more valuable than a put only slightly in the money).

It can be shown that if both the call and the put share the same expiration date and the same exercise price, the following relationship—which is called the put-call parity—must hold between the prices at the time we take our original position:

$$\text{value of stock} + \text{value of put} - \text{value of call}$$
$$= \text{present value of exercise price}$$

The following example elucidates this fundamental relationship. Suppose the exercise price of a European call equals the exercise price of a European put, which amounts to $60. The expiration date is one year from now. The current stock price is $49, and the prevailing interest rate is 10 percent. Suppose that the stock will be either $63 or $38 on the expiration date and that we pursue the following offsetting strategy: (1) buy the stock, (2) buy the put, and (3) sell the call. The payoffs at expiration are as follows:

Initial Transaction	Payoffs on the expiration date	
	Stock price rises to $63	Stock price falls to $38
Buy stock	$63	$38
Buy put	$0	$22 = $60 − $38
Sell call	−$3 = −($63 − $60)	$0
Total	$60	$60

Note that if the stock price rises, the call is in the money and the investor will let the put expire; if the stock price falls, the put will be in the money and the call will expire without being exercised. In either case we end up with $60. Thus, combining both strategies, as we did in the example, eliminates all risk.

This example gave us the payoffs at expiration; however, we have ignored the earlier investment. To remedy this, suppose that we originally paid $6.55 for the put and received $1.00 for selling the call. Thus, we have paid:

$$\text{stock purchase (\$49.00)} + \text{purchase of put (\$6.55)} - \text{sale of call (\$1.00)} = \$54.55$$

In other words, the investor pays $54.55 today and is guaranteed $60.00 in one year or he or she will simply earn the interest rate of 10 percent. The prices in our example allow no possibility of arbitrage or a "free lunch." Conversely, if the put sold for only $5.00, the initial investment would be $53.00 and the investor would have a nonequilibrium return of 13.21 percent over the year. Thus, we conclude that in order to avoid arbitrage, the put-call parity must hold:

$$\$49.00 + \$6.55 - \$1.00 = \$54.55 = \$60.00/1.10$$

In the example the call and put options were both European. An American put must sell for more than $60.00 – $49.00, or $11.00, because if the price were, say, only $6.55, one would buy the put, buy the stock, and exercise immediately, which would result in an immediate arbitrage profit of –$6.55 – $49.00 + $60.00, or $4.45.

A Two-State Option Model

Heretofore we discussed in qualitative terms the fact that the values of call and put options are a function of the expiration date, exercise price, stock price, interest rate, and variability of the underlying asset. Let us now move on to an option valuation done in quantitative terms. This is done by using the famous Black-Scholes option-pricing model, which is a rather imposing model (Black and Scholes, 1965). The derivation of this model is beyond the scope of the text; however, some intuitive understanding can be obtained by first introducing a simpler, two-state model as an example to demonstrate that the combination of a call and a stock can eliminate all risk. This is a two-state model because we let the future stock price be one of only two values. We are able to duplicate the call by eliminating the possibility that the stock price can take on values other than the two chosen.

To explain the two-state model, consider the following example. Suppose the market price of a stock is $60 and it will be either $70 or $50 at the end of the year. In addition, we assume the existence of a call option for 100 shares of this stock with a one-year expiration date and a $60 exercise price. The prevailing interest rate at which investors can borrow is 10 percent. We examine two possible trading strategies: (1) buy the call on the stock or (2) buy 50 shares of the stock and borrow a duplicating amount. The duplicating amount is the amount of borrowing necessary to make the future payoff from borrowing and buying the stock just as would be done if making the future payoff from buying a call on the stock. In the example, the duplicating amount of borrowing is $2,500/1.10 = $2,273. Note that with a 10 percent interest rate, principal and interest at the end of the year amount to $2,273(1.10) = $2,500.

At the end of one year, the future payoffs of the two trading strategies are as follows:

Initial	Future payoffs	
transactions	If stock price is $70	If stock price is $50
(1) Buy a call (100 share contract)	100($70 – $60) = $1,000	0
(2) Buy 50 shares of stock.	50($70) = $3,500	50($50) = $2,500
Borrow $2,273	– ($2,273)(1.10) = –$2,500	–$2,500
Total from strategy (2)	$1,000	0

In our example the future payoff of the "buy a call" strategy is duplicated by the strategy of buying a stock and borrowing. These two strategies are equivalent as far as market traders are concerned. Consequently, they must have the same cost. The cost of buying 50 shares of stock while borrowing $2,273 is $727 (buy 50 shares of stock at $60, or $3,000, minus borrow $2,273 at 10 percent). Thus, the call must be priced at $727 since it gives the same return.

The Black-Scholes Model

A duplicating strategy such as discussed here will not work in the real world over a one-year time frame because there are many more than two possibilities for next year's stock price. Naturally, however, the number of possibilities will be reduced as the time period shortens.

In fact, it is plausible to assume that there are only two possibilities for the stock price over the next infinitesimal instant. Black and Scholes demonstrated mathematically that a specific combination of stock purchase and borrowing can indeed duplicate a call over an infinitesimal instant. Because the stock price will change over the first instant, another combination of stock purchase and borrowing is necessary to duplicate the call over the second instant, and so on. By adjusting the combination from moment to moment, the model can continually duplicate the call. This process reflects the basic intuition behind the model.

The Black-Scholes (B-S) model is:

$$C = SN(d_1) - Ke^{-rt}N(d_2) \tag{5}$$

where:

$$
\begin{aligned}
C &= \text{value of a call} \\
d_1 &= [\ln(S/K) + (r + 0.5\sigma^2)t]/\sqrt{\sigma^2 t} \\
d_2 &= d_1 - \sqrt{\sigma^2 t} \\
S &= \text{current stock price} \\
K &= \text{exercise price of call} \\
r &= \text{continuous risk-free rate of return (annualized)} \\
\sigma^2 &= \text{variance (per year) of the continuous return on the} \\
&\quad \text{stock} \\
t &= \text{time (in years) to expiration date} \\
e &= \text{conventional symbol for the number 2.71828 (known} \\
&\quad \text{as the basis of natural logarithms)} \\
\ln &= \text{conventional symbol for a natural logarithm} \\
N(d) &= \text{probability that a standardized, normally distributed,} \\
&\quad \text{random variable will be less than or equal to } d
\end{aligned}
$$

The underlying assumptions of the B-S model are:

1. The option is European.
2. The stock pays no dividends.
3. The stock price is continuous (that is, there are no jumps).
4. The market operates continuously.
5. The stock price is log normally distributed.
6. Transaction costs and taxes are zero.
7. There are no penalties for, or restrictions on, short selling (selling of securities that the seller does not yet have but expects to cover later at a lower price).

These assumptions appear severe; however, when they do not hold, a variation of the model will often work. The formula can, for instance, be fine-tuned to account for dividends. Experience shows that the model does well in computing the value of a call option, particularly when it is fine-tuned.

The attraction of the B-S model is that four of the necessary parameters are observable: S, K, r, and t. Only one of the parameters, σ^2, must be estimated. Another attraction of the model involves the parameters that are not needed. First, the model does not depend on the expected return of the stock since the call depends on the stock price and that price already balances the investors' divergent assessments of the stock's expected return. Second, the investor's risk aversion does not affect the value of a call option. Thus, the model can be used by anyone, regardless of willingness to bear risk.

The use of equation (5) first calls for the insertion of parameters into the basic formulae for d_1 and d_2, which is straightforward. Next, we determine the values $N(d_1)$ and $N(d_2)$. These values can be best explained with the help of Figure 6.2, which shows a normal distribution with an expected value of 0 and a standard deviation of 1. This is often referred to as a standardized normal distribution. The shaded area of Figure 6.2 represents cumulative probability. Because the probability is 61.79 percent that a drawing from the standardized normal distribution will be below .3046, we say that $N(.3046) = .6179$. In other words, the cumulative probabilty of .3046 is .6179. The next paragraph further elucidates this concept.

Figure 6.2
Graph of Cumulative Probability

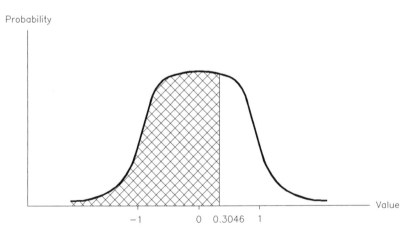

What is the probability that a drawing from a standardized normal distribution will be below 0? Since this distribution is symmetric, the answer is 50 percent. Statisticians say that the cumulative probability of 0 is 50 percent, or $N(0) = 50$ percent. Similarly, $N(.3046) = .6179$ means that there is a 61.79 percent probability that a drawing from the standardized normal distribution will be below 0.3046; or, $N(0.5628) = 0.7123$ means that there is a 71.23 percent probability that a drawing from the standardized normal distribution will be below .5628. More generally, $N(d)$ is the notation that a drawing from the standardized normal distribution will be below d, or $N(d)$ is the cumulative probability of d.

We can establish the cumulative probability from Appendix 4. Consider, for example, that $d = 0.35$. This can be found in the appendix as 0.3 in the first vertical column and 0.05 on the first horizontal row. The value in the table for $d = 0.35$ is 0.1368. To determine the cumulative probability, we make the following adjustment:

$$N(0.35) = 0.50 + 0.1368 = 0.6368$$
$$N(-.35) = 0.50 - 0.1368 = 0.3632$$

Unfortunately, Appendix 4 only handles two significant digits. If, for instance, $d = 0.3542$, we must interpolate to find $N(0.3542)$. Thus $N(0.35) = 0.6368$ and $N(0.36) = 0.6406$. Because $N(0.35) = 0.6368$ and $N(0.36) = 0.6406$, the difference between the values is 0.0038. Since 0.3542 is 42 percent of the way between 0.35 and 0.36, we interpolate as:

$$N(0.3542) = 0.6368 + 0.42(0.0038) = 0.6384$$

With this explanation we can now apply the B-S model to an example. Let us price a European call with the following characteristics:

$$
\begin{aligned}
\text{stock price} &= \$110 \\
\text{strike price} &= \$100 \\
\text{time to expiration} &= 120 \text{ days} \\
\text{stock-price variance} &= 0.20 \\
\text{risk-free interest rate} &= 0.05
\end{aligned}
$$

Thus, $S = \$110$, $K = \$100$, $t = 1/3$, $\sigma^2 = 0.20$, and $r = 0.05$. We first compute:

$$d_1 = \{\ln(\$110/\$100) + [0.05 + (1/2)(0.20)](1/3)\}/[(0.20)(1/3)]^{0.5}$$
$$= 0.5628, \text{ or approximately } 0.56$$
$$d_2 = 0.5628 - [(0.20)(1/3)]^{0.5} = 0.3046, \text{ or approximately } 0.30$$

Consequently:

$$N(d_1) = 0.7123$$
$$N(d_2) = 0.6179$$

Thus:

$$C = [\$110N(d_1)] - \$100e^{-(0.05)(1/3)}N(d_2) = \$110(0.7123)$$
$$- \$100e^{-(0.05)(1/3)}(0.6179) = \$17.58$$

Suppose that today the option call had a closing value of $16.00. In other words, the estimated price of $17.58 is greater than the $16.00 actual price, implying that the call option is underpriced. A trader believing in the B-S model would buy a call. However, the disparity between the model's estimate and the market price may reflect an error in the model's estimate of variance. In the real world, an option trader would know S, K, and t exactly, while U.S. Treasury Bills are normally viewed as riskless, so that r may be obtained from a current quote from, for instance, the *Wall Street Journal*. The problem lies in establishing the variance of the stock's return between the purchase and expiration dates. Unfortunately, this represents the future, so the correct value of the variance is not available. Therefore, traders frequently estimate the variance from past data. In addition, some traders may use intuition to adjust their estimate if, for example, an expected upcoming event currently appears to be increasing the volatility of the stock.

3. INTEREST RATE OPTIONS

Options may be considered a form of insurance against adverse movements in asset prices. For example, if a corporation needs to sell bonds at a future date to raise capital, a put option on a bond gives it the right to sell the bond at a fixed price. The premium one pays for the option is like a premium one has to pay for an insurance policy.

Let us consider the following put option on a bond. A firm buys an option to sell a six-month, zero-coupon bond with a face value of $10,000,000.00 in three months' time at a strike price of $.97; the premium is $25,000.00. The spot date of the contract is June 10, and the maturity is 92 days. Thus, the underlying asset is a bond that will have a maturity of 182 days, 92 days after June 10. The strike price at which the option may be exercised is $.97 per $1.00 of principal.

The payoff of the option depends on the bond's price in 3 months' time. If, for instance, the price falls to $.96, the option will be exercised and a profit is made. Since the option is to sell at $.97, the bonds can be bought for $.96 and sold for $.97, yielding a profit of $.01 per bond. However, if the bond price rises to, say, $.98, the bonds would have to be bought for more than the strike price; consequently the option is not exercised and the payoff is zero. The payoffs for the two cases, excluding the option premium, are as follows:

$$(strike\ price - bond\ price)principal\ amount = gross\ payoff$$

If the price falls:

$$(\$.97 - \$.96)10,000,000.00 = \$100,000.00$$

If the price rises:

$$(\$.97 - \$.98)10,000,000,00 = \$0$$

The option premium is usually paid up front at the date of the contract (June 10). The net profit from the option position should take into account the interest on the premium. Suppose the interest rate is 7 percent. Thus, the interest is $.07(92/365)\$25,000.00 = \$441.10$. This makes the respective profit and loss after paying the premium:

gross payoff – compounded premium = net profit from put option
Case 1: $100,000.00 – $25,441.10 = $74,558.90
Case 2: $0.00 – $25,441.10 = –$25,441.10

For this example, the position of a hedger who needs to sell $10 million of zero coupon bonds and buys the put option in order to provide protection against a fall in the market price is as follows. Before accounting for the premium, the hedger receives:

cash from sales of bonds + gross payoff from put option = sales proceeds
Case 1: $9,600,000.00 + $100,000.00 = $9,700,000.00
Case 2: $9,800,000.00 + $0.00 = $9,800,000.00

In other words, the hedger is guaranteed a sale proceeds of $9,700,000.00; however, if the price rises to more than $.97, the hedger can sell for the market price ($.98) and the proceeds will amount to $9,800,000.00. After paying the premium, the net position for the hedger is as follows:

cash from sales of bonds + net profit from put option = net sales proceeds
Case 1: $9,600,000.00 + $74,558.90 = $9,674,558.90

Case 2: $9,800,000.00 – $25,441.10 = $9,774,558.90

This shows that the hedger guarantees minimum sales proceeds of $9,674,558.90 and more if the market price goes above $.97.

The next example of an interest rate option deals with interest rate guarantees. An interest rate guarantee (IRG) is an agreement to enter a forward rate agreement (FRA) at time T and a fixed rate k. An FRA is an agreement to exchange a fixed-rate payment at a rate k for a LIBOR payment on an underlying loan with a specific principal for the period T to $T + m$. Specifically, the interest rate option in the example is known as a caplet, which is an option to enter a long FRA.

Let us consider a caplet with a maturity of 6 months; the underlying loan has a maturity of 6 months, so the final maturity is in 12 months' time. The underlying loan has a notional principal of $10,000,000. We call this a notional principal, since with an FRA, no loan principal changes hands; however, the interest payments are determined by the size of the underlying principal, P. The option pays the difference between the 6-month $LIBOR and a strike rate of 7 percent discounted to time T. The option premium, which is usually paid up front on the spot date, is 30 basis points, or $(0.30)(0.01)($10,000,000) = $30,000$, since one basis point is equal to .01 percent. Assume that the spot date of the option contract is June 10. Thus, the settlement day is December 10 and the loan maturity date is 12 months from June 10. It is noted that the next business day (Monday) is used if the settlement and loan maturity dates fall on either a Saturday or Sunday. In the example, we assume that this is not the case.

The payoff of the caplet depends on the underlying interest rate in 6 months' time. If it is higher than the strike rate of 7 percent, the option will be exercised and the firm will receive a payoff from the option, but if it is lower than 7 percent, no payoff will be received. Ignoring, for the time being, the premium that has to be paid, the payoffs are:

$$(i – k)P(N/M)(DF) \qquad (6)$$

where:

i = LIBOR
N = number of days between interest reset days (182 in the example)
M = the money market day count convention (360 for $LIBOR)
DF = discount factor = $1/[1 + i(N/M)]$
k and P are as previously defined

Let us determine the payoffs to the firm if $LIBOR turns out to be 5, 6, 7, 8, or 9 percent. There is no need to compute the payoff for 5, 6, or 7 percent, since it is always zero (the option is not exercised). Thus, we compute DF for 8 and 9 percent. For 8 percent, it is:

$$DF = 1/[1 + 0.08(182/360)] = 0.9611$$

For 9 percent, it is:

$$DF = 1/[1 + 0.09(182/360)] = 0.9565$$

Next, we calculate the payoffs with the help of equation (6). For 8 percent, it is:

$$(0.08 - 0.07)(\$10,000,000.00)(182/360)(0.9611) = \$48,588.94$$

For 9 percent, it is:

$$(0.09 - 0.07)(\$10,000,000.00)(182/360)(0.9565) = \$96,712.78$$

In order to compare the premium of $30,000.00 payable on the spot date with the payoffs listed here we need to compound it at the current $LIBOR for 6 months, which we assume to be 7.05 percent for the example. The compounded premium amounts to $30,000.00[1 + 0.0705(182/360)] = $31,069.25. The net profits/losses can now be determined as the difference of the option payoff and the compounded premium. They are as follows.

> 5 percent: –$31,069.25
> 6 percent: –$31,069.25
> 7 percent: –$31,069.25
> 8 percent: $48,588.94 – $31,069.25 = $17,519.69
> 9 percent: $96,712.78 – $31,069.25 = $65,643.53

The net profit/loss made on the caplet changes the amount the borrower has to borrow at time T. For instance, if $LIBOR turns out to be 9 percent, the net profit of $65,643.53 made on the option reduces the required loan to $9,934,356.47. Interest on this loan at 9 percent is $452,013.22, leaving a repayment at the loan maturity date of $10,386,369.69. The effective rate on a $LIBOR basis is then:

$$3.86\%(360/182) = 7.64\%$$

We could also compute the breakeven LIBOR at which a zero net profit is made. To do so, we equate the compounded premium with the payoff, where LIBOR is i percent or:

$$\$31,069.25 = (i - 7\%)(182/360)(\$10,000,000.00) \{1/[1 + i(N/M)]\} \quad (7)$$

From equation (7) we determine that the breakeven rate is $i = 7.6$ percent.

The reader is encouraged to analyze a floorlet in the same manner as done here for a caplet. A floorlet is defined as an option to enter a short FRA.

4. LOOKING FOR HIDDEN OPTIONS

In project evaluation we normally determine a project's net present value (NPV) or internal rate of return (IRR). With the NPV approach, we discount a project's cash flows during its expected life at an appropriate discount rate (cost of capital), which yields the NPV; if the NPV is zero or positive, the project is accepted. The IRR method computes the discount rate (IRR) that makes the project's cash flows during its expected life equal to zero; if the IRR is equal to or greater than the cost of capital, the project is accepted. Both approaches treat risk either through expected values of cash flows or risk loading of the discount rate (Chapter 3).

With the NPV and IRR methods we value a project today, assuming that future decisions will be optional. In most cases we do not yet know what these decisions will be because much information remains to be discovered. The following example shows that if a company is able to delay an investment or operating decisions until the release of additional information, it may be worth doing so. In other words, the company has an option.

Suppose an oil company is considering the purchase of an oil field in Indonesia. The property is listed for $25,000 and initial drilling costs are estimated at $600,000. The company expects that 10,000 barrels of oil can be extracted annually over 20 years. With oil prices at $21.00 per barrel and extraction costs at $16.50 a barrel, the company expects a net margin of $4.50 per barrel. In addition, the company assumes that its cash flow per barrel will remain at $4.50 during the 20 years of extraction, since it budgets capital in real terms. The company's cost of capital is 10 percent. For simplicity we assume that the company has enough tax credits from bad years in the past that it can ignore taxes on any profits from the oil field. Should the company buy the property?

With the NPV method we compute the present value of the investment:

$$-\$25,000.00 - \$600,000.00 + 10,000(\$4.50)(8.5136) = -\$241,888$$

Note that the factor 8.5136 is the present worth factor (pwf) of Appendix 2. Since the NPV is negative, the oil company should not buy the oil field. Although this approach is based on standard capital-budgeting techniques, it is not recommended for this particular situation since for oil prices, the upcoming year is unique. Due to a possible technological breakthrough, in one year cars using strong batteries rather than fuel could be sold on a large scale. If this development proved successful, oil prices would reduce to $10 per barrel in real terms for many years. On the other hand, the Organization of Petroleum Exporting Countries (OPEC) is considering a long-term agreement that would raise oil prices to $35 per barrel in real terms during the next 20 years. Full information on both developments will be released in exactly one year, and each development is judged to have a probability of about 50 percent.

If oil prices fall to $10 per barrel, the NPV of the project will be even more negative than today. However, if they rise to $35 a barrel, the NPV of the oil field would be:

$$-\$25,000.00 - \$600,000.00 + 10,000(\$18.50)(8.5136) = \$950,016.00$$

Thus, this development would result in a significant profit; its expected value is (0.50)$950,016 or $475,008. The company expects to be able to sell the land for $5,000 if oil prices fall to $10, in which case there would be a loss of $20,000.00. The expected value of the loss is (0.50) ($20,000.00), or $10,000.00. Since the expected value of the profit far outweighs the expected value of the loss, the right decision for the company is to (1) purchase the land, and (2) delay the drilling decision until next year, when full information on both developments will be available.

This example demonstrates that it pays to look for hidden options. The price of the land is considered the premium of a call option, while the cost of drilling is the exercise price. The high potential return should oil prices rise to $35 is clearly worth the risk to pay the premium of $25,000. Once the land has been bought, the company has an option to buy an active oil field at an exercise price of $600,000. Generally, one should not exercise a call option immediately. In the example, the company delays exercise until relevant information about future oil prices has been released. Companies will shortchange their projects if the NPV (or IRR) calculations ignore flexibility because such a consideration of options is beneficial.

SUGGESTIONS FOR FURTHER READING

Black, F., and M. Scholes. "The Behavior of Stock Prices." *Journal of Business*, 38 (January 1965): 34–105.

Cox, J., and M. Rubinstein. *Options Markets*. Englewood Cliffs, NJ: Prentice-Hall, 1985.

Geske, R. "The Valuation of Compound Options." *Journal of Financial Economics*, 7 (December 1984): 1511–24.

McMillan, L. G. *Options as a Strategic Investment*. New York: New York Institute of Finance, 1986.

Whaley, R. "On the Valuation of American Call Options on Stocks with Known Dividends." *Journal of Financial Economics*, 9 (June 1981): 209–12.

CHAPTER 7

Warrants and Convertibles

Life is what happens when you are making other plans.
—John Lennon

A warrant gives the holder the right, but not the obligation, to buy shares of common stock at a fixed (exercise) price for a given period of time. Typically, a warrant is issued in a package with privately placed bonds; afterward it becomes detached and is traded separately. A convertible is a financial instrument that gives the holder the right to exchange a bond for common stock. In other words, it is a combination of a straight bond and a call option.

There are many plausible and implausible arguments for issuing bonds with warrants and convertible bonds. One plausible argument for such bonds deals with risk. That is, bonds with warrants and convertible bonds are associated with risky companies. Naturally, lenders can lend less (or not at all) to risky companies, require high yields, or impose restrictions on such debt. When dealing with risky firms, we can, however, also issue bonds with "equity kickers." In this case we protect against risk by giving the lenders the chance to benefit from it and by reducing the conflicts between bondholders and stockholders concerning risk management.

In this chapter we will examine the basic features of warrants and convertibles. The difference between warrants, convertibles, and call options will be analyzed in detail. Next, we will learn how to value warrants and convertible bonds. We then move on to a discussion of the reasons for issuing them. Finally, the reader will get an appreciation of the circumstances under which warrants and convertibles are converted into common stock.

1. WARRANTS

Warrants are securities that give the holder the right, but not the obligation, to buy shares of common stock directly from a firm at a fixed price and during a given period of time. The fixed price and given period of time are referred to as exercise price and exercise period, respectively. A significant proportion of private placement bonds and a smaller proportion of public issues are sold with warrants. In addition, warrants are sometimes given to investment bankers as compensation for underwriting services. They can also be attached to new issues of common or preferred stock, although this seldom happens. Because warrants are usually issued in combination with privately placed bonds, they are frequently referred to as equity kickers.

From our definition of warrants, it is evident that they are similar to call options. A call option is an option to buy an underlying asset such as a stock, a debt instrument, or a stock index. The differences in contractual features between call options traded on the Chicago Board Options Exchange and warrants are small. For instance, warrants have longer maturity periods; in fact, some are perpetual, meaning that they never expire. As we will see in the following section, the effect of a warrant on a company is, however, different from that of a call option.

Like call options, warrants are usually protected against stock splits. That is, they specify that the exercise price and number of shares must be adjusted for stock splits and stock dividends. Suppose, for example, that the share of a company was selling for $150 on the day a warrant was obtained. The warrant gives the holder the right to buy 100 shares of the company at an exercise price of $120 during a given period of time. Suppose also that the next day, the share splits in a proportion of five for one. Each share would drop in price to $30, and the probability that it would rise over $120 in the near future is rather remote. To protect the warrant holder from such an occurrence, warrants are typically adjusted for such splits. In the case of a five-for-one split, the exercise price would become $120/5, or $24. In addition, the warrant contract would now include 500 shares instead of the original 100.

As an example of a warrant, we consider how, in July 1983, MCI Communications raised $1 billion by selling packages of bonds and warrants. The package consisted of one 9.5 percent subordinated note due in 1993 and 18 warrants, each of which gave the right to purchase one share of common stock for $55 at any time before August 1988. At the time of issue, the price of the common stock was $42, or 76 percent of the exercise price. The package was issued at $1,000. The MCI warrants were detachable; that is, they could be traded separately as soon as the issue was distributed. The MCI issue had two special features. First, after 1986 the company had the right to repurchase each warrant for $17 as long as the stock price exceeded $82.50. This is, in fact, a mini-option hidden inside the main option, which empowers MCI to "force" the warrant holders to exercise the warrant. Second, to do so, the holder was given a choice to either pay $55 in cash or hand over bonds with a face value of $55. Thus, if the bond is worth more than $1,000, it is better to use cash; however, if it is worth less than $1,000, it pays to hand over the bond. This is another mini-option hidden inside the main option.

The MCI warrant can be classified as a five-year American option with an exercise price of $55. Similar to the discussion in Section 2 of Chapter 6, we state that the upper and lower boundaries of warrant values are the price of the stock and the difference between this price and the exercise price, respectively. In addition, based on the same arguments as in Chapter 6, we note that the factors that determine a warrant's value are the expiration date, exercise price, stock price, interest rate, and variability of the underlying asset. Specifically, other things being equal:

1. the value of a warrant must be at least as great as the value of another warrant with a shorter term to expiration;
2. the higher the exercise price, the lower the value of a warrant;
3. the higher the stock price, the more valuable the warrant will be;
4. the higher the interest rate, the more valuable the warrant will be; and
5. the greater the variability of the underlying asset, the more valuable the warrant will be.

2. THE DIFFERENCE BETWEEN WARRANTS AND OPTIONS

Warrants are similar to call options from the holder's point of view. That is, a warrant, like a call option, gives the holder the right to buy common stock at a specified price. From the company's point of view, however, warrants are different from call options on the company's common stock. The reason is that warrants are issued by companies, while call options are sold by individuals. Thus, a company must issue new shares of stock when a warrant is exercised, and consequently, the number of shares outstanding will become larger. In contrast, when a call option is exercised, there is no change in the number of shares outstanding.

Let us consider the following simple example in order to analyze how warrants affect the value of a company. Suppose Mr. Smith and Mr. Jones are two investors who bought ten ounces of gold for $4,500; each contributed half the cost, or $2,250. They incorporated, printed two stock certificates (one for each of them), and called the company Gold Company. The gold is the company's only asset. We further assume that Mr. Smith later decides to sell Ms. Adams a call option issued on his share. The call option gives Ms. Adams the right to buy Mr. Smith's share for $2,500 within the next year. Should the price of gold rise above $500 per ounce, the company would be worth more than $5,000 and Smith and Jones's shares each would be worth more than $2,500. If Ms. Adams decides to exercise her option, Mr. Smith must give her his stock certificate and receive $2,500.

How would the company be affected if Ms. Adams exercises her option? In this situation there will still be two shares; however, one share will now be owned by Mr. Jones and the other one by Ms. Adams. If the price of gold rises to $600 an ounce, each share will be worth $3,000 and Ms. Adams will profit by $500.

Now suppose that Mr. Smith does not sell Ms. Adams a call option. Instead, he and Mr. Jones decide that the Gold Company will issue a warrant and sell it to Ms. Adams. The warrant will give her the right to receive a share of the company at an exercise price of $2,500. If Ms. Adams decides to exercise the warrant, the company will issue another stock certificate and give it to her in exchange for $2,500. From Ms. Adams's point of view, the call option and the warrant seem the same since their exercise prices are identical ($2.500). In addition, it is still to Ms. Adams's benefit to exercise the warrant if the price of gold exceeds $500 per ounce. However, due to dilution, Ms. Adams makes less in the warrant situation than in the call option situation.

Suppose that the price of gold rises to $600 an ounce and Ms. Adams exercises her warrant. Thus, Ms. Adams will pay the company $2,500, and the company will print a stock certificate for her. The certificate represents a one-third claim on the company's gold. The value of the company increases since Ms. Adams contributed $2,500 to it. The new value of the firm is equal to the value of gold plus Ms. Adams's contribution, or $6,000 + $2,500 = $8,500. Since Ms. Adams has a one-third claim on the company's value, her share is worth $2,833.33, and her gain is $2,833.33 − $2,500 = $333.33 which is less than the $500 profit she made in the call option situation. The reason for this lower profit is dilution or the creation of another share. In the call option case, Ms. Adams contributes $2,500 and receives one of the two outstanding shares. That is, she receives a share worth $3,000 and her gain is $3,000 − $2,500 = $500.

In summary, Ms. Adams's gain is:

With exercise of the call option: $6,000/2 − $2,500 = $500
With exercise of the warrant: ($6,000 + $2,500)/(2 + 1) − $2,500 = $333.33

Warrants and convertible bonds cause (1) the number of shares to increase and (2) the company's net income to be spread over a larger number of shares, thereby decreasing the earnings per share.

A company can hurt warrant holders through its actions. For instance, Smith and Jones could hurt Adams by paying themselves a large dividend funded by the sale of a substantial amount of gold. The value of the company would decrease and the warrant would now be worth much less.

3. VALUATION OF WARRANTS

Based on the previous example, we now move on to express the gains from exercising a call and a warrant in more general terms. The gain on a call is given by equation (1).

$$\text{Gain from exercising a single call} = \\ (\text{firm's value net of debt})/n - \text{exercise price} \quad (1)$$

where:

$$n = \text{the number of shares outstanding}$$

The firm's value net of debt is defined as the total firm value less the value of debt. Note that the ratio following the equals sign in equation (1) represents the value of a share of stock.

The gain on a warrant can be written as:

$$\text{Gain from exercising a single warrant} = (\text{firm's value net of debt} \\ + \text{exercise price} \times m)/(n + m) - \text{exercise price} \quad (2)$$

where:

$$n = \text{as previously defined} \\ m = \text{the number of warrants outstanding}$$

The ratio after the equals sign in equation (2) represents the value of a share of stock after the warrants have been exercised. The numerator of the ratio is the firm's value net of debt after the warrants' exercise. It is the sum of the firm's value net of debt before the warrants' exercise plus the proceeds the firm gets from the exercise. Our discussion uses the plausible assumption that all warrants that are in the money will be exercised. The denominator, $(n + m)$, is the number of shares outstanding after the warrants' exercise.

Note that equation (2) can also be expressed in two other ways:

(Firm's value net of debt)$/(n + m)$ – (exercise price $\times\ n)/(n + m)$

or

$$[n/(n + m)][(\text{firm's value net of debt})/n - \text{exercise price}] \qquad (3)$$

Equation (3) relates the gain on a call to the gain on a warrant. The term between the second square brackets is equation (1). Consequently, the gain from exercising a warrant is a proportion of the gain from exercising a call in the firm without warrants. The proportion is $n/(n + m)$, or the ratio of the number of shares in the firm without warrants to the number of shares after all the warrants have been exercised. It should be clear that this ratio is always less than 1 and that the gain on a warrant is always less than the gain on an identical call in a firm without warrants.

Chapter 6 discussed the manner in which we can determine the value of a call option with the Black-Scholes model. We can use this model to value a warrant by first calculating the value of an identical call. Next, we establish the value of the warrant by multiplying the call price by $n/(n + m)$.

4. CONVERTIBLE BONDS

A convertible bond gives the holder the right to exchange it for a given number of shares of stock anytime up to, and including, the maturity date of the bond. Thus, a convertible bond is similar to a bond with warrants. However, a bond with warrants can be separated into distinct securities, while a convertible bond cannot. The difference between a convertible preferred stock and a convertible bond is that the former has a infinite maturity date while the latter has a finite one.

The example of a warrant in Section 1 related to MCI Communications. In 1983 MCI issued not only warrants, but also $400 million of 7 3/4 percent convertible bonds due in 2003. In fact, the MCI issue consisted of a convertible subordinated debenture (unsecured bond). That is, there are no specific assets reserved to pay off the holders in the event of default. The term *subordinated* implies that the bond is a junior debt; in the event of default, its holders will be at the end of the line of creditors.

The 7 3/4 percent convertible bonds could be converted into 19.18 shares of common stock at any time. Thus, the owner of such a bond had a 20-year option to return it to MCI and receive 19.18 shares of MCI stock in exchange. The number of shares received for each bond is called the conversion ratio. In the case of the MCI bond, the ratio was 19.18. In order to receive 19.18 shares of MCI stock, one has to surrender bonds with a face value of $1,000. Thus, in order to receive one share, you have to surrender a face amount of $1,000/19.18, or $52.14. This amount is called the conversion price. In other words, any person who bought the bond for $1,000 in order to convert it into 19.18 shares paid the equivalent of $52.14 per share. At the time of issue, the price of MCI stock was $44. Therefore, the conversion price was 18.50 percent higher than the stock price. This percentage is referred to as the conversion premium. It reflects the fact that the conversion option in MCI convertible bonds was out of the money, which is typical.

Convertibles are usually issued at their face value, or 100 percent of par. The underlying bond of a convertible is worth less than 100 percent because a convertible consists of a bond plus an option and the option has a value. For most convertibles, the value of the bond that must be surrendered (the exercise price of the option) increases over time since the value of the bond can be expected to increase over the period between issue and maturity. Normally, convertibles are protected against stock splits or dividends. When MCI split its stock two for one, the conversion ratio was increased from 19.18 to 38.37 and the conversion price fell to $1,000/38.37, or $26.06.

The MCI issue of a convertible is fairly typical. Variations of this issue include situations where the conversion price steps either up or down over time. In addition, companies have issued convertibles that can be exchanged for other bonds. So-called flip-flop bonds give the investor the option to change back and forth a number of times.

Conversion ratio, conversion price, and conversion premium are terms often used in the financial world. It should be noted that conversion price and conversion premium implicitly assume that the convertible bond is selling at par. If the bond is selling at another price, the terms have little meaning. The conversion ratio, however, has a meaningful interpretation regardless of the price of the bond.

5. VALUATION OF CONVERTIBLE BONDS

The price of a convertible bond depends on its bond value, conversion value, and option value. The bond value is what the bond would sell for if it could not be converted. The conversion value is what the bond would sell for if it had to be converted immediately. The value of a convertible bond usually exceeds both the bond and the conversion values since holders of convertible bonds need not convert immediately. By waiting, they can take advantage of whichever value is greater in the future, the bond value or the conversion value. This option to wait has value, and therefore, the value of the convertible is normally higher than the bond value and higher than the conversion value. We will now discuss the three components that determine the value of a convertible bond.

Bond Value

The bond value depends on the general level of interest rates and the default risk. Let us discuss how to determine the bond value of the MCI convertible bonds. Suppose we do this at a time when similar nonconvertible issues are yielding 12 percent and that the MCI convertible has a remaining maturity of 20 years. In this situation, the bond value is obtained by discounting the $77.5 coupon (7 3/4 percent of $1,000) and the final $1,000 principal repayment at 12 percent:

$$\text{Bond value} = 7.4694(\$77.5) + 0.1037(\$1,000) = \$682.58$$

The discount factors of 7.4694 and 0.1037 are the pwf and single payment present worth factor (sppwf) of Appendix 2.

The bond value of a convertible bond is a minimum value. That is, the price of MCI's convertible could not have gone lower than the bond value. The bond value portion of a convertible depends on the market's assessment of default risk. Bond value increases if a company performs well. On the other hand, it falls if the company does not. In the worst case, when the company is worthless, its bonds also become worthless.

Conversion Value

Conversion value is what the value of the bond would be if holders converted immediately. It is usually established by multiplying the stock price by the number of shares into which each bond can be converted. After the two-for-one split, the MCI bond can be converted into 38.37 shares. Thus, if the stock price is $20, the conversion value is 38.37 × $20 = $767.40. The conversion value increases along with the value of a firm.

A convertible bond can never sell for less than its conversion value because if it did, investors could buy the convertible, exchange it for stock, and sell the stock. Their profit would be equal to the difference between the conversion value and the price of the convertible.

When a company does well, the conversion value exceeds the bond value; the investor would choose to convert if forced to make an immediate decision. Hence, the convertible's value should be at least equal to its conversion value. On the other hand, the bond value will exceed the conversion value if the company does poorly. The holders of the convertible would hold on to their bonds if forced to make an immediate choice either for or against conversion. In this case, the bond value is the effective lower bound.

Option Value

From the discussion of bond and conversion values we can conclude that the value of a convertible bond must be at least the greater of the bond value and the conversion value. Normally, the value of a convertible is higher than the greater of these two values since the holders of a convertible have the option to wait and see whether the bond value or the conversion value will be greater in the future. Naturally, such an option must have a value. Thus, the value of a convertible bond equals the greater of the bond value or conversion value, to which is added the option value.

Let us consider the following simple example in order to examine the circumstances that will make it advantageous to holders of convertible bonds to convert to common stock. Suppose that Company XYZ has outstanding 2,000 shares of common stock and 200 bonds and that each bond has a face value of $1,000 at maturity. The bonds are discount bonds and pay no coupons. Further suppose that at maturity, each bond can be converted into 10 shares of newly issued common stock. The holders of the convertible bonds will receive $200 \times 10 = 2,000$ shares of common stock if they convert to common stock. The total number of outstanding shares becomes these 2,000 shares plus the 2,000 originally outstanding shares, or 4,000 shares. If we denote the value of Company XYZ by V, we can note that the converting bondholders own 50 percent of V.

If the holders of the convertible bonds do not convert, they will receive $200 \times \$1,000 = \$200,000$, or V, whichever is less. They will receive V if Company XYZ is unable to pay the debt and they can legally claim the assets of the firm. This action may result in liquidation and bankruptcy. To state that they will receive V if V is less than $200,000 is a simplification. In most cases they would receive less than V since there would be legal fees involved in the liquidation and bankruptcy.

The choice for the holders of the convertible bonds of Company XYZ is obvious: they should convert if 50 percent of V is greater than $200,000. It is clear that this will be true whenever V is greater than $400,000. The payoff to the convertible bondholders and stockholders is as follows.

If V is smaller than or equal to $200,000, bondholders do not convert and receive V, while stockholders receive nothing.

If V is greater than \$200,000 and smaller than or equal to \$400,000, bondholders will not convert and receive \$200,000, and the stockholders' equity will equal $V - \$200,000$.

If V is greater than \$400,000, the bondholders will convert and own 50 percent of V and the stockholders will own the remaining 50 percent.

4. REASONS FOR ISSUING WARRANTS AND CONVERTIBLES

Various studies have shown that companies that issue warrants and/or convertible bonds have one or more of the following characteristics.

1. They tend to have high growth rates and better-than-average financial leverage.
2. Their bond ratings are lower than those of other firms.
3. Convertibles are usually subordinated and unsecured.

In short, companies that issue warrants and/or convertibles are normally riskier than companies that do not use these instruments, which generally serve as a way to attract capital for firms that are considered riskier than average.

A firm may prefer convertible debt because this debt pays a lower interest rate than (the otherwise-identical) straight debt. For instance, if the interest rate is 9 percent on straight debt, the rate on convertible debt may be 8 percent. Investors accept the lower interest rate in view of the potential gain from conversion.

Although the interest rate of convertible debt is lower than that of straight debt, a company issuing convertible debt does not necessarily benefit from this. If the company's stock price later rises so that conversion is indicated, the company will be obligated to sell the convertible holders a chunk of the equity at a below-market price. This loss may be much higher than the benefit related to the lower interest rate. Naturally, if the company's stock price later falls or does not rise enough to justify conversion, the company will be glad it issued convertibles. In short, the company is worse off having issued convertible debt if the underlying stock subsequently does well; it is better off if the underlying stock subsequently does poorly. Since it is difficult to predict future stock prices, it is difficult to argue whether issuing convertible debt is preferred to straight debt.

Let us now compare convertible debt with common stock. Suppose a company issues convertible debt and subsequently does poorly. In this situation, the convertible bonds provided an expensive type of financing because the company could instead have issued common stock at high prices. If, however, the company subsequently prospers, the convertible bonds will have provided an inexpensive financing. Again, since it is difficult to predict future stock prices in an efficient market, we cannot argue either for or against common stock or convertibles.

We may conclude that convertible bonds may be neither less nor more expensive than other instruments. A convertible bond is a package of straight debt and an option to buy common stock. The difference between the market value of a convertible bond and the value of a straight bond is the price investors pay for the call option feature. This is a fair price in an efficient capital market (see Section 3 of Chapter 5 for a discussion of an efficient capital market). Generally, if a company prospers, issuing convertible bonds will turn out to be less beneficial than issuing straight bonds and more beneficial than issuing common stock. In contrast, if a firm does poorly, issuing convertible bonds will turn out to be better than issuing straight bonds and worse than issuing common stock.

In sum, the relatively low coupon rate on convertible bonds may be a convenience for rapidly growing companies facing heavy capital expenditures. These companies may be willing to provide the conversion option and run the risk of losing a chunk of equity in the future in order to reduce immediate cash requirements for debt service. Without the conversion option, lenders may require high interest rates to compensate for the probability of default. This would force the company to raise still more capital for debt service, which could lead to financial distress and, eventually, to the possibility of bankruptcy. Paradoxically, lenders that protect themselves against default by increasing interest rates may actually increase the probability of financial distress.

Another argument for using convertible bonds and bonds with warrants is in cases where it is difficult to assess the risk of the issuing company. Consider, for instance, a small company with an untried product line that wishes to issue some junior unsecured debt. All a potential lender knows is that if things go well, he or she will get his or her money back; however, if things go wrong, the potential lender may end up with nothing. In other words, since the company is in a new line of business, it is difficult to assess the chances of success or failure. Consequently, we do not know what the fair rate of interest should be. The potential lender may also be worried about the possibility that once the loan has been made, the management of the small company will be tempted to run extra risks. It may borrow additional senior debt or decide to expand its operations—and go bankrupt in the process. This could even be encouraged if a rather high interest rate is demanded.

What can the management of the small company do to protect potential lenders against a faulty estimate of the risk and to assure them that its intentions are good? It can give them a piece of the action by issuing convertibles. Lenders often do not mind a company running unanticipated risks as long as they share in potential gains as well as losses.

Finally, companies are often granted a call option on a bond. Typically, when the bond is called, its holder has about 30 days to choose between (1) converting the bond to common stock at the conversion ratio and (2) surrendering the bond and receiving the call price in cash. It is clear that if the conversion value of the bond is greater than the call price, bondholders would do well to convert rather than to surrender. If, however, the conversion value is less than the call price, surrender is better than conversion. If the conversion value is greater than the call price, the call is said to force conversion.

Normally, bondholders would like the stockholders to call the bonds in cases where the bond's value is below the call price since the shareholders would thus give the bondholders extra value. Alternatively, bondholders would like the stockholders not to call the bonds if the value of the bonds rises above the call price since they would thus be entitled to hold onto a valuable asset. Financial managers of companies with a call option on a bond should, therefore, do whatever bondholders do not want them to do. The policy that maximizes shareholders' value and minimizes bondholders' value is to call the bond when its value is equal to the call price.

SUGGESTIONS FOR FURTHER READING

Black, F., and M. Scholes. "The Pricing of Options and Corporate Liabilities." *Journal of Political Economy*, 81 (May–June 1973): 637–54.

Ingersoll, J. E. "A Contingent-Claims Valuation of Convertible Securities." *Journal of Financial Economics*, 4 (May 1977a): 289–322.

————"An Examination of Corporate Call Options on Convertible Securities." *Journal of Finance*, 32 (May 1977b): 463–78.

Merton, R. "On the Pricing of Corporate Debt: The Risk Structure of Interest Rates." *Journal of Finance*, 29 (May 1974): 449–70.

Modigliani, F., and M. Miller. "The Cost of Capital, Corporation Finance and the Theory of Investment." *American Economic Review*, 48 (June 1958): 261–97.

Schwartz, E. S. "The Valuation of Warrants: Implementing a New Approach." *Journal of Financial Economics*, 4 (January 1977): 79–93.

CHAPTER 8

The Relationship between
Risk and Return

Wisdom is ofttimes nearer when we stoop than when we soar.
—William Wordsworth

This chapter starts with a discussion of the use of expected values and standard deviations of individual stocks. In this context the concepts introduced in Chapter 3 are particularly useful. Next, the difference between the standard deviation of an individual stock and the standard deviation of a portfolio is examined. The standard deviation of an individual stock is not a good measure of how the standard deviation of a portfolio changes when an individual stock is added to it. Therefore, the standard deviation of an individual security is not a good measure of its risk for a diversified portfolio.

With diversification, individual risky stocks can be combined so that a combination of individual stocks (i.e., the portfolio) is almost always less risky than any of the individual securities. Thus, diversification is effective at reducing risk. Consequently, we are interested in the impact of an individual standard deviation on the risk of a portfolio rather than measuring the risk of an individual security. More precisely, in the case of a portfolio, the risk of an individual security is related to how the risk of the portfolio changes when the security is added to it.

The standard deviation of a portfolio drops as more securities are added; however, it does not drop to zero due to the nondiversifiable risk related to market fluctuations. In addition, the variance of the return on a portfolio with many securities is more dependent on the covariances between individual securities than on the variances of the individual stocks.

The capital asset–pricing model (CAPM) demonstrates that the risk of an individual security is well represented by its beta coefficient. In statistical terms, the beta gives us the tendency of an individual stock to vary with the market, as reflected in the Standard & Poor's Corporate Index. A stock with a beta of 1 tends to move up and down in the same percentage as the market, while a stock with a beta higher than 1 will tend to move up and down more than the market. We will demonstrate how to determine the beta.

After a discussion of CAPM, the concept of an efficient portfolio is introduced. An efficient portfolio implies that each of its investments must work equally hard so that if one security has a greater marginal effect on the portfolio's risk than another, it must also have a proportionately greater expected return.

An alternative to the CAPM is the arbitrage-pricing model. Whether the latter model will provide a better handle on risk and return than CAPM depends on whether a number of practical problems can be resolved in the future. Until this can be done, CAPM is likely to remain the dominant theory of risk and return.

It is advisable to establish specific rates of return requirements for different types of investments. Thus, each project should be compared to a financial asset of comparable risk. Unless a company is considering projects with the same risk, to choose the same discount rate for all projects is incorrect.

Finally, we discuss financial leverage, the cyclical nature of revenues, and operating leverage. The relationship between each of these concepts and the beta coefficient gives additional insight into the nature of risk.

1. INDIVIDUAL SECURITIES

Let us consider the following two examples to illustrate the riskiness of financial assets. First, suppose an investor buys $100,000 of short-term government bonds with an expected return of 10 percent. The rate of return of this investment can be estimated rather precisely: it is defined as being risk free, and the investment decision is referred to as a decision under certainty. Next, suppose the investor buys a $100,000 stock of a recently organized firm with the sole purpose of prospecting for oil in the North Sea. In this case, the investor's return cannot be estimated precisely. After having analyzed the investment, one might conclude that in a statistical sense, the expected rate of return is 30 percent, but the actual rate of return could range from, for instance,

+500 percent to –100 percent. The stock is a relatively risky one because there is a danger of actually earning less than the expected return. Thus, investment risk relates to the probability of this danger. The greater the chance of low or negative returns, the riskier the investment. This brings us to the concept of probability.

Probability is defined as the chance that an event will occur. To illustrate the probability of an event, we consider the example of Table 8.1. Columns 1 and 2 of the table recognize three states of the economy: boom, normal, and recession, with related probabilities of 0.3, 0.4, and 0.3, respectively. Since these states are the only ones considered, their probabilities must add up to 1.0. Columns 3 and 4 show the possible rates of return (dividend yield plus capital gain or loss) that one might earn in the next year on $100,000 in the stock of either company A or company B. Company A produces computer equipment for a rapidly growing data transmission industry with profits rising and falling with the business cycle and an extremely competitive market. Company B is an utility company with city franchises that protect it from competition. Its sales and profits are, therefore, relatively stable and predictable. The table shows that there is a 30 percent chance of an economic boom, in which case both companies will have high earnings and pay high dividends and/or capital gains. There is a 40 percent chance of a normal economy and moderate returns and a 30 percent probability of a recession, in which case both companies will have low earnings and dividends as well as capital losses. The riskier a stock or the higher the

Table 8.1
Probability Distributions of Two Companies, A and B

State of Economy	Prob. of State	ROR[1]		Product	
		A	B	A (2) x (3)	B (2) x (4)
(1)	(2)	(3)	(4)	(5)	(6)
Boom	0.3	90%	30%	27%	9%
Normal	0.4	15	15	6	6
Recession	0.3	(60)	0	(18)	0
	____ +			____ +	____ +
	1.0			$\hat{k} = 15\%$	$\hat{k} = 15\%$

[1]ROR = rate of return if state in Column (1) occurs.

probability that a firm will fail to pay expected dividends, the higher the expected return must be to induce one to invest.

Columns 5 and 6 of Table 8.1 present the result of multiplying each possible outcome by its probability of occurrence. The sum of these products represent the weighted average of outcome, where the weights are the probabilities and the weighted average is the expected rate of return, $\hat{k}$, called "k-hat."

Equation (1) represents the definition of the expected rate of return, or $\hat{k}$:

$$\hat{k} = P_1 k_1 + P_2 k_2 + \ldots + P_n k_n = \sum_{i=1}^{n} P_i k_i \qquad (1)$$

where

P_i = the probability of the ith outcome
k_i = the ith possible outcome

Using the data in Table 8.1, we calculate $\hat{k}$ as follows:

Company A: $\hat{k} = P_1(k_1) + P_2(k_2) + P_3(k_3) = 0.3(90\%) + 0.4(15\%)$
$+ 0.3(-60\%) = 15\%$

Company B: $\hat{k} = 0.3(30\%) + 0.4(15\%) + 0.3(0\%) + 15\%$

So far we have assumed that only three states of the economy can occur (boom, normal, or recession). Naturally, we could assume that the state of the economy ranges from a fantastic boom to a deep depression, with various possibilities in between (e.g., moderate boom, small boom, slight recession, recession, depression). If we were to consider an unlimited number of possibilities between a fantastic boom and a deep recession, the discrete probability distribution of column 2 of Table 8.1 would become a continuous probability distribution with the sum of the probabilities still equaling 1.0. In that case, the probability of obtaining exactly a rate of return of 15 percent for the normal state of economy with companies A and B would be much smaller than 40 percent since there are now many possible outcomes instead of just three. In fact, as covered in detail in statistics courses, when dealing with continuous probability distributions, it is more appropriate to ask what the probability is of obtaining at least some specified rate of return than to ask what the probability is of obtaining exactly that rate. Consequently, we introduce the probability density, which indicates the probability of obtaining at least some specified rate of return.

Figure 8.1 shows the continuous probability distributions of the rates of return of companies *A* and *B*. In this figure we have changed the assumptions so that there is essentially a zero probability that the return of company *A* will be more than 90 percent or less than -60 percent, or that the return of company *B* will be more than 30 percent or less than 0 percent; however, virtually any return within these limits is possible.

Figure 8.1 shows that the tighter the probability distribution, the more likely it is that the actual outcome will be close to the expected value, and therefore, the less likely it is that the actual return will be far below the expected return. In other words, the tighter (or more peaked) the probability distribution, the lower the risk assigned to a stock. Because company *B* has a relatively tight probability distribution, its actual return is likely to be closer to its 15 percent expected return than is that of company *A*.

To measure risk we need a measure of the tightness of the probability distribution. One such measure is the standard deviation, the symbol for which is σ (sigma). The smaller the σ, the tighter the probability distribution, and, consequently, the smaller the risk of a given investment. To calculate σ, we first compute the variance, σ^2, which is defined as:

Figure 8.1 Continuous Probability Distributions of Rates of Return of Companies *A* and *B*

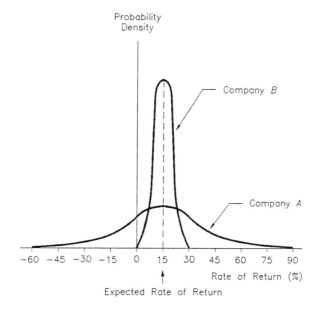

$$\text{Variance} = \sigma^2 = \sum_{i=1}^{n} (k_i - \hat{k})^2 P_i$$

(2)

where the symbols are as defined previously. Taking the square root of the variance gives the standard deviation. Table 8.2 shows the computations used to arrive at the σ of company A in Table 8.1. Using the same procedure, we find the σ of company B to be 11.62 percent. Since company A has a larger σ, it is the riskier stock according to this measure of risk.

One type of continuous probability distribution, which emerges commonly enough, is a symmetrical distribution that is bell-shaped and shows some tendency to have a few cases at some distance from the mean in each direction; that is, the frequencies do not stop abruptly. We call this the normal type. Other types are unsymmetrical; rarely, a J-shaped or U-shaped distribution occurs. Figure 8.2 shows the probability ranges for a normal distribution. We can now make the following specific observations about this figure:

1. The area under a normal curve equals 100 percent.
2. Half of the area under a normal curve is to the left of the mean, $\hat{k}$, indicating that there is a 50 percent probability that the actual outcome will be less than the mean, and half is to the right of $\hat{k}$, indicating a 50 percent probability that it will be greater than the mean.
3. Of the area under the curve, 68.26 percent is within $\pm 1\sigma$ of the mean, indicating that the probability is 68.26 percent that the actual outcome will be within the range of either $\hat{k} - 1\sigma$ or $\hat{k} + 1\sigma$. Figure 8.2 illustrates this point and shows the situation for $\pm 2\sigma$ and $\pm 3\sigma$.

Table 8.2
Calculating Company A's Standard Deviation

$k_i - \hat{k}$	$(k_i - \hat{k})^2$	$(k_i - \hat{k})^2 P_i$
$90 - 15 = 75$	5,625	1,687.5
$15 - 15 = 0$	0	0.0
$-60 - 15 = -75$	5,625	1,687.5
		$\sigma^2 = 3{,}375.0$
		$\sigma = \sqrt{\sigma^2} = 58.09\%$

Note: The variance is 3,375.0 if the standard deviation is expressed as a percentage. If we write $\sigma = 0.5809$, the variance is 0.3375.

4. For a normal distribution, the larger the value of σ, the greater the probability that the actual outcome will vary widely from the expected outcome.

We saw that for company A, $\hat{k}$ = 15.00 percent and σ = 58.09 percent. Thus, there is a 68.26 percent probability that the actual return for company A will be in the range of 15.00 ± 58.09 percent, or from −43.09 to 73.09 percent. For company B, the 68.26 percent range is 15.00 ± 11.62 percent, or from 3.38 to 26.62 percent. In other words, there is only a small probability that the return of company B will be significantly less than expected, and hence, the stock is not very risky. For the average company listed on the New York Stock Exchange, the standard deviation has been about 30 percent in recent years.

A person who chooses a less risky investment is risk averse. The average investor is risk averse, at least with regard to his or her own money. What are the implications of risk aversion for stock prices and rates of return? To answer this question, we analyze the situation of the stocks of companies A and B in Table 8.1. Suppose each stock sold for $100 per share and each had an expected rate of return of 15 percent. There would be a preference for company B since investors are risk averse. People with money to invest would buy the stock of company B rather than company A, and stockholders of company A would start selling their stock and using the proceeds to buy the stock of company B. Buying pressure would drive up the price of the stock of company B, and selling pressure would simultaneously cause the stock price of company A to decline. These price changes, in turn, would cause

Figure 8.2
Probability Ranges for a Normal Distribution

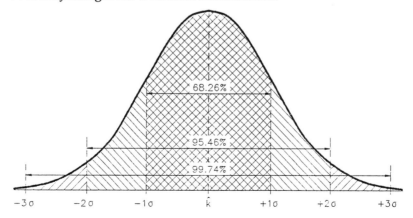

changes in the expected rates of return on the two stocks. Suppose, for example, that the price of company B was bid up from $100 to $140 and the price of the stock of company A declined from $100 to $80. This would cause the expected return of company B to fall to 10 percent, while the expected return of company A would rise to 20 percent. The difference in return, 10 percent, is a risk premium representing the compensation investors require for assuming the additional risk of company A. This example illustrates an important principle: in a market dominated by risk-averse investors, riskier stocks should have higher expected returns, as estimated by the average investor, than less risky stocks; if this situation did not hold, stock prices will change in the market to force it to occur.

2. PORTFOLIOS

If we examined the historical risk and return of highly diversified portfolios typified by the Standard & Poor's (S&P) composite index, we would find that the historical standard deviation of the S&P composite is much lower than the historical standard deviations of individual stocks. In fact, the average historical standard deviation of individual stocks is more than twice that of highly diversified portfolios.

The difference between the standard deviation of an individual stock and the standard deviation of a portfolio is due to diversification. That is, with diversification, individual stocks can be combined in such a way that a combination of individual stocks, the portfolio, is almost always less risky than any of the individual securities. Since the returns of individual securities are not usually perfectly correlated to each other, a certain amount of risk is thus eliminated through diversification. Although diversification is rather effective at reducing risk, the risk of holding stock cannot be completely eliminated thereby.

Covariance (COV) is a statistic that measures the relationship between the return on one stock and the return on another. For the example problem of Table 8.1, we computed for each of the companies A and B the expected rate of return (15 percent for each), the deviation of each possible return from the expected return (for company A, in column 1 of Table 8.2), and the standard deviation (58.09 percent for company A and 11.62 percent for company B). The deviations of each possible return from the expected return for company B are $(30 - 15) = 15$, $(15 - 15) = 0$, and $(0 - 15) = -15$ for the boom, normal, and recession states of the economy, respectively.

Using the information about expected returns and deviations of each possible return from the expected return, we can compute covariance in two steps, as follows.

1. For each state of the economy, multiply together company A's deviation from its expected return and company B's deviation from its
   expected return.
2. Compute the weighted average value of the three states. This average is the covariance.

Carrying out step 1 for the example problem of Table 8.1 gives the
following:

State of the economy	Company A $(k_i - \hat{k})$	Company B $(k_t - \hat{k})$	Product of deviations
Boom	75%	15%	0.1125
Normal	0	0	0
Recession	−75	−15	0.1125

Indicating the actual returns of companies A and B by R_A and R_B and
the covariance of R_A and R_B by $\mathrm{cov}(R_A, R_B)$, we compute the $\mathrm{cov}(R_A, R_B)$
with step 2:

$$\mathrm{cov}(R_A, R_B) = (0.30)(0.1125) + (0.40)(0) + 0.30(0.1125) = 0.0675$$

The ordering of the two variables is unimportant. That is, $\mathrm{cov}(R_A, R_B)$
= $\mathrm{cov}(R_B, R_A)$. In this example, we have a situation where company A's
return is above its average when company B's return is above its
average, and A's return is below its average when B's return is below
its average. This is an indication of a positive relationship between the
two returns. Consequently, we found a positive value for the covariance. We would have found a negative covariance if company A's return
were generally above its average when company B's return was below
its average and company A's return was generally below its average
when company B's return was above its average.
   Suppose there was no relationship between the two returns of companies A and B. In this case, knowing whether the return of company
A was above or below its expected return would tell us nothing about
the return of company B. In the covariance formula, then, there will be
no tendency for the terms to be positive or negative, and on average,
they will tend to offset and cancel out each other. Consequently, the
covariance will be zero.
   From this discussion of covariance, it is clear that this statistic appears
to capture what we are looking for. If the returns are positively related
to each other, they will have a positive covariance. If, on the other hand,
they are negatively correlated to each other, they will have a negative

covariance. Like the variance, the covariance is stated in squared deviation units. It is, therefore, difficult to put it in perspective. This problem can be solved by calculating the correlation.

We calculate the correlation (corr) of R_A with R_B or, corr(R_A, R_B) by
dividing the covariance by the product of the standard deviations of
both companies. For the example problem in Table 8.1, we have:

$$\text{corr}(R_A, R_B) = 0.0675/(0.5809)(0.1162) = 1.0000$$

The sign of the correlation between two variables must be the same
as that of the covariance between the two variables since the standard
deviation is always positive. If the correlation is positive, we say that
the variables are positively correlated. If it is negative, we say that the
variables are negatively correlated. The variables are uncorrelated if the
correlation is zero. It can be demonstrated that, due to the standardizing
procedure of dividing by the two standard deviations, the correlation
is always between +1 and −1. As with covariance, the ordering of the
two variables is unimportant. That is, corr(R_A, R_B) = corr(R_B, R_A). Later
in this chapter we will see that variance and covariance are the building
blocks of the beta coefficient.

As shown in equation (3), the expected return on a portfolio, $\hat{k}_p$, is the
weighted average of the expected returns on the individual stocks in
the portfolio, where the weights represent the fraction of the total
portfolio invested in each stock:

$$\hat{k}_p = w_1\hat{k}_1 + w_2\hat{k}_2 + \ldots + w_n\hat{k}_n = \sum_{i=1}^{n} w_i\hat{k}_i \qquad (3)$$

where:

$\hat{k}$ = expected return on stock i
w_i = the weight allocated to stock i
n = number of stocks in the portfolio

The weight given to stock i is the proportion of the portfolio's dollar
value invested in stock i; the weights must add up to 1.0. For instance,
a $100,000 portfolio consisting of $50,000 in stock A with an expected
return of 15 percent, $25,000 in stock B with an expected return of 20
percent, and $25,000 in stock C with an expected return of 30 percent
has an expected return of:

$$0.50(15\%) + 0.25(20\%) + 0.25(30\%) = 20\%$$

Now consider two stocks, each with an expected return of 15 percent like the stocks of companies A and B in the example problem in Table 8.1. The expected return on a portfolio consisting of these two stocks must be 15 percent, regardless of the proportions of the two stocks. This result implies that we cannot reduce the expected return by investing in a number of securities. Rather, the expected return on the portfolio is simply a weighted average of the expected returns on the individual securities in the portfolio.

Contrary to a portfolio's expected return, the standard deviation of a portfolio is not the weighted average of the individual stocks' standard deviations. To elucidate this point, we first determine the variance of a portfolio composed of two securities.

The variance (var) of a portfolio consisting of two securities, A and B, is given by equation (4).

$$\text{var(portfolio)} = w_A^2\sigma_A^2 + 2w_Aw_B\sigma_{A,B} + w_B^2\sigma_B^2 \qquad (4)$$

where:

w_A and w_B	= the proportions of the total portfolio in the assets A and B, respectively
σ_A^2 and σ_B^2	= the variance of A and B, respectively
$\sigma_{A,B}$	= the covariance between the two securities—another way of writing $\text{cov}(R_A, R_B)$

Equation (4) indicates that the variance of a portfolio of two securities depends on both the variances of the individual securities and the covariance between the two securities. The variance of a security measures the variability of an individual's security return. Covariance measures the relationship between the two securities. For given variances of the individual securities, a positive covariance between the two increases the variance of the entire portfolio, while a negative covariance between the two decreases the variance of the entire portfolio. This result is obvious; if one of the securities tends to go up when the other goes down, or vice versa, the two securities will offset each other. This is what was called a hedge in Chapters 4 and 5, and it will cause the risk of the entire portfolio to be low. However, if both securities rise and fall together, we are not hedging. Consequently, the risk of the entire portfolio will be higher.

Assuming that an individual with $1,000 invests $600 in company A (Table 8.1) and $400 in company B, $w_A = 0.6$ and $w_B = 0.4$, we compute the variance of the return of the portfolio consisting of two stocks with the help of equation (4) as follows:

$$0.36(0.3375) + 2(0.6)(0.4)(0.0675) + 0.16(0.0135) = 0.1561$$

Note that the variance of the portfolio is higher than the variance of the stock of company B since both securities rise and fall together. Naturally, this is not the type of portfolio we should have if we wish to reduce risk through diversification. The standard deviation of the portfolio, which we call σ_p, is calculated by taking the square root of its variance:

$$\sigma_p = \sqrt{(0.1561)} = 0.3951$$

Of course, the standard deviation of a portfolio is not the weighted average of the individual stocks' standard deviations. For instance, we found that the standard deviations of the stocks of companies A and B were 58.09 percent and 11.62 percent, respectively. Their weighted average is $0.6(0.5809) + 0.4(0.1162) = 0.3950$. The difference between 0.3951 and 0.3950 is small due to the small size of the portfolio.

Diversification

Does the fact that the variance of the portfolio in Table 8.1 is higher than the variance of the stock of company B mean that diversification does not work? It does not, because, first, the portfolio is too small, and second, it consists of two securities that rise and fall together. To elucidate the second point, we consider the following example.

Ms. Jones is considering investing in the common stock of company ABC and in a risk-free asset such as a treasury bond. Suppose she chooses to invest a total of $1,000, $400 of which is to be invested in company ABC and $600 to be placed in the risk-free asset. The relevant parameters are as follows.

	Company ABC	Treasury bond
Return	15%	10%
Standard deviation	0.25	0.00

The expected return on her portfolio, consisting of one risky asset and one riskless one is the weighted average of the two returns, or $(0.40 \times 0.15) + (0.60 \times 0.10) = 0.12$.

Assume that the first and third terms of equation (4) correspond to the variance of company ABC and the variance of the treasury bonds, respectively. By definition, a risk-free asset has no variability. Thus, in Ms. Jones's case, both the second and third terms are zero. The variance of her portfolio is, therefore, equal to $(0.40)^2(0.25)^2 = 0.01$, which is smaller than the variance of company ABC.

Diversification works because prices of different stocks do not move exactly together. In an extreme case, consider a little known collection agency with earnings that have fluctuated a lot in the past, a record of not paying dividends, and stock that is not very liquid. In other words, we would expect that the agency was risky and, therefore, its required rate of return should be relatively high. In reality, however, its rate of return had been low in relation to those of most other companies, indicating that investors regarded it as a low-risk company despite its uncertain profits and nonexistent dividend stream. The reason is that a stock from the collection agency provides diversification. The firm's stock price will thus rise during recessions, while other stocks will tend to decline. Consequently, including the agency's stock in a portfolio of more robust stocks will tend to stabilize returns on the entire portfolio.

If the stocks' returns move countercyclically to each other—that is, when X's returns fall by a certain percentage, those of Y rise by the same percentage, and vice versa—then the portfolio is riskless. In statistical terms, we say that the returns on stocks X and Y are perfectly negatively correlated, with a correlation equal to -1.0. The correlation can range from $+1.0$, denoting that the two variables move up and down in perfect synchronization, to -1.0, denoting that the variables move in exactly opposite directions. Returns on two perfectly positively correlated stocks would move up and down together, and a portfolio consisting of two such stocks would be exactly as risky as the individual stocks.

There is plenty of statistical evidence showing that the larger the size of the portfolio (in terms of diversification of stocks), the smaller its risk. Figure 8.3 shows how portfolio risk is affected by portfolio size. It was drawn by forming increasingly larger portfolios of randomly selected NYSE stocks. Thus, standard deviations are plotted for an average one-stock portfolio, two-stock portfolio, and so on, up to a portfolio consisting of 1,500-plus common stocks, as listed on the NYSE when the figure was prepared (1995).

Figure 8.3 shows that:

1. The σ of an average one-stock portfolio is approximately 28.0 percent.
2. The σ of a portfolio consisting of all stocks (called a market portfolio) is about 15.1 percent.
3. The riskiness of a portfolio consisting of average NYSE stocks generally tends to decrease and to asymptotically approach a limit as the size of the portfolio increases.

Figure 8.3
Effects of Portfolio Size on Portfolio Risk for Average Stocks

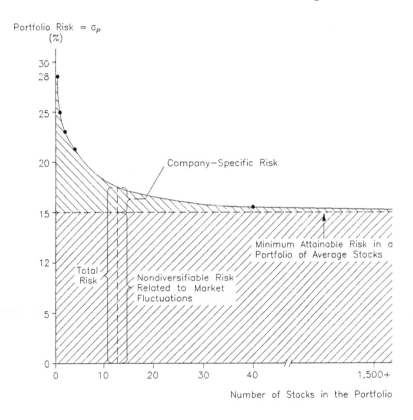

4. Almost half (28.0 percent – 15.1 percent) of the riskiness of an average individual stock can be eliminated if the stock is held in a reasonably well-diversified portfolio, say one consisting of about 45 stocks.
5. It is virtually impossible to diversify away the effects of broad stock market movements.

The part of a stock risk that cannot be eliminated is called non-diversifiable, systematic, or market risk; the part that can be eliminated is called diversifiable, unique, unsystematic, or company-specific risk. Market risk is caused by factors that affect most companies (high interest rates, recessions, inflation, and so on), while company-specific risk stems from events unique to a particular firm (lawsuits, strikes, the losing of major contracts, and so on). Total risk is the sum of market and company-specific risks.

Equation (4) can be expressed in the format of a matrix, as given in Table 8.3. The matrix consists of four boxes, and we can add the terms in the boxes to obtain equation (4), the variance of a portfolio composed of two securities, A and B. The term in the upper left-hand corner involves the variance of A, and the one on the lower right involves the variance of B. The other two boxes contain the term involving the covariance. These boxes are identical, indicating that in equation (4), the covariance is multiplied by 2.

The box approach is easily generalized to more than two securities in order to compute the variance (and standard deviation) of a portfolio of many assets. Table 8.4 presents a matrix for a portfolio of n assets. We can make the following observations about the matrix of Table 8.4.

1. σ_i is the standard deviation of stock i and $\text{cov}(R_i, R_j)$ is the covariance between i and j where $i = j = 1, 2, ..., n$.
2. Terms involving the standard deviation of a single security appear on the diagonal.
3. Terms involving covariance between securities appear off the diagonal.
4. The matrix has $n \times n = n^2$ boxes.
5. The term in the box with, for instance, a horizontal dimension of 2 and a vertical dimension of 3 is $w_3 w_2 \text{cov}(R_3, R_2)$ where w_3 and w_2 are the percentages of the entire portfolio that are invested in the third and second asset, respectively, and $\text{cov}(R_3, R_2)$ is the covariance between the returns on the third asset and those on the second asset.
6. The term in the box with a horizontal dimension of 3 and a vertical dimension of 2 is $w_2 w_3 \text{cov}(R_2, R_3)$.
7. Since $\text{cov}(R_3, R_2)$ is equal to $\text{cov}(R_2, R_3)$ the boxes mentioned in items 5 and 6 have the same value: the second and third securities make up one pair of stocks.
8. Every pair of securities appears twice in the table, once in the lower left-hand side and once in the upper right-hand side.
9. The term in the boxes with a horizontal dimension equal to the vertical dimension contain $w_i^2 \sigma_i^2$ (with $i = 1, 2, ..., n$) where σ_i^2 is the variance of the return on the ith stock.

Table 8.3
Matrix Approach to Computing
the Variance of a Portfolio of Two Assets

	Security A	Security B
Security A	$w_A^2 \sigma_A^2$	$w_A w_B \sigma_{AB}$
Security B	$w_A w_B \sigma_{AB}$	$w_B^2 \sigma_B^2$

Table 8.4

Matrix Approach to Computing the Variance of a Portfolio of n Assets

Stock	1	2	3	....	n
1	$w_1^2 \sigma_1^2$	$w_1 w_2 \text{cov}(R_1,R_2)$	$w_1 w_3 \text{cov}(R_1,R_3)$		$w_1 w_n \text{cov}(R_1,R_n)$
2	$w_2 w_1 \text{cov}(R_2,R_1)$	$w_2^2 \sigma_2^2$	$w_2 w_3 \text{cov}(R_2,R_3)$		$w_2 w_n \text{cov}(R_2,R_n)$
3	$w_3 w_1 \text{cov}(R_3,R_1)$	$w_3 w_2 \text{cov}(R_3,R_2)$	$w_3^2 \sigma_3^2$		$w_3 w_n \text{cov}(R_3,R_n)$
.					
.					
.					
n	$w_n w_1 \text{cov}(R_n,R_1)$	$w_n w_2 \text{cov}(R_n,R_2)$	$w_n w_3 \text{cov}(R_n,R_3)$		$w_n^2 \sigma_n^2$

10. The number of diagonal terms (number of variance terms) is the same as the number of stocks in the portfolio.
11. The number of off-diagonal terms (number of covariance terms) rises much faster than the number of diagonal terms. For instance, a portfolio of 100 securities has 9,900 covariance terms.
12. The variance of a portfolio's returns is the sum of the terms in all boxes.
13. In view of items 11 and 12, the variance of the return of a portfolio with many stocks depends more on the covariances between individual stocks than on the variances of the individual stocks.

In this exposition we have discussed two principal themes of this chapter.

1. The standard deviation of a portfolio drops as more securities are added to the portfolio; however, it does not drop to zero due to nondiversifiable risk related to market fluctuations (Figure 8.3).
2. The variance of the return on a portfolio with many securities is more dependent on the covariances between individual securities than on the variances of the individual stocks.

To enhance our understanding of these two points, we alter the matrix in Table 8.4. Specifically, we assume that:

1. all securities possess the same variance, which we indicate by $\overline{\text{var}}$;
2. all covariances are the same, which we write as $\overline{\text{cov}}$; and
3. all securities are equally weighted in the portfolio.

Table 8.5 is the matrix of variances and covariances under these three simplifying assumptions. Since there are n assets in the portfolio, the weight of each asset is $1/n$. Note that all the diagonal terms are identical, as are all the off-diagonal terms. There are n diagonal terms, involving variance, and $n(n-1)$ off-diagonal terms, involving covariance. As with Table 8.4, the variance of the portfolio is the sum of the terms in the boxes of Table 8.5.

Summing across all the boxes in Table 8.5, we compute the variance of the portfolio as follows.

$$\text{var(portfolio)} = n(1/n)^2\overline{\text{var}} + n(n-1)(1/n)^2\overline{\text{cov}}$$

or:

$$\text{var(portfolio)} = (1/n)\overline{\text{var}} + [(n-1)/n]\overline{\text{cov}} \qquad (5)$$

Equation (5) is a weighted average of the variance and covariance terms since the weights, $(1/n)$ and $[(n-1)/n]$ sum to 1.

Table 8.5
Special Case of a Matrix Approach to Computing the Variance of a Portfolio of n Assets

Stock	1	2	3	....	n
1	$(1/n)^2\overline{\text{var}}$	$(1/n)^2\overline{\text{cov}}$	$(1/n)^2\overline{\text{cov}}$		$(1/n)^2\overline{\text{cov}}$
2	$(1/n)^2\overline{\text{cov}}$	$(1/n)^2\overline{\text{var}}$	$(1/n)^2\overline{\text{cov}}$		$(1/n)^2\overline{\text{cov}}$
3	$(1/n)^2\overline{\text{cov}}$	$(1/n)^2\overline{\text{cov}}$	$(1/n)^2\overline{\text{var}}$		$(1/n)^2\overline{\text{cov}}$
.					
.					
.					
.					
n	$(1/n)^2\overline{\text{cov}}$	$(1/n)^2\overline{\text{cov}}$	$(1/n)^2\overline{\text{cov}}$		$(1/n)^2\overline{\text{var}}$

Note: The case is special since (1) all the securities of the portfolio possess the same variance, indicated by $\overline{\text{var}}$, (2) all pairs of securities of the portfolio possess the same covariance, indicated by $\overline{\text{cov}}$, and (3) all securities are held in the same proportion $(1/n)$.

This above expression shows that when we increase the number of stocks in the portfolio without limit, the variance of the portfolio becomes:

$$\text{variance of portfolio (when } n \rightarrow \infty) = \overline{cov} \qquad (6)$$

Equation (6) holds because (1) the weight of the variance term in equation (5), $(1/n)$, goes to 0 as n goes to infinity, and (2) the weight of the covariance term, $[(n-1)/n]$, which can also be written as $1 - 1/n$, goes to 1 as n goes to infinity. Equation (6) shows that, in the special case of Table 8.5, the variances of the individual stocks disappear as the number of stocks becomes large. However, the covariance term remains. In other words, the variance of the portfolio becomes the average covariance, which is equal to $\overline{cov}$ since all covariances of Table 8.5 are the same. The variances of the individual securities are diversified away, but the covariance terms cannot be.

The shape of Figure 8.3 would have been similar if the vertical axis had represented variance instead of standard deviation. For the special case of Table 8.5, the dashed horizontal line indicating the difference between diversifiable and nondiversifiable risk in this figure would have a vertical coordinate of $\overline{cov}$. Thus, the portfolio's variance never drops to zero. Rather, it reaches a floor of $\overline{cov}$, which is the covariance of each pair of securities. Although beyond the scope of this book, it can be demonstrated that this risk reduction also applies to the general case where variances and covariances are *not* equal.

For our special case, we have:

total risk of individual stock = nondiversifiable risk of portfolio + diversifiable risk of portfolio

or

$$\overline{var} = \overline{cov} + (\overline{var} - \overline{cov})$$

Total risk, which is $\overline{var}$ in our special case, is the riskone bears by holding on to one stock only. The nondiversifiable risk is the risk one still bears after achieving full diversification, which is $\overline{cov}$. To an individual who selects a diversified portfolio, the total risk of an individual stock is not important. When considering the addition of stock to a diversified portfolio, he or she cares instead about that portion of the risk that cannot be diversified away. This risk can be viewed as the contribution of a stock to the risk of an entire portfolio.

Each additional security added to the portfolio continues to reduce risk since the variance of the portfolio will asymmetrically approach $\overline{cov}$. Does this mean that one can never achieve too much diversification? The answer is no, since in the real world, there is a cost to diversification. That is, commissions per dollar invested fall as one makes larger purchases in a single stock. However, one must purchase fewer shares of each stock when buying more different stocks. By comparing the costs and benefits of diversification, it can be argued that a portfolio of about 30 securities achieves optimal diversification (see Statman 1987).

The typical investor is risk averse. A risk-averse investor prefers to avoid fair gambles or gambles with a zero expected return. He or she can be induced to take fair gambles only if they are sweetened so that they become unfair to the investor's advantage. For instance, one may have to raise the odds of winning from 50:50 to 75:25 or higher. Because risk-averse investors avoid unnecessary risk, such as the unsystematic risk of a stock, they choose well-diversified portfolios.

Conceptually, the risk of an individual stock relates to how the risk of a portfolio changes when the security is added. In this case, the standard deviation of an individual stock is not a good measure of its risk. In fact, a security with a high standard deviation may not necessarily have a high impact on the standard deviation of a large portfolio. In contrast, a security with a low standard deviation may have a high impact on a large portfolio's standard deviation. This apparent paradox is the basis of the well-known capital asset–pricing model.

3. CAPITAL ASSET PRICING MODEL

The capital asset–pricing model (CAPM) is based on the proposition that any stock's required rate of return equals the risk-free rate of return plus a risk premium, where risk reflects diversification. Stock held as part of a portfolio is less risky than the same stock held in isolation. The concept of CAPM is that the risk and return of an individual security should be analyzed in terms of how that security affects the risk and return of the portfolio in which it is held. We have seen that the higher the riskiness of an individual security, the higher the expected return required to induce the investor to buy it. How should the riskiness of an individual stock be assessed if the investor is concerned about the riskiness of a portfolio? According to the CAPM, the relevant riskiness of an individual stock is its contribution to the riskiness of a well-diversified portfolio. The riskiness of an individual stock might be high if held by itself, but if most of its risk can be eliminated by diversification, then its relevant risk may be small. Different stocks will affect the portfolio differently, so different stocks have different degrees of relevant risk. To measure this relevant risk we define an average stock as one that tends to move up and down in step with the general market as measured by some index such as the S&P 500, Dow Jones Industrials, or the NYSE.

A stock has, by definition, a beta (β) equal to 1.0 if its price moves up or down, by percentage, in accordance with the market's movement. A portfolio of such ($\beta = 1.0$) stocks will move up or down exactly with the broad market averages, and its riskiness is the same as that of the averages. A $\beta = 0.5$ value means that a stock moves up or down by half as much as the market moves up or down, or the stock is half as volatile as the market. A portfolio of $\beta = 0.5$ stocks is half as risky as a portfolio of $\beta = 1.0$ stocks. On the other hand, if $\beta = 2.0$, the stock is twice as volatile as an average stock, and a portfolio of such stocks will be twice as risky as an average portfolio. The β coefficients of thousands of companies are calculated and published by organizations like Value Line and Merrill Lynch. Most stocks have betas in the range of 0.50 to 1.50, and the average of all stocks is, by definition, 1.0. In general, a β coefficient is calculated by using data from some past period and assuming that the stock's relative violatility will be the same in the future as it was in the past. Next, a statistical technique called regression analysis is used to calculate the coefficient. The beta of a set of securities is the weighted average of the individual securities' betas. For instance, a $100,000 portfolio consisting of $50,000 in stock A, with a $\beta = 0.60$; $25,000 in stock B, with a $\beta = 0.70$; and $25,000 in stock C, with a $\beta = 1.50$; has a portfolio β equal to $0.50(0.60) + 0.25(0.70) + 0.25(1.50) = 0.85$. Suppose stock B is sold and replaced by stock D, with a $\beta = 1.10$. This action will increase the portfolio's β from 0.85 to 0.50 (0.60) + 0.25(1.10) + 0.25(1.50) = 0.95. Adding a stock with a $\beta = 0.20$ instead of stock D would reduce the riskiness of the portfolio.

More precisely, the beta coefficient is defined as follows.

$$\beta_i = \text{cov}(k_i, k_M)/\sigma^2(k_M) \qquad (7)$$

where:

β_i = the stock's beta coefficient (the i signifies the ith company's beta)

k_i = return on the stock of company i

k_M = the expected rate of return on the market (or on an "average" stock)

$\sigma^2(k_M)$ = the variance of the market

Although both cov(k_i, k_M) and β_i can be used as measures of the contribution of security i to the risk of the portfolio, β_i is more commonly used. One useful property of the β_i is that the average beta across all securities, when weighted by the proportion of each security's market value to that of the market portfolio, is 1, or:

$$\sum_{i=1}^{n} w_i\beta_i = 1 \qquad (8)$$

where:

> n = number of stocks in the portfolio
> w_i = proportion of the ith security's market value to that of the market portfolio
> β_i = as previously defined

The higher the riskiness of an individual stock, the higher the expected return required to induce the investor to buy it. In other words, the expected return on a security is positively related to its risk. Consequently, the expected return on a security should be positively related

Figure 8.4
Relationship between Expected Return on an Individual Security and Beta of the Security

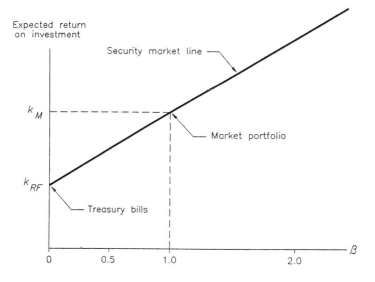

to its beta as illustrated in Figure 8.4. The upward-sloping line in this figure is called the security-market line (SML).

We can make the following observations about Figure 8.4.

1. The expected return on a stock with $\beta = 0$ is the risk-free interest rate, k_{RF}, since a stock with zero beta has no relevant risk.
2. Equation (8) tells us that the average beta across all stocks, when weighted by the proportion of each stock's market value to that of the market portfolio, is 1. The beta of the market portfolio is 1 since the market portfolio is formed by weighing each stock by its market value. The expected return for any stock with $\beta_i = 1$ is the expected return on the market portfolio, k_M, since all stocks with the same beta have the same return.
3. The beta cannot be less than zero. Suppose we could find a stock with a negative beta. The stock would, therefore, offer a lower expected return than treasury bills, which are risk free, since the stock with a negative beta would be very desirable. If we invested in both the stock with a negative beta and the market portfolio in the proper proportions, we could reduce risk dramatically. This is, alas, impossible in the real world.
4. The relationship between expected return and beta corresponds to a *straight* line. Securities lying under the SML are overpriced, and their prices must fall until their expected returns lie on the SML. Similarly, securities lying above the SML are underpriced, and their prices must rise until their expected returns lie on the SML. In other words, if the SML were curved, many stocks would be mispriced. Although stocks may be mispriced in the short run, in the long run stocks would be held only when prices changed so that the SML became straight. Thus, linearity would be achieved.
5. Relying on our high school algebra, we note that a line can be described algebraically if we know its slope and intercept. The slope of the SML is $(k_M - k_{RF})$ because the expected return of any stock with $\beta = 1$ is k_M. Figure 8.4 shows that the intercept of the SML is k_{RF}.

The final observation enables us to write the SML algebraically as follows: expected return on a stock = risk-free interest rate + β(difference between expected return on the market and risk-free interest rate), or

$$\hat{k} = k_{RF} + \beta(k_M - k_{RF}) \tag{9}$$

Equation (9) is called the CAPM. Note that if $\beta = 0$, $\hat{k} = k_{RF}$, as mentioned in the first observation, and if $\beta = 1$, $\hat{k} = k_M$, as mentioned in the second.

Consider, for example, the stock of company *ABC* with a beta of 1.5 and that of company *XYZ* with a beta of 0.8. The risk-free interest rate is 7.0 percent, and the difference between the expected return on the market and the risk-free rate is 8.5 percent. The expected returns on the two stocks are as follows.

expected return for *ABC*: 7% + 1.5(8.5%) = 19.75%
expected return for *XYZ*: 7% + .8(8.5%) = 13.8%

Let us now consider a portfolio formed by investing equally in our stocks of companies *ABC* and *XYZ*. Based on equation (3), the expected return on the portfolio is 0.5(19.75 percent) + 0.5(13.80 percent) = 16.78 percent. As we have seen, the beta of a portfolio is simply a weighted average of the two stocks, or .5(1.5) + .5(.8) = 1.15. Under the CAPM, the expected return on the portfolio is 7 percent + 1.15(8.50 percent) = 16.78 percent. The same result is obtained in two different ways. Until now, our discussion of the CAPM considered individual stocks. The result obtaining the expected return on the portfolio in two different ways demonstrates that equation (9) and Figure 8.4 hold for portfolios as well. Thus, CAPM holds for individual stocks as well as for portfolios.

Based on statistics kept by the University of Chicago since 1926, financial analysts in the United States often assume $(k_M - k_{RF}) = 8.5$ percent. Others have taken a value for $(k_M - k_{RF})$ based on the most recent 15, 25, or 40 years. For instance, if you do not believe that another world war will take place during the next 20 years, there is no reason to include the effect of World War II on $(k_M - k_{RF})$ by going back to 1926. Values for $(k_M - k_{RF})$ may also vary from country to country.

In arriving at equation (9), two assumptions were made but not fully spelled out:

1. Investment in U.S. Treasury Bills is risk free. Although it is true that there is little chance of default with treasury bills, they do not guarantee a real return. That is, there remains a risk of inflation. However, if inflation is low, this assumption will not be violated too severely. In addition, Chapter 9 shows how to include an inflation premium in k_{RF} in cases where inflation is significant.
2. Investors can borrow money at the same rate of interest as they can lend it. In the real world, brokers generally do charge low interest, with many rates being only slightly above the risk-free rate. This is so, since (a) procedures for replenishing the account similar to those described in Section 1 of Chapter 4 (a margin account) have developed over many years, and (b) the broker holds the stock as collat-

eral, resulting into little default risk. In particular, the broker can sell the stock in order to satisfy the loan if margin contributions are not made on time. In contrast, corporations often borrow using illiquid assets such as plant and equipment as collateral. The costs to the lender of initial negotiation, ongoing supervision, and working out arrangements in case of financial distress or bankruptcy can, therefore, be substantial. Consequently, it is difficult to argue that individuals must borrow at higher rates than can corporations.

In conclusion, these assumptions are not crucial. With a little modification, the CAPM can handle them. Chapter 9 explains other problems related to beta in a discussion of the use of CAPM to determine the cost of retained earnings.

The original formulation of CAPM was based on an analysis of how investors can construct an efficient portfolio. An efficient portfolio means that each investment must work equally hard so that if one security has a greater marginal effect on the portfolio's risk than another security, it must also have a proportionately greater expected return. This means that if we plot each security's expected return against its marginal contribution to the risk of the efficient portfolio (or its beta, as in Figure 8.4), we will find that the securities lie along a straight line, or SML. In other words, a portfolio is efficient if there is a straight-line relationship between each security's expected return and its marginal contribution to portfolio risk.

The Arbitrage-Pricing Model

An alternative to the CAPM is the arbitrage pricing theory (see Ross 1976). In essence, this theory assumes that (1) each stock's return depends on several independent influences, or "factors," and (2) the return must obey the simple relationship of equation (10).

$$\text{expected return on stock} = a + b_1(\text{factor 1}) + b_2(\text{factor 2}) + b_3(\text{factor 3}) + \ldots \tag{10}$$

where:

$b_1, b_2, b_3, \ldots$ = parameters indicating the stock's sensitivity to each of the factors

The arbitrage-pricing model states that it must be possible to construct a diversified portfolio that has zero sensitivity to each factor provided there is a sufficient number of stocks. In other words, such a portfolio would be risk free. The model also states that each stock's risk premium depends on (1) the risk premiums associated with each factor, and (2) the previously mentioned parameters, in the following manner:

$$\text{risk premium on stock} = b_1(k_1 - k_{RF}) + b_2(k_2 - k_{RF})$$
$$+ b_3(k_3 - k_{RF}) + ... \qquad (11)$$

where:

$k_1, k_2, k_3, ...$ = risk premiums associated with each factor
$b_1, b_2, b_3, ...$ = as previously defined
k_{RF} = risk-free interest rate

Arbitrage-pricing theory does not identify the factors of equation (10). The return on the market portfolio could be a factor, fuel price may be a factor, or there could be an interest rate factor. Some stocks will be more sensitive to a particular factor than others. For instance, Shell Oil would be more sensitive to an oil factor than Apple Computers. Thus, if factor 1 relates to unexpected changes in oil prices, b_1 would be higher for Shell Oil than Apple. The theory argues that if the expected risk premium on a given stock is higher than the risk premium computed with equation (11), smart investors will sell other stocks and buy the high-premium stock. The pressure of their demand then would force an increase in the price of the stock and a fall in its return and risk premium until equation (11) held. Alternatively, if the expected risk premium on a given stock falls lower than the risk premium computed with equation (11), investors will sell it and buy a group of other fairly priced stocks with the same average sensitivity to each factor. The new portfolio would be equally exposed to changes in the factors; however, it would offer a higher expected return.

In conclusion, the arbitrage-pricing model offers an alternative to CAPM for dealing with risk and return. CAPM is the best-known model of risk and return. Whether the arbitrage-pricing theory will provide a better handle on risk and return depends on whether it is possible to (1) identify the factors affecting stock returns, (2) measure the expected return on each of these factors, and (3) determine the parameters of equation (10) ($b_1, b_2, b_3, ...$). Until these practical problems are solved, CAPM is likely to remain the dominant theory of risk and return.

Determination of the Beta Coefficient

In Chapter 3 it was argued that it is advisable to establish requirements for specific rates of return for different types of investments.

Thus, each project should be compared to a financial asset of comparable risk. Specifically, this means that if a project's beta differs from that of the company, the project's net present value (NPV) should be calculated with a discount rate commensurate with its own beta. This is important because companies often refer to a corporate discount rate, benchmark, cutoff rate, or hurdle rate. Unless all projects that a corporation is considering have the same risk, choosing the same discount rate for all projects is not correct.

The β coefficients of thousands of companies are published by organizations like Value Line and Merrill Lynch and computed by using a statistical technique called regression analysis. Let us now consider in more detail the determination of the beta coefficient of a proposed project with the following example. Suppose a publishing firm, Books Inc., is considering the acceptance of a project in computer software. Books Inc. views the software venture's risk differently from the risk of the rest of its business. It should, therefore, discount the project at a rate commensurate with the risk of software companies. Thus, Books Inc. determines the beta related to computer software. It has collected the following information about a computer software company (called Computer Software) comparable to its computer software venture and the S&P 500 Index for the last four years.

Year	Computer Software ROR[1]	S&P 500 Index (ROR)
1	10%	3%
2	12	5
3	15	10
4	17	13

[1]ROR = rate of return.

We compute beta in six steps, as follows.
Step 1: calculate the average return on each asset:

average return on Computer Software company: $(0.10 + 0.12 + 0.15 + 0.17)/4 = 0.1350$
average return on market portfolio: $(0.03 + 0.05 + 0.10 + 0.13)/4 = 0.0775$

These results are given at the end of columns 2 and 4 of Table 8.6.

Step 2: for each asset, calculate the deviation of each return from the asset's average return computed in step 1. These deviations are given in columns 3 and 5.

Step 3: multiply the deviation of Computer Software's return by the deviation of the market's return. This is presented in column 6 (note that step 3 is analogous to the calculation of covariance presented earlier in the chapter).

Step 4: compute the squared deviation of the market's return. This is given in column 7 (step 4 is analogous to the calculation of variance presented earlier in the chapter).

Step 5: determine the sum of column 6 and the sum of column 7. (The sums are 0.0042 and 0.0064, respectively.)

Step 6: divide the sum of column 6 by the sum of column 7. This is the beta of Computer Software (see also Table 8.6). Thus:

$$\text{beta} = (0.0042)/(0.0064) = 0.6563$$

This calculation of the beta seems straightforward. There are, however, a number of potential pitfalls. First, the sample size (that is, four

Table 8.6
Beta Calculation

(1)	(2)	(3)	(4)	(5)	(6)	(7)
Year	ROR[1] on Computer Software	Computer Software's deviation from average return	ROR on market portfolio	Market portfolio's deviation from average return	(Deviation of Computer Software) × (deviation of market portfolio)	Squared deviation of market portfolio
1	0.10	-0.0350	0.03	-0.0475	0.0017	0.0023
2	0.12	-0.0150	0.05	-0.0275	0.0004	0.0008
3	0.15	0.0150	0.10	0.0225	0.0003	0.0005
4	0.17	0.0350	0.13	0.0525	0.0018	0.0028
	Avg = 0.1350		Avg = 0.0775		Sum = 0.0042	Sum = 0.0064

Beta of Computer Software: $(0.0042)/(0.0064) = 0.6563$

[1]ROR = rate of return

years) may be too small. Second, betas may vary over time. Third, betas are affected by changing business risk and financial leverage. The first two problems can be overcome by using more sophisticated statistical techniques, while the third problem can be lessened by adjusting for changes in business and financial risks. In addition, it may have been prudent for Books Inc. to consider beta estimates of a number of comparable firms rather than just one.

Suppose that the risk-free interest rate is 6 percent, $(k_M - k_{RF}) = 8.5$ percent, and Books Inc. is an all-equity firm (that is, it has no debt). As we will learn in Chapter 9, equation (9) can also be used to determine the cost of equity for Books Inc. Thus, this cost is 6.00 percent + 0.6563(8.50 percent) = 11.58 percent. To determine whether the proposed project should be accepted or rejected, Books Inc. can now determine its NPV (or IRR) by using the discount rate of 11.58 percent.

Naturally, this six-step procedure can also be used to determine the beta of a company. In this case, we would take a sample of the rates of return of the company (rather than those of a comparable company, such as Computer Software company in the example) and the S&P 500 Index. The beta of a company is determined by the company's characteristics. Three important characteristics are the financial leverage, the cyclical nature of revenues, and the operating leverage.

Financial leverage is defined as the extent to which fixed income securities (debt and preferred stock) are used in a company's capital structure. To keep our discussion simple, we will ignore preferred stock (discussed in Chapter 9). To explain the concept of financial leverage, we consider a company balance sheet, which, in an oversimplified version, looks as follows.

Asset value (A)	Debt value (D)
	Equity value (S)

Asset value (A)	Firm value (V)

Note that $V = D + S$ and $A = V$. The stockholders own the company's equity and share the asset value with the debt holders, who receive part of the cash flows generated by the company's assets and bear part of the asset's risks.

Let us assume that we bought all of the company's securities. That is 100 percent of its debt and 100 percent of its equity. In this case, we would not share the risks with anyone else, and every dollar the company paid out would go to us. In other words, the beta of our debt-plus-equity portfolio would be equal to the company's asset beta. Ignoring tax complications such as debt interest—generating tax savings (see Chapter 9), the beta of our hypothetical portfolio would be

$$\beta_a = \beta_p = \beta_d \, D/(D + S) + \beta_s \, S/(D + S) \tag{12}$$

where:

β_a = the asset's beta
β_p = the portfolio's beta
β_d = the debt's beta
β_s = the equity's beta
all other terms are as previously defined

Equation (12) tells us that the asset's beta is the weighted average of the debt and equity betas.

Business risk is reflected by the company's asset beta, while the difference between a company's equity and asset betas reflects financial risk. From the oversimplified balance sheet we can conclude that the company's business risk is not affected by using more (or less) debt and correspondingly less (or more) equity. However, more debt means more financial risk. In other words, if a company decided to use more (or less) debt and correspondingly less (or more) equity, there would be no change in the company's asset beta and no change in the beta of a portfolio of all the company's debt and equity securities. In contrast, the equity beta would change.

The terms of equation (12) can be rearranged to obtain equation (13).

$$\beta_s = \beta_a + (\beta_a - \beta_d) \, D/S \tag{13}$$

Equation (13) shows that a company's equity beta increases if debt increases. Since financial risk reflects the difference between a company's equity and asset betas, and the asset beta does not change if a company decides to use more debt, we can conclude that financial leverage creates financial risk.

Debt holders of large, blue-chip companies bear much less risk than stockholders. The debt betas of these companies are often assumed to be zero, although this may not be true at times when prices of long-term government and corporate bonds fluctuate significantly, as in periods of volatile interest rates (such as occurred in the early 1980s).

Companies normally do well in the expansion phase of the business cycle and poorly in the contraction phase. Consequently, the revenues of some companies are quite cyclical. Empirical evidence shows that high-tech firms, automotive firms, and retailers fluctuate with the business cycle. By contrast, railroads, utilities, airlines, and food industries are less dependent on the cycle. Highly cyclical stocks have high betas, since the beta is by definition the standardized covariability of a stock's return with the market's return (see equation (7)). For the same reason, lowly cyclical stocks have low betas.

Let us now move on to operating leverage. To explain the concept of operating leverage, we introduce the classification of fixed versus incremental costs as applied to investment analyses, where we consider the economic results of changes from preestablished and/or existing conditions. Fixed costs are those that will continue unchanged, whether or not a given change in operations or policy is adopted. Incremental costs—sometimes called variable costs—arise as a result of a change in operations or policy. Thus, fixed costs do not change as the quantity of output rises or falls; however, incremental costs increase (or decrease) as the quantity of output rises (or falls). Examples of fixed costs are the wages of workers under contract and property taxes. Examples of incremental costs are sales commissions, costs of raw materials, and some labor and maintenance costs. Incremental costs should not be confused with marginal costs, which are a special case of the former. That is, a marginal cost is the increment cost of one added unit of output.

Operating leverage (OL) is defined as:

$$OL = [(\text{change in } EBIT)/EBIT] \times [\text{sales}/(\text{change in sales})]$$

where:

$$EBIT = \text{earnings before interest and taxes}$$

Thus, operating leverage measures the percentage change in EBIT for a given percentage change in sales or revenues. It can be shown that operating leverage increases as fixed costs increase and as incremental costs decrease. Companies whose costs are mostly fixed are said to have high operating leverage.

The cash flow generated by a productive asset can be represented as:

$$\text{cash flow} = \text{revenue} - \text{fixed cost} - \text{incremental cost}$$

The asset's present value (PV) can be broken down in the same manner:

$$PV(\text{asset}) = PV(\text{revenue}) - PV(\text{fixed cost}) - PV(\text{incremental cost})$$

or:

$$PV(\text{revenue}) = PV(\text{fixed cost}) + PV(\text{incremental cost}) + PV(\text{asset})$$

Debt holders in the project are those who receive the fixed costs and the holders of levered equity in PV (revenue) are those who receive the net cash flows from the asset.

Similarly to the argument used to arrive at equation (12), we state that the beta of the value of the revenues is a weighted average of the beta of its component parts, or

$$\beta_r = \beta_{fc}\, PV_{fc}/PV_r + \beta_{ic}\, PV_{ic}/PV_r + \beta_a\, PV_a/PV_r \qquad (14)$$

where:

$$
\begin{aligned}
\beta_r &= \text{the revenue's beta} \\
\beta_{fc} &= \text{the fixed cost's beta} \\
\beta_{ic} &= \text{the incremental cost's beta} \\
\beta_a &= \text{the asset's beta} \\
PV_{fc} &= \text{the fixed cost's present value} \\
PV_r &= \text{the revenue's present value} \\
PV_{ic} &= \text{the incremental cost's present value} \\
PV_a &= \text{the asset's present value}
\end{aligned}
$$

By definition, the fixed-asset beta is zero. The party that receives the fixed costs holds a safe asset. Since the betas of the revenues and incremental costs respond to the same underlying variable (the rate of output), these betas should be approximately the same. Consequently, since $\beta_{fc} = 0$ and $\beta_r = \beta_{ic}$, equation (14) becomes, after some rearranging of its terms:

$$\beta_a = \beta_r(PV_r - PV_{ic})/PV_a$$

or:

$$\beta_a = \beta_r(1 + PV_{fc}/PV_a) \qquad (15)$$

where:

all symbols are as previously defined

Expression (15) shows that, given the cyclicality of revenues as reflected in β_r, the asset beta increases when the ratio of the present value of fixed costs to the present value of the project increases. Indeed, empirical evidence suggests that companies with high operating leverage do have high betas.

The analogy between financial and operating leverage is almost exact. That is, the beta of the stock increases when the ratio of debt to equity increases, and the beta of the asset rises when the ratio of the value of the fixed costs to the value of the asset rises. Finally, equation (15) is helpful for judging the relative risks of alternative technologies or designs for producing the same project. Other things being equal, the alternative with the higher project beta is the one with the higher ratio of fixed costs to project value.

SUGGESTIONS FOR FURTHER READING

Breeden, D. T. "An Intemporal Asset Pricing Model with Stochastic Consumption and Investment Opportunities." *Journal of Financial Economics*, 7 (September 1979): 265–96.

Chen, N. F., R. Roll, and S. A. Ross. "Economic Forces and the Stock Market: Testing the APT and Alternative Pricing Theories." *Journal of Business*, 59 (July 1986): 383–403.

Foster, G. *Financial Statement Analysis*. Englewood Cliffs, NJ: Prentice-Hall, 1986.

Levy, H., and M. Sarnat. *Portfolio and Investment Selection: Theory and Practice*. Englewood Cliffs, NJ: Prentice-Hall, 1984.

Modigliani, F., and G. A. Pogue. "An Introduction to Risk and Return." *Financial Analysis Journal*, 30 (March–April 1974): 69–88.

Ross, S. A. "The Arbitrage Theory of Capital Asset Pricing." *Journal of Economic Theory*, 13 (December 1976): 341–60.

Schall, L. D. "Asset Valuation, Firm Investment and Firm Diversification." *Journal of Business*, 45 (January 1972): 11–28.

Statman, M. "How Many Stocks Make a Diversified Portfolio?" *Journal of Financial and Quantitative Analysis*, 22, no. 3 (September 1987): 353–63.

CHAPTER 9

The Relationship between Risk and Cost of Capital

> There are some minds like either convex or concave mirrors, which represent objects such as they receive them, but they never receive them as they are.
>
> —Joseph Joubert

Decisions regarding whether to invest in fixed assets, namely, capital-budgeting decisions, involve discounted cash flow analysis. We estimate a project's cash flows, find their present value (PV), and if the PV of the inflows exceeds the cost of the project, we undertake the investment. This chapter deals with determining the proper discount rate for use in calculating the PV of the cash inflows, or the cost of capital. We will also discuss how to take account of risk when determining the cost of capital.

A firm's cost of capital (COC) is determined by the organization's cost of debt, cost of preferred stock, and cost of common equity (retained earnings plus common stock). We start out by making a number of observations that apply to the use of COC. This is followed by a discussion of components that determine a company's cost of capital, the weighted average of the component costs, and the weighted average cost of capital.

Managers often add "fudge" factors to discount rates to offset worries about political risks, environmental risks, and so on. However, the use of such cushions is not advocated. The discussion of fudge factors leads us to important observations about the effect on the discounted present value of a project of delays in (1) project completion and (2) time required to reach a certain percentage of full capacity.

There are two ways of incorporating project risk into the capital budgeting process. One is the certainty equivalent method, which establishes the smallest certain return for which we would exchange the risky cash flow. This approach is difficult to implement in practice. We will focus, therefore, on the risk-adjusted discount rate approach, under which differential project risk is dealt with by changing the discount rate. Average risk projects are discounted at the firm's weighted average cost of capital, above-average risk projects are discounted at a higher cost of capital, and below-average risk projects are discounted at a rate below the firm's weighted average cost of capital.

Capital budgeting and the COC are actually interrelated. That is, we cannot determine the COC until we determine the size of the capital budget, and we cannot establish the size of the capital budget until we determine the COC. Thus, the COC and the capital budget must be determined simultaneously. This is done with the concepts of schedules of marginal costs of capital and investment opportunities.

We will also learn about the effect of corporate taxes on the debt and the equity of a firm and the relationship between the weighted average cost of capital and corporate taxes. In addition, the effect of personal taxes on the value of a firm is examined. Personal taxes as well as financial distress costs reduce advantages related to debt financing or the tax shield. Examples of financial distress and related selfish strategies followed by stockholders of firms near bankruptcy are provided. It is impossible to determine the optional debt level, since costs of financial distress are hard to quantify. However, based on experience, we arrive at the important factors to be considered when faced by decisions of the effect of financial distress on the debt level. Finally, we analyze the relationship between the beta factor and leverage.

1. GENERAL OBSERVATIONS ABOUT THE COST OF CAPITAL

The first observation concerns whether to use one value for the COC for all future time periods or different values for different times in the future. Normally, we associate a higher COC with investments subject to more risk. It is logical that investments with more chance of failure can demand a higher rate of return than investments with less chance. Consequently, the use of one value for the COC for all future time periods may seem unrealistic if the uncertainty or riskiness of future returns is expected to vary over time.

It can be shown, however, that the use of one value for COC is valid if the risk is expected to change over time at a constant rate. In this situation, we can find a constant COC that provides an unambiguous measure of return under risk. For instance, if the COC applicable to the first year return of an investment is 10 percent and thereafter is expected to increase as the result of risk increasing at an annual constant rate, we can find one constant COC applicable to the returns of all years of the investment's expected life and which is equivalent to the increasing annual COCs. We will learn more about this in the next section.

Significant changes in risk from one year to another are not characteristic of the typical pattern of cash flows experienced in most investment analyses. In addition, situations where we are able to specify the exact change in risk from one year to another with a high degree of accuracy are exceptional. We will, therefore, use a COC that is constant over all future time periods. The use of a constant COC simplifies the analysis of capital investments significantly. In fact, the application of different COCs is ordinarily too cumbersome for anything other than expository purposes.

The second observation concerns the manner in which the rate of interest was introduced in Appendix 2. Specifically, it discusses the rate of interest as a way of expressing the price ratio between current and future claims. This is sometimes referred to as the agio, or premium, concept of interest. The term *premium* suggests that current dollars trade for future dollars at better than one-for-one. In line with the practical approach followed in this book, we will not consider the interest rate against a detailed background of productive transformations between the present and future as such a treatment involves complex principles of intertemporal choice or the allocation of resources for consumptive and productive purposes over time.

The third observation concerns the real risk-free rate of interest, r^*, which is defined as the interest rate that would exist on a riskless security if no inflation were expected. It may be thought of as the interest rate which would exist on short-term U.S. Treasury Securities in an inflation-free world. It is difficult to measure the real risk-free rate precisely; most experts in the United States think that it has fluctuated in the range of 1 to 4 percent in recent years.

The nominal, or quoted, risk-free rate of interest, r_{RF}, is the real risk-free rate plus a premium for expected inflation: $r_{RF} = r^* + IP$, where IP = inflation premium. Strictly speaking, the nominal risk-free rate means the interest rate on a totally risk-free security or one that has no risk of default, maturity risk, liquidity risk, or risk of loss should inflation increase. Naturally, such a security does not exist. A U.S. Treasury Bill or a short-term security issued by the U.S. government is, however, free of most risks. T-bonds or longer-term securities issued by the U.S. government are free of default and liquidity risks but are exposed to some risk due to changes in the general level of interest rates. If the term "risk-free rate" is used without the modifier "real" or "nominal," people generally mean the nominal risk-free rate, which includes an inflation premium equal to the expected inflation rate over the life of the security. T-bill and T-bond rates are generally used to approximate the short- and long-term risk-free rates, respectively.

2. A COMPANY'S COST OF CAPITAL

A company can finance new projects by borrowing, issuing preferred stocks, using its retained earnings, and/or issuing common stocks. Financing new projects only by borrowing is normally not recommended since at some point the firm will find it necessary to use one of the other forms of financing to prevent the debt ratio (the ratio of total debt to total assets where total debt includes both current liabilities and long-term debt) from becoming too large. Creditors prefer low debt ratios because the lower the ratio, the greater the cushion against creditor's losses in the event of liquidation. Financing new projects by issuing too many preferred stocks is also not desirable since it is risky to guarantee a given dividend to many persons. A firm should, therefore, be considered an ongoing concern, and the COC used in capital budgeting should be established as a weighted average of the various types of funds it generally uses, regardless of the specific financing used to fund a particular project.

We introduce the following notation:

k_d = interest rate on a firm's new debt; it is the before-tax cost of debt

$k_d (1 - T)$ = the after-tax cost of debt, where T is the firm's marginal tax rate

k_p = the cost of preferred stock

k_s = the cost of retained earnings (or internal equity); it is identical to the required rate of return on common stock

k_e = the cost of external equity obtained by issuing new common stock as opposed to retained earnings

WACOC = the weighted average cost of capital

Cost of Debt

We use the after-tax cost of debt, $k_d(1 - T)$, to calculate the WACOC. It is the interest rate on debt, k_d, less the tax savings that result because the interest is deductible, which is the same as k_d multiplied by $(1 - T)$, where T is the firm's marginal tax rate. In other words, the government pays part of the cost of debt because the interest is deductible. In the United States, the federal tax rate for most corporations is 34 percent, while most are also subject to state income taxes, making the marginal tax rate on most corporate incomes about 40 percent. For instance, if a company can borrow at an interest rate of about 10 percent and has a marginal (federal plus state) tax rate of 40 percent, then its after-tax cost of debt is:

$$k_d(1 - T) = 10\%(1.0 - 0.4) = 10\% \ (0.6) = 6\%$$

The following observations can be made regarding the cost of debt:

1. for a firm with losses, the tax rate is zero, so that the after-tax cost of debt equals k_d;
2. the cost of debt is the interest rate on new debt, not that on already outstanding debt, since our primary concern is the use of the COC in capital-budgeting decisions rather than a rate at which a firm has borrowed in the past (which is a sunk cost); and
3. this discussion of the cost of debt ignores flotation costs (the costs incurred for new issuances on debt) since the vast majority of debt is privately placed and, consequently, has no flotation cost; however, if bonds are publicly placed and do involve flotation costs, the after-tax cost of debt is determined by:

$$M(1 - F) = \sum_{t=1}^{n} [INT(1 - T)/(1 + k_D)^t] + M/(1 + k_D)^n$$

where:

M = the maturity value of the bond
F = the percentage amount of the bond flotation cost
n = the number of periods to maturity
INT = the dollars of interest per period
T = the corporate tax rate
k_D = the after-tax cost of debt adjusted to reflect flotation costs

Cost of Preferred Stock

The cost of preferred stock, k_p, used to compute the COC, is defined as the preferred dividend, D_p, divided by the net issuing price, P_n, or the price the firm receives after deducting flotation costs: $k_p = D_p/P_n$. Thus, if a firm has preferred stock that pays a $10.00 dividend per share and sells for $100.00 per share in the market, and if it incurs a flotation (or underwriting) cost of 2.5 percent, or $2.50, per share, then it will net $97.50 per share. Consequently, the firm's cost of preferred stock is $k_p = \$10.00/\$97.50 = 10.3$ percent. No tax adjustments are made when computing k_p because preferred dividends, unlike interest expense, are not deductible.

Cost of Retained Earnings

The cost of retained earnings, k_s, is the rate of return stockholders require on equity capital that the firm obtains through earnings, or that part of current earnings not paid out in dividends and hence available for reinvestment. Thus, it refers to the income statement item, "addition to retained earnings." It does not refer to its balance sheet item, "retained earnings," since this item consists of all the earnings retained in the business throughout its history. The earnings remaining after interest payments to bondholders and dividends to preferred stockholders belong to the common stockholders and serve to compensate them for the use of their capital. A firm may pay out the earnings in the form of dividends or retain and reinvest them in the business. If the management of a firm decides to retain earnings, there is an opportunity cost involved since shareholders could have received them as dividends and invest the money in real estate, bonds, or other stocks. Consequently, the firm is expected to earn on its retained earnings at least as much as the shareholders could earn on alternative investments of comparable risk. Thus, the cost of a company's retained earnings is the minimum acceptable, or required, rate of return on its stock, considering both its riskiness and the returns available on other investments.

Whereas debt and preferred stock are contractual obligations with easily determined costs, it is not easy to measure k_s. In practice, three methods are commonly used to determine k_s: the bond yield plus risk premium approach, the discounted cash flow approach, and the capital asset–pricing model (CAPM) approach.

The bond yield plus risk premium approach is an ad hoc, subjective procedure consisting of calculating a firm's long-term debt and adding a risk premium of three to five percentage points. For instance, according to this approach, a well established computer firm with bonds yielding 9 percent has a cost of retained earnings determined as follows:

$$k_s = \text{bond yield} + \text{risk premium} = 9\% + 4\% = 13\%$$

A riskier firm may have bonds yielding 12 percent, and therefore, its estimated cost of equity will be:

$$k_s = 12\% + 4\% = 16 \text{ percent}$$

It makes sense that a firm with risky, low-rated, and hence, high inter-est–rate, long-term debt also will have risky, high-cost equity. It is clear that the 4 percent risk premium and the estimated value of k_s based on this premium are judgmental estimates. The range of three to five percentage points for the risk premium is based on empirical work in the United States (Harris and Ravic, 1991).

According to the discounted cash flow approach, the k_s is determined by the following equation:

$$V_S = \sum_{t=1}^{t=\infty} D_t / (1 + k_s)^t$$

where:

V_S = the present value of stock
t = indicates the year
D_t = dividend in year t (expected to be paid at the end of year t)
∞ = indicates that the value of t is infinitely large

It can be shown that if dividends are expected to grow at a constant rate, g, the expression for V_S reduces to the following formula:

$$V_S = D(1 + g)/(k_s - g) = D_1/(k_s - g) \tag{1}$$

where:

D = the stocks' last dividend (which has already been paid)
D_1 = the estimated dividend one year hence

Equation (1) may be written as:

$$k_s = (D_1/V_S) + \text{expected } g$$

Thus, the cost of retained earnings equals an expected dividend yield, D_1/V_S, plus a capital gain, g.

It is relatively easy to determine the expected dividend yield; how-ever, the establishment of the proper growth rate is difficult if growth rates in earnings and dividends have not been relatively stable. In other words, the projection of the growth rate cannot be based on a firm's historic growth if it has been abnormally low or high due to general economic fluctuations or a unique situation. Merrill Lynch, Salomon Brothers, and other organizations make forecasts of earnings and dividend growth based on projected sales, profit margins, and competitive factors. In addition, publications such as *Value Line* provide growth rate factors for a range of companies. One could, therefore, obtain several available forecasts of a company's dividend growth rate, average them, and use the average as a proxy for the growth expectations of investors in general.

To illustrate the discounted cash flow approach, consider a firm's stock that sells for $25.00; its next expected dividend is $1.25, and its expected dividend growth rate is 7 percent. The firm's expected and required rate of return, and, hence, its cost of retained earnings is:

$$k_s = (\$1.25/\$25.00) + 7\% = 5\% + 7\% = 12\%$$

This figure of 12 percent is the minimum rate of return that management is expected to earn to justify retaining earnings and plowing them back into the business rather than paying them out to stockholders as dividends.

The CAPM approach determines k_s with the help of the following equation:

$$k_s = k_{RF} + (k_M - k_{RF})\beta_i \tag{2}$$

where:

k_{RF} = the risk-free rate, generally taken to be either the U.S. Treasury Bond rate or the short-term U.S. Treasury Bill rate

k_M = the expected rate of return on the market (or on an average stock)

β_i = the stock's beta coefficient (the i signifies the ith company's beta)

Thus, the CAPM estimate of k_s consists of the risk-free rate, k_{RF}, and a risk premium, $k_M - k_{RF}$, scaled up or down to reflect the particular stock's risk as measured by its beta coefficient.

The meaning of β_i was discussed in detail in Chapter 8. The parameter indicates the relationship between the return on a portfolio of stocks and the return on the market, while β_i indicates the relationship between the return of the ith stock of the portfolio and the average return on the market.

Note the similarity between equation (2) and equation (9) of Chapter 8. This similarity should be of no surprise if we remember that k_s is identical to the required rate of return on common stock. Although the CAPM approach appears to yield precise estimates of k_s, in practice there are several problems: (1) it is difficult to estimate the beta that investors expect the firm to have in the future, (2) there is controversy about whether to use long- or short-term treasury yields for k_{RF}, and (3) a firm's true investment risk is not measured by its beta if its stockholders are not well diversified and, consequently, are more concerned with total risk rather than market risk.

To illustrate the CAPM approach, suppose that for a given stock, $\beta_i = 0.7$, $k_{RF} = 7$ percent, and $(k_M - k_{RF}) = 8.5$ percent. Hence, the stock's k_s is calculated as follows:

$$k_s = 7\% + (8.5\%)0.7 = 7\% + 6\% = 13\%$$

Had β_i been 1.7, indicating that the stock was riskier than average, its k_s would have been

$$k_s = 7\% + (8.5\%)(1.7) = 7\% + 14.5\% = 21.5\%$$

For an average stock:

$$k_s = k_M = 7\% + (8.5\%)(1.0) = 15.5\%$$

Cost of Newly Issued Common Stock

The cost of new common equity or external equity capital, k_e, is higher than the cost of retained earnings, k_s, because of flotation costs involved in selling new common stock. A firm's existing stockholders expect it to pay a stream of dividends, D_t, which will be derived from existing assets with a per-share value of V_S. Likewise, new investors expect to receive the same stream of dividends, but the funds available in assets will be less than V_S because of flotation costs. Funds obtained from the sale of new stock must be invested at a return high enough so as not to impair the D_t stream of existing stockholders. In other words, funds obtained from the sale of new stock must provide a dividend stream whose present value equals the price the firm will receive:

$$V_S(1 - F) = \sum_{t=1}^{t=\infty} D_t / (1 + k_e)^t = V_N \tag{3}$$

where:

V_S = the present value of an existing stock
V_N = the present value of a newly issued stock
F = the percentage flotation cost incurred in selling the new stock issue
D_t = dividend to be paid to existing and new stockholders at the end of year t
k_e = cost of new outside equity

When growth is constant, equation (3) reduces to:

$$V_S(1 - F) = D_1/(k_e - g)$$

or:

$$k_e = [D_1/V_S(1 - F)] + g \qquad (4)$$

Note that $V_S(1 - F)$ is the net price per share received by the firm when it issues new common stock. Equation (4) may also be written as:

$$k_e = [(D_1/V_S)/(1 - F)] + g = [\text{dividend yield}/(1 - F)] + g$$

Let us consider again the example of the discounted cash flow approach to computing k_s. That is, a firm's stock sells for $25.00, and its next expected dividend and dividend growth rate are $1.25 and 7 percent, respectively. The flotation cost is 10 percent. The cost of retained earnings and the cost of new outside equity are, respectively:

$$k_s = (\$1.25/\$25.00) + 7\% = 12\%$$
$$k_e = [\$1.25/\$25.00(1 - 0.10)] + 7\% = 12.56\%$$

Investors require a return of $k_s = 12$ percent on the stock; however, the firm must earn more than 12 percent due to flotation costs. Specifically, the firm's expected dividend can be maintained and the price per share will not decline if the firm earns 12.56 percent on funds obtained from new stock. If the firm earns less than 12.56 percent, then earnings, dividends, and growth will fall below expectations, causing the stock's price to decline. If it earns more than 12.56 percent, however, the stock's price will rise.

Another way of looking at the flotation adjustment is as follows. Consider a company with $1,000,000 of assets and no debt. It earns a 14 percent return ($140,000) on its assets, and it pays all earnings out as dividends, so its growth rate is zero. The company has 10,000 shares of stock outstanding so its earnings per share (EPS) and dividends per share (DPS) are EPS = DPS = $14, and V_S = $100. Thus k_s = ($14/$100) + 0 = 14 percent.

Now suppose the company can get a return of 14 percent on new assets. Should it sell new stock to acquire new assets? If it sold 10,000 new shares of stock for $100 per share and incurred a 10 percent flotation cost on the issue, the company would net $100 − 0.10($100) = $90 per share, or $900,000 in total. Next, the company would invest the $900,000 and earn 14 percent ($126,000). Its new total earnings would be $140,000 from the old assets plus $126,000 from the new, or $266,000 in total, and the company would now have 20,000 of stock outstanding. Thus, its EPS and DPS would fall from $14.00 to $13.30, because the new EPS and DPS are: EPS = DPS = $266,000/20,000 = $13.30. Since the company's EPS and DPS would decline, the stock's price would also decline from V_S = $100 to $13.30/0.14 = $95 because investors have put up $100 per share but the company has received and invested only $90 per share. The $90 must, therefore, earn more than 14 percent to provide investors with a 14 percent return on the $100 they put up. Had the company earned a return of k_e based on equation (4), we would have:

k_e = [$14/$100(0.90)] + 0 = 15.56%
New total earnings = $140,000 + $900,000(0.1556) = $280,000
New EPS and DPS = $280,000/20,000 = $14
New price = $14/0.14 = $100 = original price

Thus, if the return on the new assets is based on the k_e of equation (4), then EPS, DPS, and the stock price will remain constant.

Weighted Average Cost of Capital

The WACOC is a weighted average of the component costs of debt, preferred stock, and common equity. Consider, for instance, a firm with a capital structure consisting of 45 percent debt, 1 percent preferred stock, and 54 percent common equity (retained earnings plus common stock). Suppose its before-tax cost of debt, k_d, is 10 percent; its marginal tax rate is 40 percent; its cost of preferred stock, k_p, is 11 percent; its cost of common equity from retained earnings, k_s, is 13 percent, and all of its new equity will come from retained earnings. We now determine the firm's WACOC as follows:

$$\text{WACOC} = w_d k_d (1 - T) + w_p k_p + w_s k_s = 0.45(10\%)(0.6) + 0.01(11\%)$$
$$+ 0.54(13\%) = 10\%$$

The variables w_d, w_p, and w_s are the weights used for debt, preferred, and common equity, respectively. They are based on the accounting values shown on the firm's balance sheet (book values). Theoretically, the weights should be based on the market values of the different securities; however, book value weights can be used as a proxy for market value weights if the two are reasonably close.

Each firm has an optimal capital structure, defined as the capital structure with the lowest WACOC. Such a capital structure is the combination of debt, preferred equity, and common equity that causes its stock price to be maximized. The concept of optimal capital structure is based on a capital structure policy which involves a trade-off between risk and return. That is, using more debt raises the riskiness of a firm's earnings; however, a higher debt ratio generally leads to a higher expected rate of return. In other words, higher risk associated with greater debt tends to decrease the stock's price, but the higher expected rate of return increases it. The optimal capital structure is the one that strikes the optimal balance between risk and return, and by doing so, maximizes the stock's price.

Financial leverage, which is the extent to which fixed-income securities (debt and preferred stock) are used in a firm's capital structure, affects the firm's expected earnings per share (EPS), their riskiness, and, consequently, its stock price. As a result of using financial leverage, an additional risk is placed on common stockholders. This additional risk, called the financial risk, is the portion of the stockholders' risk over and above the basic business risk (see Chapter 8 for a detailed discussion of financial risk).

The following example illustrates how financial leverage affects a company's EPS and stock price. Suppose a company's annual sales are $400,000; its fixed costs are $80,000; its variable costs are 60 percent of sales, or $240,000; and its marginal tax rate, T, is 40 percent. The company's total assets are worth $400,000. We consider two cases:

1. Debt-assets ratio (D/A ratio) = 0, or there is zero debt and 20,000 shares outstanding.
2. D/A ratio = 50 percent; the interest rate, k_d, is equal to 12 percent; and there are 10,000 shares outstanding.

Thus, in the first case, the company is capitalized with 0 debt and 100 percent equity, while in the second case, the company is capitalized with 50 percent debt and 50 percent equity.

We determine the EPS for these two cases with equation (5):

$$\text{EPS} = (\text{sales} - \text{fixed costs} - \text{variable costs} - \text{interest})$$
$$(1 - T)/\text{shares outstanding} \qquad (5)$$

For $D/A = 0$, equation (5) becomes:

$$EPS = (\$400{,}000 - \$80{,}000 - \$240{,}000 - 0)(0.6)/20{,}000 = \$2.40$$

For $D/A = 50$ percent, we have:

$$EPS = (\$400{,}000 - \$80{,}000 - \$240{,}000 - \$24{,}000)(0.6)/10{,}000 = \$3.36$$

Let us assume that the company pays all its earnings out as dividends, so EPS = DPS; moreover, no retained earnings will be plowed back into the business, and consequently, growth in EPS and DPS will be zero. Suppose the risk-free rate of return, k_{RF}, is 6 percent; the required return on an average stock, k_M, is 10 percent; the beta pertaining to the D/A = 0 case is 1.50; and the beta pertaining to the D/A = 50 percent case is 2.35. The application of equations (2) and (1) gives, for $D/A = 0$:

$$k_s = 6\% + (10\% - 6\%)1.50 = 12.0\%$$
$$V_S = DPS/k_s = \$2.40/0.120 = \$20.00$$

For $D/A = 50$ percent:

$$k_s = 6\% + (10\% - 6\%)2.35 = 15.4\%$$
$$V_S = DPS/k_s = \$3.36/0.154 = \$21.82$$

Next, we determine the price earnings (P/E) ratio and WACOC for each of the cases considered. For $D/A = 0$:

P/E ratio $= V_S/EPS = \$20.00/ \$2.40 = 8.33$
WACOC $= w_d k_d(1 - T) + w_s k_s = (D/A)(k_d)(1 - T) + (1 - D/A)k_s = 0 + k_s$
    $= 12.0\%$

For $D/A = 50$ percent:

P/E ratio $= V_S/EPS = \$21.82/\$3.36 = 6.49$
WACOC $= (D/A)(k_d)(1 - T) + (1 - D/A)k_s = 0.5(12\%)(0.6) + 0.5(15.4\%)$
    $= 3.6\% + 7.7\% = 11.3\%$

This example illustrates that changing a company's capitalization from 0 debt and 100 percent equity to 50 percent debt and 50 percent equity decreases the WACOC from 12.0 percent to 11.3 percent, increases the EPS from \$2.40 to \$3.36, and increases the company's estimated stock price from \$20.00 to \$21.82. In other words, using financial leverage is to the advantage of the company, since it increases the company's stock price. How far should the company go with substituting debt for equity? The answer is that the company should choose the capital structure that will maximize the price of its stock. To elucidate this concept, we consider the same example as the one discussed above, and increase the number of cases pertaining to different D/A ratios as given in Table 9.1.

The values of columns 2 and 4 of Table 9.1 are given, while the values of the other columns are calculated in the same manner as we computed them for $D/A = 0$ and $D/A = 50$ percent. For instance, for $D/A = 20$ percent, we have:

$$EPS = (\$400{,}000 - \$80{,}000 - \$240{,}000 - \$6{,}800)(0.6)/16{,}000 = \$2.75$$
$$k_s = 6\% + (10\% - 6\%)1.65 = 12.6\%$$
$$V_S = \$2.75/0.126 = \$21.83$$
$$P/E \text{ ratio} = \$21.83/\$2.75 = 7.94$$
$$WACOC = 0.2(8.5\%)(0.6) + 0.8(12.6) = 11.10$$

Table 9.1
Estimates of Stock Price and Cost of Capital for a Company According to Different D/A Ratios

D/A (%)	k_d (%)	Exp. EPS and DPS[1]	Est. β	k_s^2 (%)	V_S^3	P/E[4]	WA-COC[5] (%)
(1)	(2)	(3)	(4)	(5)	(6)	(7)	(8)
0	-	$2.40	1.50	12.0	$20.00	8.33	12.00
10	8.0	2.56	1.55	12.2	20.98	8.20	11.46
20	8.5	2.75	1.65	12.6	21.83	7.94	11.10
30	9.0	2.97	1.80	13.2	22.50	7.58	10.86
40	10.0	3.20	2.00	14.0	22.86	7.14	10.80
50	12.0	3.36	2.35	15.4	21.82	6.49	11.30
60	15.0	3.30	2.75	17.8	18.54	5.62	12.52

[1]The company pays all its earnings out as dividends, so EPS = DPS.
[2]$k_s = [k_{RF} + (k_M - k_{RF})\beta]$, with $k_{RF} = 6\%$ and $k_M = 10\%$.
[3]Estimated price.
[4]Resulting P/E ratio.
[5]Weighted average cost of capital.

Table 9.1 shows that at a 40 percent debt ratio, the expected stock price is maximized and the WACOC is minimized. Thus, the optimal capital structure calls for 40 percent debt and 60 percent equity. The company should set its target capital structure at these ratios; it should move toward this target when new securities offerings are made if the existing ratios are off target. As we will see later in this chapter, the capital structure consisting of 40 percent debt and 60 percent equity is not the truly optimal capital structure since costs of financial distress (which are hard to quantify) and personal taxes, are not considered. Thus, the 40 percent debt, 60 percent equity capital structure is optimal given the information about k_{RF} and k_M and the data of the first, second, and fourth columns of Table 9.1.

The following observations are made about the figures of Table 9.1:

1. Column 2 shows that the company's cost of debt varies if different percentages of debt are used in its capital structure; the higher the percentage of debt, the riskier the debt, and, consequently, the higher the interest rate lenders will charge.
2. Column 3 demonstrates that the expected EPS is maximized at a D/A ratio of 50 percent; however, this does not mean that the company's optimal capital structure calls for a 50 percent debt, since the optimal capital structure is the one that maximizes the price of the company's stock, which always calls for a D/A ratio smaller than the one that maximizes expected EPS.
3. The beta coefficients of column 4 measure the relative volatility of the company's stock as compared with that of an average stock (Section 3 of Chapter 8 discusses the manner in which beta coefficients are established); it has been demonstrated both empirically and theoretically that a company's beta increases with its degree of financial leverage.
4. Column 5 shows that the values of k_s increase when the estimated beta coefficients increase (by definition of k_s); note that $(k_M - k_{RF})$ is not equal to 8.5 percent, as is often the case in the United States (see Chapter 8), since the example pertains to a European country.
5. As mentioned above, the values of column 6 are computed to establish the optimal capital structure—the one that results in the highest estimated stockprice.
6. The P/E ratios of column 7 demonstrate that, other things held constant, they will decline as the riskiness of a company increases; the P/E ratios are computed as a check on the reasonableness of the other data of Table 9.1, and they can be compared for consistency with those of zero-growth competitive companies with varying amounts of financial leverage.

7. Column 8 shows that as the D/A ratio increases, the costs of both debt and equity rise and the increasing costs of the two components begin to offset the fact that larger amounts of the lower-cost component are being used; at 40 percent debt, WACOC hits a minimum; it rises after that as the D/A ratio is increased.

Fudge Factors

In everyday usage, "risk" often means "bad outcome." That is, managers think of the risks of a project as a list of things that can go wrong. This list may include the political, legal, and environmental risks discussed in Chapter 1. Alternatively, a geologist looking for oil may worry about the "risk of a dry hole." Managers often add fudge factors to discount rates to offset worries such as these. This approach is not advocated since (1) the list of things that can go wrong appear to reflect diversifiable risks (Section 3, Chapter 8), which would not affect the expected rate of return demanded by investors; and (2) the need for fudge factors usually arises because managers fail to give bad outcomes their due weight in cash flow forecasts. In the latter case, we could argue that managers try to offset their mistake by adding a fudge factor to the discount rate.

Consider, for example, a project, X, that will produce a net annual cashflow of $1 million (M) in perpetuity. We regard it as average risk, suitable for discounting at a 10 percent company cost of capital. Thus, its present value (PV) is $1,000,000/0.10 = $10,000,000. Now, however, we discover that the company's engineers are behind schedule in making the technology required to comply with U.S. government environmental standards. The company engineers are "confident" they will be able to comply with these standards, but they admit to a small chance they will not, in which case the project will not be implemented. We still consider the most likely outcome as $10 M, but we also see some chance that project X will generate zero cash flow. Consequently, the project will be worth less than $10 M.

Rather than working with a fudge factor, we propose to work with present values representing unbiased forecasts, which give due weight to all possible outcomes. Managers making unbiased forecasts are correct on average.

Let us assume that the initial prospects of project X, $10 M, are based on the following three possible outcomes and related probabilities.

Possible PV	Probability	Probability-weighted PV
$12 M	0.25	$3 M
10 M	0.50	5 M
8 M	0.25	2 M

The most likely PV is the sum of the probability-weighted PV, or $3 M + $5 M + $2 M = $10 M. This is an unbiased PV. If technology uncertainty introduces the chance of a zero PV, we have to revise the possible outcomes and related probabilities of project X. We decide, therefore, on the following outcomes.

Possible PV	Probability	Probability-weighted PV
$ 12 M	0.25	$3 M
10 M	0.40	4 M
8 M	0.25	2 M
0 M	0.10	0 M

The most likely PV is now $9 M.

Naturally, we can now establish the right fudge factor to add to the discount rate to apply to the original net cash flow of $1 M. It is 0.0111, since $1 M/0.1111 = $9 M. However, we had to consider possible present values in order to get the fudge factor, and once we have done so, we need no fudge factor.

In this example we considered different cash flows related to a project and each of these cash flows had a given probability. Different cash flows often arise due to a delay in project completion and/or attainment of full-capacity production. Appendix 5 examines the effect of delays on the present value of a project. Although the average reader may not be interested in the mathematics of Appendix 5, its conclusions are important. They are:

1. The effect of delays in project completion on the discounted present value of a project is significantly smaller than the effect of delays in time required to reach a certain percentage of full capacity.
2. The smaller the value of the parameter of the function depicting the time profile output of a project, or the longer the time required to reach a certain percentage of full capacity, the more sensitive is the discounted present value of a project to changes in the value of this parameter.
3. An increase in the time required to complete a project and/or an increase in the time required to reach a certain percentage of full capacity may turn a project from a profitable venture to a nonprofitable undertaking.
4. Generally, changes in the value of the aforementioned parameter and/or start-up time have a stronger impact on the present discounted value of a project if the fixed costs are small (start-up time is the time at which production starts, as measured from the beginning of the investment outlay).

The practical value of the approach of Appendix 5 is in converting such vague questions as, "How far off are we?" "Should we cash in our chips on this one and go to something else?" and "How can we pull this one out of the hole in time for an acceptable payoff?" into quantitative terms that can serve as the basis for informed decision and action.

3. CERTAINTY EQUIVALENCE

Differential project risk can be taken into account by considering different risk premiums, different dividend streams or different betas in, respectively, the bond yield plus risk premium, discounted cash flow, and CAPM approaches to establishing the cost of retained earnings. The risk-adjusted discount rate approach deals with differential project risk by changing the discount rate. A firm may also use its weighted average cost of capital for average risk projects, while below-average risk projects are discounted at a rate below the firm's weighted average cost of capital and above-average risk projects are discounted at a higher cost of capital.

Another method for incorporating project risk into the capital budgeting decision process is the certainty equivalent approach. According to this approach we ask ourselves, "What is the smallest certain return for which we could exchange a risky cash flow?"

The certainty equivalence of a project is defined by equation (6).

$$\sum_{t=1}^{T} [CEQ_t/(1+k_{RF})^t] = \sum_{t=1}^{T} [a_t C_t/(1+k_{RF})^t] \tag{6}$$

where:

t = index denoting a specific year of the expected life of the project
T = number of years of the project's expected life
CEQ_t = certainty equivalence in year t
k_{RF} = the risk-free rate
a_t = the ratio of the certainty equivalent cashflow to its expected value in year t, or $a_t = CEQ/C_t$
C_t = the risky cash flow in year t

To elucidate the use of certainty equivalence, we consider the following simple example. Suppose that the forecast value of a risky cash flow is $1,500 and that we are willing to trade it for a safe cash flow of $1,200. In that case, $1,200 is the certainty equivalence of the risky cash flow.

That is, we are indifferent between an $1,200 safe return and an expected, but risky, cash flow of $1,500. Since, by definition, we are indifferent between the two cash flows, the present value of the $1,500 forecast cash flow must be the same as the present value of a certain $1,200. Assuming a risk-free rate of 7 percent, we compute the present value (PV) of $1,500 as follows.

$$PV(1{,}500) = CEQ_1/(1 + k_{RF}) = \$1{,}200/1.07 = \$1{,}121.50$$

Note that the expression $CEQ_1/(1 + k_{RF})$ is the term on the left-hand side of the equals sign of equation (6), where $T = 1$. We could have gotten the same answer by discounting $1,500 at a risk-adjusted rate. Thus, $PV(1{,}500) = \$1{,}500/(1 + r) = \$1{,}121.50$, where the risk-adjusted rate, r, is equal to 0.337, or 33.7 percent. In other words, we have two equivalent expressions for PV; that is, $PV = C_1(1 + r) = CEQ_1/(1 + k_{RF})$.

The certainty equivalent approach is difficult to implement in practice. We will focus, therefore, on the risk-adjusted discount rate approach. However, certainty equivalence enhances our understanding that the use of one value for the COC is valid if the risk is expected to change over time at a constant rate.

Specifically, when we discount at a constant, risk-adjusted rate, which we call r, we implicitly make a special assumption about the coefficient a_t. To see this, we consider a project offering cash flows in two years. If the certainty equivalent and risk-adjusted discount rate expressions are indeed equivalent, they should give the same present value for each cash flow, or $C_1/(1 + r) = a_1C_1/(1 + k_{RF})$ and $C_2/(1 + r)^2 = a_2C_2(1 + k_{RF})^2$. Consequently, $a_1 = (1 + k_{RF})/(1 + r)$, and $a_2 = [(1 + k_{RF})/(1 + r)]^2 = (a_1)^2$. In general terms, we can write that for a project offering cash flows in T years, $a_t = [(1 + k_{RF})/(1 + r)]^t = (a_1)^t$. The use of a constant risk-adjusted discount rate to value the cash flow for each period is justified only if the value of a_t decreases over time at a constant rate.

To enhance our understanding of the use of one COC, we consider a project requiring $40 today $(t = 0)$ and offering expected cash flows of $110 per year for six years. The risk-free rate is 7 percent, the market risk premium is 12 percent, and the estimated beta is 0.6. With the help of equation (2), we determine the risk-adjusted discount rate as follows.

$$0.07 + (0.12 - 0.07)\,0.6 = 0.10, \text{ or } 10\%$$

Table 9.2 shows what we implicitly assume about the values of a_t. That is, we are effectively making a larger deduction for risk from the later cash flows by using a constant discount rate. The larger deduction is reflected in lower values for a_t. Notice also that a_t decreases at a constant compound rate of about 2.7 percent per year. In other words, any risk-adjusted discount rate recognizes that more distant cash flows have more risk. This is true since the discount rate compensates for the risk borne per year. The more distant the cash flows, the greater the number of years and the larger the total risk adjustment.

4. MARGINAL COST OF CAPITAL AND INVESTMENT OPPORTUNITY SCHEDULES (IOSs)

As a company tries to attract more new dollars, the cost of each dollar will at some point rise. In other words, the weighted average cost of capital (WACOC) depends on the amount of new capital raised; the WACOC will, at some point, rise if more and more capital is raised during a given period. This is so since (1) flotation costs cause the cost

Table 9.2
Example Demonstrating the Certainty Equivalence Implied by the Constant Risk-Adjusted Discount Rate

(1)	(2)	(3)	(4)	(5)	(6)
Period	C_t	PV	CEQ_t	a_t	PV of CEQs
0	(400)	(400)	(400)	1.000	(400)
1	110	100	107	0.973	100
2	110	91	103	0.936	90
3	110	82	100	0.909	82
4	110	75	98	0.891	75
5	110	68	95	0.864	68
6	110	62	94	0.855	63
		NPV = 78			NPV = 78

Note: The heading of column 2 represents the expected cash flow during period t, where $t = 0, 1, 2, 3, 4, 5$, and 6 (see column 1). The heading of column 3 is the present value (PV), or $PV = C_t/(1.10)^t$. The heading of column 4 represents the certainty equivalent CEQ_t, implied by the use of the 10 percent discount, where $CEQ_t = C_t[(1 + k_{RF})/(1 + k_s)]^t$, k_{RF} = risk-free rate = 7 percent, and k_s = risk-adjusted discount rate = 10 percent. The heading of column 5 is the ratio of CEQ_t to C_t. The heading of column 6 is the PV of the CEQs at the 7 percent risk-free rate.

of new equity to be higher than the cost of retained earnings, and (2) higher rates of return on debt, preferred stock, and common stock may be required to induce investors to supply additional capital to the company, which increases its risk. The marginal cost of capital (MCC) is defined as the cost of the last dollar of new capital that the company raises; the marginal cost rises as more and more capital is raised during a given period.

A graph which shows how the WACOC changes as more and more new capital is raised during a given period is called the marginal cost of capital schedule. Figure 9.1 shows how the WACOC changes for the

Figure 9.1

Combining the MCC Schedule and the IOS to Determine the Optimal Capital Budget

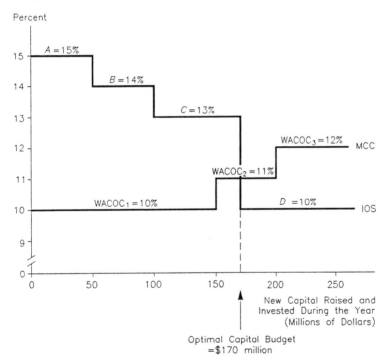

Project	Cost (in Millions)	Rate of Return
A	$50	15%
B	$50	14%
C	$70	13%
D	$80	10%

following example. From $0 to $150 M of new capital the WACOC is 10 percent, whereas just beyond $150 M, the WACOC rises to 11 percent since the cost of the debt rises. This may be due to the fact that a bank is willing to lend a company at a given interest rate up to a given limit; beyond this limit, the interest rate will be higher due to the additional risk exposure the bank is taking. At $200 M, the WACOC rises again to 12 percent, since at this point, external equity is required and the cost of external equity is higher than the cost of retained earnings. There could, of course, be still more break points, or points at which the WACOC would increase; they would occur if the interest rate continued to rise or if there was a rise in the cost of preferred and/or common stock.

A part of the capital-budgeting process involves the assessment of the riskiness of each project and its assignment to a capital cost based on its relative risk. The cost of capital assigned to an average risk project should be the MCC. Less risky projects should be evaluated with a lower cost of capital, while more risky projects should be assigned higher costs of capital. In other words, firms first measure the MCC and then scale it up or down to reflect individual projects' riskiness. Although the use of CAPM has enhanced our knowledge in measuring risk, we admit that risk cannot be measured precisely. Thus, there is no exact way of specifying how much higher or lower than the MCC the costs of capital of non–average-risk projects should be; given the present state of the art, risk adjustments are necessarily judgmental.

Since the cost of capital depends on how much capital a firm raises, the question of which WACOC it should use arises. Specifically, in the example of Figure 9.1, should we use a WACOC of 10, 11, or 12 percent? The answer is based on the concept of marginal analysis, which tells us that firms should expand output to the point where marginal revenue equals marginal cost. At that point, the last unit of output exactly covers its cost—further expansion would reduce profits and the firm would forgo profits at any lower production rate.

To apply the concept of marginal analysis, we introduce a schedule that is analogous to the MCC schedule. This is the investment opportunity schedule (IOS), which shows the rate of return expected on each potential investment opportunity. Figure 9.1 shows an IOS for projects A, B, C, and D. The first three projects all have expected rates of return that exceed the cost of capital that will be used to finance them, but the expected return on project D is less than its cost of capital. Consequently, projects A, B, and C should be accepted, and project D should be rejected. The WACOC at the point where the IOS intersects the MCC curve is defined as the corporate cost of capital—this point reflects the marginal cost of capital to the corporation.

5. THE CAPITAL-BUDGETING PROCESS

Capital budgeting consists of (1) identification of the set of investment opportunities, (2) estimation of the future cash inflows associated with each project, (3) determination of the present value (PV) of cash inflows of each project, and (4) comparison of each project's PV with its cost—and acceptance of a project if the PV of its future cash inflows exceeds its cost. To obtain the optimal capital budget, we should, in step 3, use a firm's marginal cost of capital; however, at this point in time we do not yet know this cost. Therefore, we compute the internal rate of return (IRR) of each project to develop a graph as in Figure 9.1. Specifically, the rates of return of projects A, B, C, and D in the figure are the internal rates of return, and based on these returns, we accept projects A, B, and C, and we reject project D. Chapter 3 introduced the concept of IRR. The firm's marginal cost of capital is the WACOC where the IOS intersects the MCC curve, which in the example of Figure 9.1 is 11 percent. We can now proceed with carrying out step 3 by using the weighted average cost of capital equal to the firm's marginal cost of capital. Thus, if the costs of projects A, B, and C amount to $50 M, $50 M, and $70 M, respectively (as indicated in Figure 9.1), and assuming that carrying out step 4 also results in the selection of projects A, B, and C, then the optimal capital budget is $170 M.

Up to this point we have not yet considered the determination of the optimal capital budget when among the identified set of investment opportunities there are some mutually exclusive projects. Consider, for example, that we have identified projects A, B, C, D, and E and that projects B and C are mutually exclusive and each have an IRR larger than the marginal cost of capital. In this case, we develop two graphs as in Figure 9.1, one for projects A, B, D, and E, and one for projects A, C, D, and E. Next, we determine the marginal cost of capital related to each graph and the corresponding sum of net present values of projects with an IRR larger than the marginal cost of capital. Project B is selected if the sum of net present values of the projects including project B is larger than the sum of net present values including project C. Naturally, if the former sum is smaller than the latter, we select project C.

The previous discussion of establishing the optimal capital budget was given for a rather small set of identified investment opportunities in order to keep the presentation simple. However, the methodology can be applied to any number of identified investment opportunities.

Although the procedures set forth in the preceding paragraphs are conceptually correct and an understanding of their underlying logic is important, management often uses a more judgmental, less quantitative, process for establishing the final capital budget. Typically, the financial vice president of a company acquires reasonably good estimates of the MCC schedule and the IOS from the treasurer and director of capital budgeting, respectively. These two schedules are then combined, as in Figure 9.1, to get a reasonably good approximation of the company's marginal cost of capital (the cost of capital at the intersection of the IOS and MCC schedules). The corporate MCC is then scaled up or down for each division to reflect the division's risk characteristics and capital structure, which is included if a company finances different assets in different ways. For instance, one division may have most of its capital tied up in special-purpose machinery, which is not very well suited as collateral for loans, while another division may have a lot of real estate, which is good collateral. As a result, the division with the real estate has a higher debt capacity than the division with the machinery, and consequently, an optimal capital structure that contains a higher percentage of debt.

Suppose, for instance, that the corporate MCC is 11.0 percent. The financial vice president may then decide to assign a factor 0.9 to a stable and low-risk division, but a factor of 1.1 to a more risky division. Therefore, the cost of capital of the low-risk division is 0.9(11.0 percent) = 9.9 percent, while that for the more risky division is 1.1(11.0 percent) = 12.1 percent. Next, each project within each division is classified into one of three groups—high risk, average risk, and low risk—and the same factors, 0.9 and 1.1, are used to adjust the divisional MCCs. For example, a low-risk project in the low-risk division would have a cost of capital of 0.9(9.9 percent) = 8.9 percent, and a low-risk project in the more risky division would have a cost of capital of 0.9(12.1 percent) = 10.9 percent. A high-risk project in the low-risk division would have a cost of capital of 1.1(9.9 percent) = 10.9 percent, and a high-risk project in the more risky division would have a cost of capital of 1.1(12.1 percent) = 13.3 percent. Naturally, the corporate MCC of 11.0 percent is not adjusted for an average-risk project in an average risk division.

After having established the adjusted cost of capital for each project in each division, we determine the net present value (NPV) for each project by using its risk-adjusted cost of capital. The optimal capital budget consists of all independent projects with risk-adjusted, positive NPVs plus the mutually exclusive projects with the risk-adjusted, highest positive NPVs among that group.

This approach to establishing the final capital budget has the advantage that it forces a company to think carefully about each division's relative risk, the risk of each project in each division, and the relationship between the total amount of capital raised and its cost. In addition, the company's capital budget is adjusted to reflect capital market conditions—the cost of capital to evaluate projects will increase if the cost of debt and equity rises, and projects that are marginally acceptable when capital costs are low will be ruled unacceptable when capital costs are high.

To deal with projects with different risks, we can also determine the corporate cost of capital for groups of projects with about equal risk. Thus, the first group of projects may consist of high-risk projects; the second group, of average-risk projects; and the third group, of low-risk projects. Next, we determine the IOS and MCC schedules for each group to arrive at the corporate costs of capital.

6. CORPORATE AND PERSONAL TAXES AND FINANCIAL DISTRESS

To examine how corporate taxes affect stockholders and bondholders, consider the following example. Suppose company ABC has expected earnings before interest and taxes (EBIT) of $1 M; a cost of debt, k_d, of 10 percent, and a corporate tax rate, T_c, of 34 percent. Let us consider two financing plans for company ABC. Under plan 1, ABC has no debt in its capital structure, and under plan 2, it has $4 M of debt, D. We carry out the following calculations:

	Plan 1	Plan 2
EBIT	$1,000,000	$1,000,000
Interest (k_dD)	0	(400,000)
Earnings before taxes (EBT) = (EBIT − k_dD)	1,000,000)	600,000
Taxes $(T_c = 0.34)$	(340,000)	(204,000)
Earnings after corporate taxes (EAT) = $[(EBIT − k_dD)(1 − T_c)]$	660,000	396,000
Total cash flow to both stockholders and bondholders $[EBIT (1 − T_c) + T_ck_dD]$	$660,000	$796,000

From this example we see that more cash flow reaches the stockholders and bondholders under plan 2. The difference is $796,000 − $660,000 = $136,000, which is due to the fact that the U.S. Internal Revenue Service (IRS) receives less taxes under plan 2 ($204,000) than under plan 1 ($340,000). The difference is $340,000 − $204,000 = $136,000. This difference occurs because IRS taxes earnings after interest but before corporate taxes (EBT) at the 34 percent rate, whereas interest is not subject to corporate taxes.

Tax Shields

If we ignore the effect of depreciation, the example shows that for an all-equity firm, the taxable income is EBIT and total taxes are EBIT $\times T_c$. For a levered firm, the taxable income is (EBIT $- k_dD$) and total taxes are T_c(EBIT $- k_dD$). In these expressions we define the symbols as follows: T_c = corporate tax rate, k_d = cost of debt, and D = amount of debt. Note that for the levered firm, we have cash flow going to both stockholders and bondholders equal to:

$$\text{EBIT}(1 - T_c) + T_c k_d D \tag{7}$$

and cash flow going to the stockholders equal to:

$$\text{EBIT} - k_dD - T_c(\text{EBIT} - k_dD) = (\text{EBIT} - k_dD)(1 - T_c) \tag{8}$$

Expression (7) shows that the cash flow going to the stockholders and bondholders depends on the amount of debt financing. By comparing expression (7) with the expression for earnings after corporate taxes for an all-equity firm, which is EBIT$(1 - T_c)$, we note that the difference is $T_c k_d D$. This difference is the extra cash flow going to investors (that is, stockholders and bondholders) in the levered firm. Equation (8) shows what is left for stockholders after paying corporate taxes and interest.

This discussion demonstrates a tax advantage to debt and a tax disadvantage to equity. In addition, although in the example we looked at the difference between plans 1 and 2 during a given year, it is clear that the example also applies to later years. In other words, the algebraic expressions apply to each year of the expected life of a project. Thus, the cash flow of the levered firm each year is greater than the cashflow of the all-equity firm by a factor of $T_c k_d D$, which is called the tax shield from debt. We conclude, therefore, that

$$\text{tax shield from debt} = T_c k_d D \tag{9}$$

Let us assume that all cash flows are perpetual and without growth. As long as a firm anticipates being in a positive tax bracket, it is safe to assume that equation (9) will have the same risk as the interest on the debt. Consequently, the value of the tax shield is given by equation (10).

$$\text{present value of tax shield} = T_c k_d D/k_d = T_c D \tag{10}$$

A tax shield reduces the risk of a project since the U.S. government contributes to it.

We now move on to determine the value of a levered firm. The value of an all-equity firm is the present value of EBIT$(1 - T_c)$:

$$V_U = \text{EBIT}(1 - T_c)/k_u \qquad (11)$$

where:

> V_U = the present value of an unlevered firm
> k_u = the cost of capital to an all-equity firm
> all other terms are as previously defined.

Naturally, equation (11) also assumes that the cashflows are perpetual.

The value of a levered firm is the sum of the present value of the corresponding unlevered firm and the present value of the tax shield:

$$V_L = V_U + T_c D \qquad (12)$$

where:

> V_L = the present value of the corresponding levered firm
> all other terms are as previously defined.

Note that the $T_c D$ and V_U correspond to equations (10) and (11), respectively. The reason why the definition of V_L refers to the "corresponding" levered firm is that the expressions apply to the analysis of the same firm, as in the example in the beginning of this section. Thus, V_U applies to plan 1, and V_L applies to plan 2 of company ABC. To enhance our understanding of equation (12), we can consider the following example. Suppose company XYZ, which is currently an all-equity company, is considering a capital restructuring to allow \$40,000 of debt. It anticipates generating, in perpetuity, \$30,304 in cash flow before interest and taxes. The corporate tax rate is 34 percent, and consequently, the after-tax cash flow is 0.66(\$30,304) = \$20,000. The company has a cost of debt capital of 10 percent, while unlevered firms in the same industry have a cost of equity capital of 20 percent.

The management of company XYZ wishes to know the new value of the company and the value of levered equity should it go ahead with the capital restructuring. From this information we establish that T_c = 0.34, k_u = 0.20, EBIT = \$30,304, and D = \$40,000. We now use equation (11) to determine V_U:

$$V_U = \$30,304\ (1 - 0.34)/0.20 = \$20,000/0.20 = \$100,000.$$

Next, we use equation (10) to determine T_cD:

$$T_cD = 0.34(40,000) = \$13,600.$$

With the help of equation (12), we find V_L:

$$V_L = \$100,000 + \$13,600 = \$113,600$$

Since V_L must be equal to the sum of debt, D, plus the value of levered equity, S, or $V_L = D + S$, we conclude that $S = \$113,600 - \$40,000 = \$73,600$. The example shows that the k_u of equation (11) applies to the cost of equity capital of unlevered firms in the same industry. Thus, if company XYZ were in the textile industry, we would use the k_u of textile companies; if it were an airline, we would use the k_u applying to airlines; and so on. Note that (1) in order to arrive at the value for V_L, we did not have to use the cost of debt of 10 percent, and (2) in a world with taxes, k_u is used to discount after-tax cash flows.

To simplify the presentation, we have assumed that cash flows are perpetual. It is, however, not difficult to extend equations (10) through (12) if we have a finite life. For instance, equation (10) is replaced by the following calculations if we wish to compute the value of the tax shield of a firm that has \$1 M in debt with a 7 percent coupon rate. The debt matures in two years, the cost of debt capital, k_d, is 10 percent, and the corporate tax rate, T_c, is 34 percent. The debt is amortized in equal installments over two years. Thus, we have the following situation.

Year	Loan balance	Interest	Tax shield	PV of tax shield
0	$1,000,000			
1	$500,000	$70,000	0.34($70,000)	$21,637
2	$0	$35,000	0.34($35,000)	$ 9,834
				PV = $31,471

The present value (PV) of the tax savings is:

$$PV = 0.34(\$70,000)(0.9091) + 0.34(\$35,000)(0.8264) = \$31,471$$

Note that the factors 0.9091 and 0.8264 are obtained from Appendix 2. It is clear that the calculations can be easily extended to consider debt that matures in three or more years.

Expected Return under Corporate Taxes

Using the concept of market-value balance sheets (introduced in Chapter 8), a levered firm's market-value balance sheet can be portrayed as follows.

V_U = Value of unlevered firm	D = debt
T_cD = Tax shield	S = equity

This balance sheet shows that the firm's value increases by T_cD when debt of D is added. It may surprise the reader to see the tax shield on the asset side of the balance sheet since it is not a physical asset. However, remember that an asset is any item with value, and the tax shield has value because it reduces the stream of future taxes. The value of the unlevered firm is the value of the assets without the tax benefit of leverage. The tax shield has the same risk as the debt, so its expected rate of return is k_d; however, the expected rate of return on assets is k_u, since they are risky.

For this value-market balance sheet, the expected cash flow to both stockholders and bondholders is:

$$Sk_s + Dk_d \qquad (13)$$

Expression (13) reflects the fact that the stock earns an expected return of k_s and the debt earns the interest rate k_d. We have used the symbol k_s for the cost of retained earnings; however, this is identical to the required rate of return on common stock. The expected cash flow from the left-hand side of the balance sheet can be written as:

$$V_uk_u + T_cDk_d \qquad (14)$$

In our no-growth perpetuity model, all cash flows are paid out as dividends. Consequently, the cash flows going into the firm are equal to those going to stockholders and bondholders. Hence, expressions (13) and (14) are equal:

$$Sk_s + Dk_d = V_uk_u + T_cDk_d \qquad (15)$$

Dividing both sides of equation (15) by S, subtracting Dk_d from both sides, and rearranging gives:

$$k_s = (V_U/S)k_u - (1 - T_c)(D/S)\, k_d \qquad (16)$$

We noted that $V_L = V_U + T_cD = D + S$. Hence:

$$V_U = S + (1 - T_c)D.$$

Thus, equation (16) can be rewritten as:

$$k_s = \{[S + (1 - T_c)D]/S\}k_u - (1 - T_c)(D/S)k_d$$

Bringing together the terms involving $(1 - T_c)D/S$ gives:

$$k_s = k_u + (D/S)(1 - T_c)(k_u - k_d) \tag{17}$$

Applying equation (17) to company XYZ, we get:

$$k_s = 0.20 + (\$40,000/\$73,600)\ (1 - 0.34)(0.20 - 0.10) = 0.2359$$

Let us check this calculation by discounting at k_s to establish the value of levered equity. This value is given by equation (18):

$$S = (\text{EBIT} - k_dD)(1 - T_c)/k_s \tag{18}$$

The numerator of equation (18) is the expected cash flow to levered equity after interest and taxes. The denominator is the rate at which the cash flow to equity is discounted. For company XYZ we get:

$$(\$30,304 - 0.10\ \$40,000)(1 - 0.34)/0.2359 = \$73,600$$

This is the same result we obtained earlier. The equals sign in the equation is only approximately true since the calculation is subject to rounding error (we only carried the discount rate, 0.2359, out to four decimal places).

We have defined the weighted average cost of capital (WACOC) as follows:

$$\text{WACOC} = (D/V_L)k_d(1 - T_c) + (S/V_L)k_s \tag{19}$$

For company XYZ, the WACOC is $(\$40,000/\$113,600)(0.10)(0.66) + (\$73,600/\$113,600)(0.2359) = 0.1761$. In other words, the company can reduce its WACOC from 0.20 (with no debt) to 0.1761 with reliance on debt. Using the WACOC approach, we can confirm that the value of company XYZ is $113,600 as follows:

$$V_L = \text{EBIT}(1 - T_c)/\text{WACOC} = \$30,304(0.66)/0.1761 = \$113,600.$$

Does the fact that company *XYZ* reduced its WACOC by relying on debt imply that firms should issue maximum debt? After all, equation (12) tells us that the greater the debt, the greater the value of the firm. The answer to the question is "no," because so far we have ignored personal taxes and the costs of financial distress.

Personal Taxes

Let us call the personal tax rate on interest T_i and, the personal tax rate on equity distributions (dividends) T_e. The net annual cash flow going to stockholders is:

$$(\text{EBIT} - k_d D)(1 - T_c)(1 - T_e)$$

The net annual cash flow going to bondholders is:

$$k_d D(1 - T_i)$$

Thus, the total cash flow to all stakeholders is:

$$(\text{EBIT} - k_d D)(1 - T_c)(1 - T_e) + k_d D(1 - T_i)$$

which can be rewritten as:

$$\text{EBIT}(1 - T_c)(1 - T_e) + k_d D(1 - T_i)[1 - (1 - T_c)(1 - T_e)/(1 - T_i)] \quad (20)$$

Note that the first term of expression (20) represents the cash flow on an unlevered firm after all taxes. The value of this stream must be the value of an unlevered firm, or V_U. A person buying a bond for D receives $k_d D(1 - T_i)$ after paying all taxes. Therefore, the value of the second term of expression (20) must be $D[1 - (1 - T_c)(1 - T_e)/(1 - T_i)]$. Consequently, the value of the stream in expression (20), which is the value of the levered firm, is:

$$V_L = V_U + [1 - (1 - T_c)(1 - T_e)/(1 - T_i)]D \quad (21)$$

Note that equation (21) degenerates to equation (12) if $T_e = T_i = 0$ (no personal taxes) or if $T_e = T_i$ (the introduction of personal taxes does not affect the value of a firm if equity distributions are taxed identically to interest at the personal level).

A comparison of equations (12) and (21) reveals that the gain from leverage is reduced when $T_e < T_i$. In this case, more taxes are paid at the personal level for a levered firm than for an unlevered firm. In addition, equation (21) indicates that there is no gain from leverage at all if $(1 - T_c)(1 - T_e) = (1 - T_i)$. The lack of gain arises because the lower corporate taxes for a levered firm are exactly offset by higher personal taxes.

Suppose company A&B expects a perpetual pretax earnings stream of $100,000 and faces a 34 percent corporate tax. Unlevered firms in the same industry have a cost of equity capital of 15 percent. The personal tax rate on equity distributions is 12 percent, and the personal tax on interest is 28 percent. A&B is an all-equity firm but is considering borrowing $150,000 at 10 percent.

The value of an all-equity firm is obtained with equation (11):

$$V_U = \$100,000(1 - 0.34)/0.15 = \$440,000$$

Next, we use equation (21) to compute the value of the levered firm:

$$V_L = \$440,000 + [1 - (1 - 0.34)(1 - 0.12)/(1 - 0.28)]\, \$150,000 = \$469,000$$

Thus, the advantage to leverage is $469,000 - $440,000 = $29,000. In a world of no personal taxes, the advantage to leverage would have been $T_c D = 0.34(\$150,000) = \$51,000$, much larger than $29,000.

Financial Distress

Although debt may provide tax benefits to a firm, it also exerts pressure because interest and principle payments are obligations. The firm may risk some sort of financial distress if these obligations are not met. In most cases it is difficult to arrive at a precise estimation of the costs of financial distress. Sometimes, the taint of impending bankruptcy suffices to drive away customers. For example, when the Chrysler automobile company skirted insolvency in the 1970s, a number of its loyal customers switched to other car manufacturers because of fear that parts and service would not be available were Chrysler to fail.

The ultimate distress is bankruptcy, whereby ownership of the company's assets is legally transferred from the stockholders to the bondholders. Let us consider the following simple example to examine the effect of the possibility of bankruptcy on the value of a firm. The example ignores taxes since we want to concentrate on costs related to a possible bankruptcy.

Suppose two companies, ABC and XYZ, have the cash flows shown in Table 9.3. Company ABC plans to be in business for one more year and expects a cash flow of either $100 or $50 in the coming year, depending on whether boom times or a recession will take place. Each of these possibilities has a probability of occurrence of 50 percent.

Previously issued debt requires *ABC* to make payments of $45 of interest and principal. Company *XYZ* has identical cash flow prospects but has $60 of interest and principal obligations. Table 9.3 indicates that company *XYZ* will be bankrupt in a recession. Under American law, corporations have limited liability. That is, *XYZ*'s bondholders will receive only $30 in a recession (*XYZ* has $20 in bankruptcy costs) and cannot get the additional $30 from the stockholders.

Although one normally assumes that investors are risk averse, we assume, for simplicity, that both bondholders and stockholders are risk neutral, and therefore, the cost of debt capital equals the cost of equity capital. Consequently, cash flows to both stockholders and bondholders are to be discounted at the interest rate, which we assume to be 10 percent. We evaluate the debt, *D*; the equity, *S*; and the value, *V*; of the entire firm for both *ABC* and *XYZ* as follows.

Company *ABC*

$S = [0.5(\$55) + 0.5(\$5)]/1.10$
$= \$27.27$

$D = [0.5(\$45) + 0.5(\$45)]/1.10$
$= \$40.91$

$V = S + D = \$68.18$

Company *XYZ*

$S = [0.5(\$40) + 0.5(\$0)]/1.10$
$= \$18.18$

$D = [0.5(\$60) + 0.5(\$30)]/1.10$
$= \$40.91$

$V = S + D = \$59.09$

The bondholders of company *XYZ* only receive $30 because the cash flow is only $50. Since they are likely to hire lawyers to negotiate

Table 9.3
Cash Flows of Companies *ABC* and *XYZ*

	Company *ABC*		Company *XYZ*	
	Boom times[1]	Recession[2]	Boom times[1]	Recession[2]
Cash flow	$100	$50	$100	$50
Payment of interest and principal on debt	45	45	60	30
Distribution to stockholders	$ 55	$ 5	$ 40	$ 0

[1]Probability of boom times is 50 percent.
[2]Probability of a recession is 50 percent.

or sue the company, the management of company XYZ is also likely to hire lawyers to defend itself. Additional costs will be incurred by company XYZ if the case goes to a bankruptcy court. In this simple example we assume that bankruptcy costs amount to $50 − $30 = $20. It is clear that in the real world these costs will be much higher; lawyers' fees are high. The fees related to bankruptcy costs are always paid before the bondholders get paid. If, in the example, the costs of bankruptcy were zero, the bondholders of Company XYZ would receive $50. Determining the value of the company in the same manner gives, for this case, $V = \$68.18$. In other words, the companies ABC and XYZ have the same value, even though XYZ runs the risk of bankruptcy. By comparing XYZ's value in a world with no bankruptcy costs ($V = \$68.18$) to XYZ's value in a world with such costs ($V = \$59.09$), we conclude that the possibility of bankruptcy has a negative effect on the value of the company. Although this may be overly philosophical, we observe that it is the costs associated with bankruptcy rather than the risk of bankruptcy itself that lowers the value of company XYZ.

The bondholders of company XYZ have valued the bonds in a realistic manner since they are willing to pay only $40.91, even though the promised payment of principal and interest is $60. Hence, their *promised* return is $[(\$60/\$40.91) − 1] = 46.7$ percent. In other words, the bondholders are paying a fair price provided they are realistic about the probability and costs of bankruptcy.

Suppose company XYZ was originally an all-equity firm and its stockholders wanted the company to issue debt with a promised payment of $60 and use the proceeds to pay a dividend. We saw that if there were no bankruptcy costs, the bondholders would pay $50 to buy debt with a promised payment of $60. Thus, a dividend of $50 could be paid to the stockholders. We also saw that if bankruptcy costs exist, bondholders would only pay $40.91 for the debt, in which case a dividend of $40.91 (rather than $50) could be paid to the stockholders. It is, therefore, the stockholders who bear the future bankruptcy costs.

When a firm is in financial distress, stockholders may follow selfish strategies or strategies to help themselves and hurt the bondholders. Examples of such strategies are (1) firms near bankruptcy may take great chances because they think they are using someone else's money, and (2) firms near bankruptcy may pay out extra dividends, leaving less in the firm for the bondholders in case of bankruptcy. Such selfish strategies are costly because they lower the firm's market value. Stockholders frequently make agreements with bondholders because they realize that they must pay higher interest rates as insurance against their own selfish strategies. Thus, such agreements may enable the stockholders to obtain lower rates. (Chapter 1 provided various examples of agreements between stockholders and bondholders.)

Integrating Tax Effects and Costs of Financial Distress

Modigliani and Miller (1958) have contributed much to the development of the concepts underlying capital structures. In fact, Modigliani was awarded the Nobel prize, in part for his work on capital structure. In principle, they argue that a firm's value rises with leverage in the presence of corporate taxes. Since this argument implies that firms should choose maximum debt, the theory does not predict the behavior of firms in the real world. There is plenty of statistical evidence that in the United States, internally generated cash flows have dominated as a source of financing.

The reason why Modigliani and Miller's theory does not hold in the real world is that they ignored personal taxes and costs of financial stress (including costs of selfish strategies). They were aware of these shortcomings, however, as can be seen in their original article (Modigliani and Miller 1958).

Figure 9.2 shows the integration of tax effects and financial distress costs. The diagonal straight line, AB, represents the value of a firm in a world without costs of financial distress. The curved line, AC, represents the value of the firm with these costs; it first rises, as the firm moves from all equity to a small amount of debt. In this case, the present value of the distress costs is small since the probability of distress is small. The present value of these costs then rises at an increasing rate as more and more debt is added. However, at some point, the increase in the present value of the financial distress costs from an additional dollar of debt is equal to the present value of the tax shield. This point represents the debt level that maximizes the value of the firm. Figure 9.2 represents this debt level by an optimal D. Beyond the optimal D, the financial distress costs increase faster than the tax shield and, consequently, the value of the firm reduces.

Unfortunately, no formula exists to establish the optimal debt level of a firm since it is difficult or impossible to quantify the financial distress costs. All we can do is to make the following observations to give some guidance when faced by decisions on the debt level:

1. Most firms use their industry's debt-equity ratio as an important factor for capital structure decisions.
2. Most firms prefer internal equity (i.e., retained earnings) over external equity since it is less costly.

Figure 9.2
The Integration of Tax Effects and Distress Costs

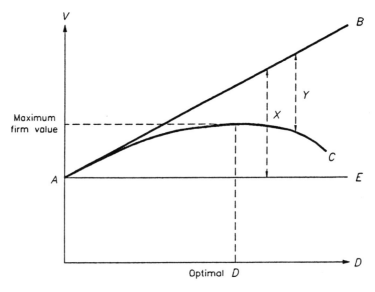

Note: V = value of firm.

D = debt.

The horizontal straight line AE represents V_U, or the value of a firm with no debt.

The diagonal straight line AB represents V_L, or the value of a levered firm $(V_L = V_U + T_cD)$.

The curved line AC represents the actual value of a firm.

The dotted arrow X indicates the present value of the tax shield on debt.

The dotted arrow Y indicates the present value of financial distress costs.

Optimal D is the optimal amount of debt.

3. If a firm has taxable income, a higher debt level will reduce corporate taxes and often increase taxes paid by bondholders.
4. If corporate tax rates are higher than bondholder tax rates, it is worthwhile to use debt.
5. Firms with less certain operating income, such as research and development organizations, have a greater chance of experiencing financial distress.
6. Firms with a large investment in tangible assets, such as equipment, land, and buildings, have a smaller chance of experiencing financial distress.

At this point, it may be worthwhile to remind the reader why we are interested in maximizing the value of a firm. In fact, it could be argued that managers should be on the lookout for the stockholders' interest and, therefore, should try to maximize stock price. Are we doing so? The answer is simple: that is, if we increase the value of a firm, we also increase the price of a stock. In other words, choosing the capital structure that gives the highest firm value results in the structure that is most beneficial to the firm's stockholders.

Coverage Ratios

Management can control the probability of financial distress by limiting the amount of interest to which the firm commits. Suppose a firm's operating income (EBIT) over the past years has a normal distribution with a mean of $1,500,000 and a standard deviation of $450,000, and suppose the firm wishes to limit interest payments to $500,000. In this case we can determine the Z value (Chapter 3) as follows:

$$Z = [500,000 - 1,500,000]/450,000 = -2.22$$

Next, we find, with the help of Appendix 1, that there is about a 1 percent chance that the firm will experience a shortfall in operating income so severe that it cannot cover its interest.

Since management is often reluctant to work with probabilities and Z tables because the concepts are difficult to understand, there is another way to view this by considering the expected coverage, namely:

$$\text{interest coverage} = 1,500,000/500,000 = 3$$

Thus, maintaining an interest coverage ratio of 3 is *equivalent to* restricting the probability of distress to about 1 percent for this firm.

Alternatively, if the firm limits interest to $750,000, the Z value is:

$$Z = [750,000 - 1,500,000]/450,000 = -1.67$$

Now there is about a 5 percent chance that the firm's EBIT will not cover its interest expense. In this case the expected coverage is:

$$\text{interest coverage} = 1,500,000/750,000 = 2$$

Thus, a coverage of 2 corresponds to a probability of distress of 5 percent for this firm.

In general, higher coverage means a lower chance of getting into financial difficulty. The various possibilities for the above mentioned example are as follows:

Expected Coverage	Chance of Shortfall
3.0	0.01
2.0	0.05
1.5	0.13
1.0	0.50

In other words, by targeting a minimum interest coverage ratio, management can control the risk of a shortfall. An expected coverage ratio of 1.0 means there is a 50:50 chance that income from operations (EBIT) will not cover interest payments. In general, the higher the coverage, the lower the likelihood of a firm being unable to cover its interest payments.

In the example, we used the interest-rate coverage ratio, or the times interest earned ratio defined as EBIT/(interest expense). Thus, we ignored principal repayments since most companies can reschedule their loans if they cannot make the principal repayments. However, we could have used the times burden covered ratio and develop a similar argument if we do not wish to ignore principal repayments. The times burden covered ratio is defined as follows:

$$\text{times burden covered} = \text{EBIT}/[\text{interest} + \text{principal repayment}/(1 - \text{tax rate})]$$

When we include principal repayment as part of a company's financial burden, we must express the figure on a before-tax basis comparable to interest and EBIT. Unlike interest payments, principal repayments are not a tax-deductible expense. In the definition of the times burden covered ratio, the before-tax burden of a principal repayment is found by dividing the repayment by 1 minus the company's tax rate. For instance, if a company is in, say, the 50 percent tax bracket, it must earn $2 before taxes to have $1 after taxes to pay creditors. (The other dollar goes to the tax collector.)

How much coverage is enough? The answer to this question depends on (1) variability and (2) vulnerability. The variability relates to how likely the firm is to experience dramatic declines in operating income (EBIT), while the vulnerability is an indication of bankruptcy cost or how much of the firm's value could be lost in the event of financial distress. In general, the higher the variability and vulnerability, the greater the target coverage ratio required.

If variability increases, how can the firm maintain the same probability of distress as before? It can do so by increasing its coverage, namely, by lowering interest payments through using less debt and more equity to finance invested capital. For instance, in the example of the firm with an expected operating income of $1,500,000 and a standard deviation of $450,000, we observed that it could limit the chance of financial distress to 5 percent with an interest rate coverage of 2. When the variability increases so that the standard deviation becomes $600,000, the firm must increase coverage to 3 to maintain the 5 percent chance of distress.

Beta and Leverage

In equation (12) of Chapter 8 we developed the following relationship:

$$\beta_a = \beta_p = \beta_d\, D/(D + S) + \beta_s\, S/(D + S) \tag{22}$$

where:

$$\begin{aligned}
\beta_a &= \text{the asset's beta} \\
\beta_p &= \text{the portfolio's beta} \\
\beta_s &= \text{the beta of levered equity} \\
D &= \text{the debt value} \\
S &= \text{the equity value}
\end{aligned}$$

Equation (22) shows that the beta of debt is multiplied by debt/(debt + equity), which is the percentage of debt in the capital structure. Similarly, the beta of equity is multiplied by the percentage of equity in the capital structure. In our discussions of levered firms, the beta of the portfolio is equal to the beta of the levered firm because the portfolio *is* the levered firm. This is what we call the firm's asset beta.

In practice, the beta of debt is very low. If we make the commonplace assumption that the beta of debt is zero, equation (22) becomes

$$\beta_a = \beta_s\, S/(D + S) \tag{23}$$

Rearranging the terms of equation (23) gives:

$$\beta_s = \beta_a(1 + D/S) \tag{24}$$

Since $S/(D + S)$ must be smaller than 1 for a levered firm, we conclude from equation (23) that $\beta_a < \beta_s$. In other words, the beta of an unlevered firm must be less than the beta of the equity in an otherwise identical levered firm. In still other words, the equity beta will always be greater than the asset beta with financial leverage.

Equation (24) applies to a world without corporate taxes. Now that we have included corporate taxes, it is worthwhile to provide the relationship between β_s and β_a in the real world. Although beyond the scope of this book, it can be shown that the relationship between the beta of the unlevered firm and the beta of the levered equity is given by equation (25).

$$\beta_s = [1 + (1 - T_c)D/S]\beta_u \qquad (25)$$

where:

β_u = the beta of the unlevered firm (i.e., the underlying asset β)
all other terms are as previously defined

Equation (25) also assumes that debt has a zero beta. Because $[1 + (1 - T_c)D/S]$ must be more than 1 for a levered firm, it follows that $\beta_u < \beta_s$.

Equation (25), the corporate tax case, is rather similar to equation (24), the no corporate tax case, since the beta of the levered firm must be greater than the beta of the unlevered firm in both cases. In other words, the intuition that leverage increases the risk of equity applies in either case. However, equations (24) and (25) are not equal. It can be shown that leverage increases the equity beta less rapidly under corporate taxes since in the world of corporate taxes, leverage generates a riskless tax shield, thus lowering the risk of the entire firm.

By rearranging the terms of equation (25) we can express the beta of an unlevered firm, β_u, in terms of the beta of the levered equity, β_s. This is done in equation (26).

$$\beta_u = [S/\{S + (1 - T_c)D\}]\beta_s \qquad (26)$$

Suppose *ABC* Inc. is considering a scale-enhancing project under which it will reduce its debt and is, therefore, interested in its discount rate as if it were an all-equity firm. *ABC's* market value of debt is $100 M, and the market value of its equity is $400 M. The debt is considered riskless, and the corporate tax rate is 34 percent. Regression analysis indicates that the beta of *ABC's* equity is 2. The risk-free rate of interest is 10 percent and the expected market premium is 8.5 percent. Thus, we have $D = \$100$ M, $S = \$400$ M, $T_c = 0.34$, $\beta_s = 2$,

k_{RF} = 0.10, and $k_M - k_{RF}$ = 8.5 percent [note that $k_M - k_{RF}$ was defined in equation (2)].

With the help of equation (26), we first determine the beta of the hypothetical all-equity firm:

$$\beta_u = [\$400\ M/\{\$400\ M + (1 - 0.34)\$100\ M\}]2 = 1.72$$

The discount rate if *ABC* were an all-equity firm is:

$$k_s = 10\% + 1.72(8.5\%) = 24.62\%$$

Chapter 8 discussed the manner in which we can determine the beta of the company. In the United States, organizations like Value Line and Merril Lynch publish β coefficients of thousands of companies with publicly traded stocks. However, if a firm's stock is not actively traded in public capital markets and the firm does not have the statistical expertise to determine the beta, we can approximate the beta using the beta of a comparable public firm. By comparable we mean a firm in the same industry, producing the same products, with similar operating strategies, and having the same leverage.

It may be difficult to find a comparable public firm with the same leverage. However, we can still use the CAPM to estimate the k_s and WACOC of a privately held company by adjusting the equity betas to make leverage comparable. This is done in two steps:

1. Unlever the comparison equity betas to remove the effects of leverage of these firms and get the underlying asset betas; and
2. Relever the average asset beta to incorporate the firm's *own* leverage position.

To elucidate this procedure, consider the following example.

The financial director of company *ABC* is trying to estimate his company's WACOC. The company is financed with equal proportion of debt and equity, pays 10 percent on its outstanding debt, and has a tax rate of 40 percent. Since *ABC* is privately held, organizations like Value Line and Merril Lynch do not estimate its equity β. The financial director is, however, aware that a competitive firm, company *XYZ*, is publicly traded and listed by Value Line. Company *XYZ* is 25 percent debt and 75 percent equity financed, pays 8 percent on its outstanding debt, and has a 40 percent tax rate. Value Line estimates that the company's stock has a β of 1.0. The risk-free rate is 7 percent, and the long-run risk premium on stocks has averaged 8.5 percent ($k_M - k_{RF}$). What are the WACOCs of companies *XYZ* and *ABC*?

For company XYZ we have:

$$k_d(1 - T) = 8\%(1 - 0.40) = 4.8\%$$
$$k_s = k_{RF} + (k_M - k_{RF})\beta = 7\% + (8.5\%)1.0 = 15.5\%$$
$$\text{WACOC} = 0.25(4.8\%) + 0.75(15.5\%) = 12.83\%$$

The underlying asset β, or unlevered β for company XYZ, is obtained with equation (26):

$$\beta_u = [0.75/\{0.75 + (1 - 0.40)0.25\}]1.0 = 0.83$$

Note that $\beta = 1.0$ reflected financial and business risks, and as we took out the financial risk, β_u should be smaller than 1.0.

The equity β of company ABC is obtained with equation (25):

$$\beta_s = [1 + (1 - 0.40)(0.50)/(0.50)]0.83 = 1.33$$

Note that ABC's β_s is higher than that of XYZ since ABC has more leverage.

We now have for company ABC:

$$k_d(1 - T) = 10\%(1 - 0.40) = 6.0\%$$
$$k_s = k_{RF} + (k_M - k_{RF})\beta = 7\% + 1.33(8.5\%) = 18.3\%$$
$$\text{WACOC} = 0.50(6.0\%) + 0.50(18.3\%) = 12.15\%$$

Note that ABC's WACOC is smaller than XYZ's WACOC since ABC has a higher tax shield due to a higher leverage.

SUGGESTIONS FOR FURTHER READING

Harris, M., and A. Ravic. "The Theory of Capital Structure." *Journal of Finance*, 46 (March 1991): 297–355.

Levine, R. "Stock Markets, Growth, and Tax Policy." *Journal of Finance*, 46 (September 1991): 1445–65.

Mayer, C. "New Issues in Corporate Finance." *European Economic Review*, 32 (June 1988): 1167–88.

Miller, M. H. "Debt and Taxes." *Journal of Finance*, 32 (May 1977): 261–75.

Modigliani, F., and M. H. Miller. "The Cost of Capital, Corporation Finance, and the Theory of Investment." *American Economic Review*, 48 (June 1958): 261–97.

———. "Corporate Income Taxes and the Cost of Capital: A Correction." *American Economic Review*, LII3 (June 1963): 433–44.

Probability of a Value of $Z = [P - E(P)]/\sigma$ Being Greater Than the Values Tabulated in the Margins

z	.00	.01	.02	.03	.04	.05	.06	.07	.08	.09
.0	.5000	.4960	.4920	.4880	.4840	.4801	.4761	.4721	.4681	.4641
.1	.4602	.4562	.4522	.4483	.4443	.4404	.4364	.4325	.4286	.4247
.2	.4207	.4168	.4129	.4090	.4052	.4013	.3974	.3936	.3897	.3859
.3	.3821	.3783	.3745	.3707	.3669	.3632	.3594	.3557	.3520	.3483
.4	.3446	.3409	.3372	.3336	.3300	.3264	.3228	.3192	.3156	.3121
.5	.3085	.3050	.3015	.2981	.2946	.2912	.2877	.2843	.2810	.2776
.6	.2743	.2709	.2676	.2643	.2611	.2578	.2546	.2514	.2483	.2451
.7	.2420	.2389	.2358	.2327	.2296	.2266	.2236	.2206	.2177	.2148
.8	.2119	.2090	.2061	.2033	.2005	.1977	.1949	.1922	.1894	.1867
.9	.1841	.1814	.1788	.1762	.1736	.1711	.1685	.1660	.1635	.1611
1.0	.1587	.1562	.1539	.1515	.1492	.1469	.1446	.1423	.1401	.1379
1.1	.1357	.1335	.1314	.1292	.1271	.1251	.1230	.1210	.1190	.1170
1.2	.1151	.1131	.1112	.1093	.1075	.1056	.1038	.1020	.1003	.0985
1.3	.0968	.0951	.0934	.0918	.0901	.0885	.0869	.0853	.0838	.0823
1.4	.0808	.0793	.0778	.0764	.0749	.0735	.0721	.0708	.0694	.0681
1.5	.0668	.0655	.0643	.0630	.0648	.0606	.0594	.0582	.0571	.0559
1.6	.0548	.0537	.0526	.0516	.0505	.0495	.0485	.0475	.0465	.0455
1.7	.0446	.0436	.0427	.0418	.0409	.0401	.0392	.0384	.0375	.0367
1.8	.0359	.0351	.0344	.0336	.0329	.0322	.0314	.0307	.0301	.0294
1.9	.0287	.0281	.0274	.0268	.0262	.0256	.0250	.0244	.0239	.0233
2.0	.0228	.0222	.0217	.0212	.0207	.0202	.0197	.0192	.0188	.0183
2.1	.0179	.0174	.0170	.0166	.0162	.0158	.0154	.0150	.0146	.0143
2.2	.0139	.0136	.0132	.0129	.0125	.0122	.0119	.0116	.0113	.0110
2.3	.0107	.0104	.0102	.0099	.0096	.0094	.0091	.0089	.0087	.0084
2.4	.0082	.0080	.0078	.0075	.0073	.0071	.0069	.0068	.0066	.0064
2.5	.0062	.0060	.0059	.0057	.0055	.0054	.0052	.0051	.0049	.0048
2.6	.0047	.0045	.0044	.0043	.0041	.0040	.0039	.0038	.0037	.0036
2.7	.0035	.0034	.0033	.0032	.0031	.0030	.0029	.0028	.0027	.0026
2.8	.0026	.0025	.0024	.0023	.0023	.0022	.0021	.0021	.0020	.0019
2.9	.0019	.0018	.0018	.0017	.0016	.0016	.0015	.0015	.0014	.0014
3.0	.0013	.0013	.0013	.0012	.0012	.0011	.0011	.0011	.0010	.0010
3.1	.0010	.0009	.0009	.0009	.0008	.0008	.0008	.0008	.0007	.0007
3.2	.0007	.0007	.0006	.0006	.0006	.0006	.0006	.0005	.0005	.0005
3.3	.0005	.0005	.0005	.0004	.0004	.0004	.0004	.0004	.0004	.0003
3.4	.0003	.0003	.0003	.0003	.0003	.0003	.0003	.0003	.0003	.0002
3.6	.0002	.0002	.0001	.0001	.0001	.0001	.0001	.0001	.0001	.0001
3.9	.0000									

Interest Tables for Discrete Compounding

A given sum of money now is normally worth more than an equal sum at some future date. The concept "money has a time value" is the basic assumption of discounting and compounding. Frequently one considers time in discrete units of one year.

We introduce the following definitions:

P = an amount of money at the present time
F = an amount of money at the end of n periods in the future
A = a constant amount paid or received at the end of each of n periods in the future ("uniform series")
n = the number of periods or times at which interest is calculated
i = the interest rate used for calculations of interest in any one of the n periods mentioned above

The definitions refer to "periods of time," which are normally years. However, "period of time" rather than "year" is preferred to eliminate redefining the symbols when other units of time are considered.

Table A2.1 presents six interest factors to use when specific data is given:

spcaf   when P is given and F is to be obtained
sppwf   when F is given and P is to be obtained
caf   when A is given and F is to be obtained
sff   when F is given and A is to be obtained
pwf   when A is given and P is to be obtained
crf   when P is given and A is to be obtained

The interpretation of the above acronyms is as follows:

spcaf = single payment compound amount factor
sppwf = single payment present worth factor
caf   = (series) compound amount factor
sff   = sinking fund factor
pwf   = (series) present worth factor
crf   = capital recovery factor

Table A2.1
Interest Factors for Discrete Discounting and Compounding

Find Given	P	F	A
P	1	$\text{spcaf} = (1+i)^n$	$\text{crf} = [1-(1+i)^{-n}]^{-1}i$
F	$\text{sppwf} = (1+i)^{-n}$	1	$\text{sff} = [(1+i)^n-1]^{-1}i$
A	$\text{pwf} = [1-(1+i)^{-n}]i^{-1}$	$\text{caf} = [(1+i)^n-1]i^{-1}$	1

The first of these six factors, spcaf, allows us to determine the value n periods hence of a present amount P if the interest rate is i. Thus, given P, i and n it allows for the computation of F. Consider the following simple, arithmetic example of the use of spcaf.

Suppose it is desired to find the sum to which $1,000.00 would grow over three years when the appropriate annual interest rate is 10%. From the spcaf formula of Table A2.1 we compute as follows:

$$
\begin{aligned}
F &= P(\text{given } P, \text{find } F, i=10\%, n=3) \\
  &= P.\text{spcaf } (i=10\%, n=3) \\
  &= P(1 + i)^n \text{ for } i=10\% \text{ and } n=3 \\
  &= \$1,000(1 + 0.10)^3 = \$1,000(1 + 0.10)(1 + 0.10)(1 + 0.10) \\
  &= \$1,000(1.331) = \$1,331.00
\end{aligned}
$$

The single payment present worth factor (sppwf) permits us to answer questions about the present value of capital available at some time in the future. Given F, i, and n, the P may be calculated from:

$$P = F.\text{sppwf} = F(1 + i)^{-n}$$

where the expression $(1 + i)^{-n}$ is a convenient way of writing $1/(1 + i)^n$.

Suppose it is desired to know the present value of a sum of $150.00 arising two years hence when the appropriate annual interest rate is 10%. Using the sppwf formula we compute:

P = F (given F, find P, i=10%, n=2)
  = F.sppwf (i=10%, n=2)
  = $F(1 + i)^{-n}$ for i=10%, and n=2
  = $150(1 + 0.10)^{-2} = \$150(0.8264)$
  = $123.96

The (series) present worth factor or pwf enables us to calculate the present value of a uniform series A. Let us consider the following problem to illustrate the application of the pwf formula.
A firm is offered the choice of a 5-year lease on a machine:

Alternative (a) $10,000.00 down and $3,000.00 per annum for 5 years.
Alternative (b) $13,000.00 down and $2,150.00 per annum for 5 years.

Annual payments are to be made at the year end, the relevant interest rate is 7%, while problems of risk, inflation, tax, etc., are ignored. Alternative (b) requires the firm to pay down $3,000.00 more at the beginning of the lease than alternative (a), but results in an annual end-year saving of $850.00 for 5 years. From the pwf formula the present values of alternatives (a) and (b) are:

(a) P = $\$10,000 + \$3,000[1 - (1 + i)^{-n}]i^{-1}$
   = $10,000 + $3,000(4.100)
   = $22,300.00
(b) P = $\$13,000 + \$2,150[1 - (1 + i)^{-n}]i^{-1}$
   = $13,000 + $2,150(4.100)
   = $21,815.00

There is a gain of net present value by taking alternative (b) equal to:

$$\$22,300.00 - \$21,815.00 = \$485.00$$

and this alternative is, therefore, preferred.
A perpetual annuity or perpetuity is a perpetual series of annual constant cash flows. An example of a perpetuity is a consol, which is an interest-bearing bond issued by the British government having no maturity date. When a regular annual series is expected to go on perpetually or $n \to \infty$ (the symbol for n tending to infinity), then the pwf formula becomes simply $P = A.i^{-1}$. This is so, since $(1 + i)^{-n}$ tends to zero when $n \to \infty$.
The (series) compound amount factor or caf permits the calculation of a future sum F given that an amount A is invested at i% at the end of

each of n equal intervals. The series of constant annual cash flows is known as an annuity.

Suppose an investor has an annuity in which a payment of $500.00 is made at the end of each year. If interest is 6% compounded annually, what is the amount after 20 years? From the caf formula this amount is as follows:

$$
\begin{aligned}
F &= A.\text{caf}(i=6\%, n=20) \\
&= \$500[(1 + 0.06)^{20} - 1](0.06)^{-1} \\
&= \$500(36.786) = \$18{,}393.00
\end{aligned}
$$

Note that the expression $(0.06)^{-1}$ is again a convenient way of writing $1/(0.06)$.

The reciprocal of the caf is the sinking fund factor or sff, which allows us to calculate the constant amount A which must be invested at the end of each period to yield an amount F at the end of the n-th period. In financial terminology, the terminal value of a constant annual investment or annuity is usually referred to as a "sinking fund". This is a fund to which periodic payments are made and then invested to accumulate to a given amount by a certain date. This is often done for the purpose of replacing a machine at the end of its expected life or the redeeming of a loan.

Consider as an example involving the use of sff, an asset with a value of $5,000.00, a service life of 5 years, and a salvage value of $1,000.00. Using the sinking-fund depreciation method we are asked to compute the required year-end sinking fund deposits if the interest rate is 6%. Using the sff formula of Table A2.1 we compute as follows:

$$
\begin{aligned}
A &= F.\text{sff}(i=6\%, n=5) \\
&= \$4{,}000i[(1 + i)^n - 1]^{-1} \\
&= \$4{,}000(0.1774) = \$709.60
\end{aligned}
$$

Note that for F a value of $4,000.00 rather than $5,000.00 is used. This is so, since the asset has a salvage value of $1,000.00. Table A2.2 shows the yearly depreciation charge, the total depreciation charge to the end of a year together with the undepreciated balance at the end of a year. According to the sinking-fund depreciation method the amount by which the asset is depreciated is the sum of (1) the amount deposited into the sinking fund at the end of the year, and (2) the amount of interest earned on the sum already in deposit in the sinking fund.

The capital recovery factor or crf permits us to calculate the equal end of period payment A for n periods which is equivalent to a present sum P. The following example illustrates the use of pwf, sppwf, and crf.

Table A2.2
Example of the Sinking-Fund Depreciation Method

Year	Deposit A	Interest Earned during Year	Yearly Depreciation Charge	Total Depreciation Charge to End of Year	Undepreciated Balance at End of Year
0	$ 0.00	$0.00	$ 0.00	$ 0.00	$5,000.00
1	709.60	0.00	709.60	709.60	4,290.40
2	709.60	.06(709.60)	752.18	1,461.78	3,538.22
3	709.60	.06(1,461.78)	797.31	2,259.09	2,740.91
4	709.60	.06(2,259.09)	845.15	3,104.24	1,895.76
5	709.60	.06(3,104.24)	895.85	4,000.00	1,000.00

Note: Asset's value = $5,000.00   Salvage value = $1,000.00
Service life = 5 years $i = 6\%$

A young economist has estimated that his annual earnings should average $20,000.00, $30,000.00, and $40,000.00 per year in succeeding decades after graduation. He hopes to graduate next month and wants an idea of the value of all his years of studying. Assuming an annual interest rate of 6%, he, therefore, decides to determine (a) the present worth (at graduation) in cash of the 30 years' earning, and (b) the equivalent uniform annual value of the 30 years' estimated income. His present worth is:

[$20,000.pwf($i=6\%$, $n=10$)] + [$30,000.pwf($i=6\%$, $n=10$).sppwf($i=6\%$, $n=10$)] + [$40,000.pwf($i=6\%$, $n=10$).sppwf($i=6\%$, $n=20$)] = $20,000 (7.360) + $30,000(7.360)(0.5584) + $40,000(7.360)(0.3118) = $147,200 + $123,294 + $91,791 = $362,288

The equivalent uniform annual value of the 30 years' estimated income is:

$362,288.crf($i=6\%$, $n=30$) = $362,288(0.07265) = $26,320

Heretofore we have adopted the convention of discounting for an annual period. Now to analyze the discounting for periods of less than a year, we introduce these following definitions:

m = the total number of years
k = the number of compounding or conversion periods per year
j = the nominal yearly interest rate to be converted n times per year

Thus, $i = j/k$ and $n = m.k$, where i and n are as defined previously.

Suppose you want to determine the amount to which $10,000.00 would grow in one year at 8% interest compounded semiannually. Thus, the nominal yearly interest rate, sometimes simply called the nominal rate, is equal to $j = 8\%$ and $n = 2$, since the interest is calculated twice a year. Consequently, the interest rate per conversion period is $i = j/k = 8\%/2 = 4\%$ and the amount F to which $10,000.00 will grow in one year at $j = 8\%$ is:

$$
\begin{aligned}
F &= \$10,000(1 + i)^2 = \$10,000(1.04)^2 \\
&= \$10,000 \text{ spcaf } (i{=}4\%, n{=}2) \\
&= \$10,820.00
\end{aligned}
$$

In other words, the $10,000.00 increased to $10,820.00 or by 8.2%. Thus the interest rate used for calculations of interest or i is 4%, the nominal yearly interest rate is 8.0%, and the effective yearly interest rate is 8.2%.

Tables A2.3 through A2.6 give values for spcaf, sppwf, pwf, and caf of Table A2.1 for given values of i and n. The crf and sff are not included since their values may be obtained by taking the reciprocal of the values for pwf and caf, respectively.

Table A2.3
Given *P*, Find *F* (spcaf)

Period	1%	2%	3%	4%	5%	6%	7%	8%	10%	12%	15%	20%
1	1.0100	1.0200	1.0300	1.0400	1.0500	1.0600	1.0700	1.0800	1.1000	1.1200	1.1500	1.2000
2	1.0201	1.0404	1.0609	1.0816	1.1025	1.1236	1.1449	1.1664	1.2100	1.2544	1.3225	1.4400
3	1.0303	1.0612	1.0927	1.1249	1.1576	1.1910	1.2250	1.2597	1.3310	1.4049	1.5209	1.7280
4	1.0406	1.0824	1.1255	1.1699	1.2155	1.2625	1.3108	1.3605	1.4641	1.5735	1.7490	2.0736
5	1.0510	1.1041	1.1593	1.2167	1.2763	1.3382	1.4026	1.4693	1.6105	1.7623	2.0114	2.4883
6	1.0615	1.1262	1.1941	1.2653	1.3401	1.4185	1.5007	1.5869	1.7716	1.9738	2.3131	2.9860
7	1.0721	1.1487	1.2299	1.3159	1.4071	1.5036	1.6058	1.7138	1.9487	2.2107	2.6600	3.5832
8	1.0829	1.1717	1.2668	1.3686	1.4775	1.5938	1.7182	1.8509	2.1436	2.4760	3.0590	4.2998
9	1.0937	1.1951	1.3048	1.4233	1.5513	1.6895	1.8385	1.9990	2.3579	2.7731	3.5179	5.1598
10	1.1046	1.2190	1.3439	1.4802	1.6289	1.7908	1.9672	2.1589	2.5937	3.1058	4.0456	6.1917
11	1.1157	1.2434	1.3842	1.5395	1.7103	1.8983	2.1049	2.3316	2.8531	3.4785	4.6524	7.4301
12	1.1268	1.2682	1.4258	1.6010	1.7959	2.0122	2.2522	2.5182	3.1384	3.8960	5.3503	8.9161
13	1.1381	1.2936	1.4685	1.6651	1.8856	2.1329	2.4098	2.7196	3.4523	4.3635	6.1528	10.699
14	1.1495	1.3195	1.5126	1.7317	1.9799	2.2609	2.5785	2.9372	3.7975	4.8871	7.0757	12.839
15	1.1610	1.3459	1.5580	1.8009	2.0789	2.3966	2.7590	3.1722	4.1772	5.4736	8.1371	15.407
16	1.1726	1.3728	1.6047	1.8730	2.1829	2.5404	2.9522	3.4259	4.5950	6.1304	9.3576	18.488
17	1.1843	1.4002	1.6528	1.9479	2.2920	2.6928	3.1588	3.7000	5.0545	6.8660	10.761	22.186
18	1.1961	1.4282	1.7024	2.0258	2.4066	2.8543	3.3799	3.9960	5.5599	7.6900	12.375	26.623
19	1.2081	1.4568	1.7535	2.1068	2.5270	3.0256	3.6165	4.3157	6.1159	8.6128	14.232	31.948
20	1.2202	1.4859	1.8061	2.1911	2.6533	3.2071	3.8697	4.6610	6.7275	9.6463	16.367	38.338
21	1.2324	1.5157	1.8603	2.2788	2.7860	3.3996	4.1406	5.0338	7.4002	10.804	18.822	46.005
22	1.2447	1.5460	1.9161	2.3699	2.9253	3.6035	4.4304	5.4365	8.1403	12.100	21.645	55.206
23	1.2572	1.5769	1.9736	2.4647	3.0715	3.8197	4.7405	5.8715	8.9543	13.552	24.891	66.247
24	1.2697	1.6084	2.0328	2.5633	3.2251	4.0489	5.0724	6.3412	9.8497	15.179	28.625	79.497
25	1.2824	1.6406	2.0938	2.6658	3.3864	4.2919	5.4274	6.8485	10.835	17.000	32.919	95.396
26	1.2953	1.6734	2.1566	2.7725	3.5557	4.5494	5.8074	7.3964	11.918	19.040	37.857	114.48
27	1.3082	1.7069	2.2213	2.8834	3.7335	4.8223	6.2139	7.9881	13.110	21.325	43.535	137.37
28	1.3213	1.7410	2.2879	2.9987	3.9201	5.1117	6.6488	8.6271	14.421	23.884	50.066	164.84
29	1.3345	1.7758	2.3566	3.1187	4.1161	5.4184	7.1143	9.3173	15.863	26.750	57.575	197.81
30	1.3478	1.8114	2.4273	3.2434	4.3219	5.7435	7.6123	10.063	17.449	29.960	66.212	237.38
35	1.4166	1.9999	2.8139	3.9461	5.5160	7.6861	10.677	14.785	28.102	52.800	133.18	590.67
40	1.4889	2.2080	3.2620	4.8010	7.0400	10.286	14.974	21.725	45.259	93.051	267.86	1469.8
45	1.5648	2.4379	3.7816	5.8412	8.9850	13.765	21.002	31.920	72.890	163.99	538.77	3657.3
50	1.6446	2.6916	4.3839	7.1067	11.467	18.420	29.457	46.902	117.39	289.00	1083.7	9100.4
55	1.7285	2.9717	5.0821	8.6464	14.636	24.650	41.315	68.914	189.06	509.32	2179.6	22645
60	1.8167	3.2810	5.8916	10.520	18.679	32.988	57.946	101.26	304.48	897.60	4384.0	56348

Table A2.4
Given *F*, Find *P* (sppwf)

Period	1%	2%	3%	4%	5%	6%	7%	8%	10%	12%	15%	20%
1	.9901	.9804	.9709	.9615	.9524	.9434	.9346	.9259	.9091	.8929	.8696	.8333
2	.9803	.9612	.9426	.9246	.9070	.8900	.8734	.8573	.8264	.7972	.7561	.6944
3	.9706	.9423	.9151	.8890	.8638	.8396	.8163	.7938	.7513	.7118	.6575	.5787
4	.9610	.9238	.8885	.8548	.8227	.7921	.7629	.7350	.6830	.6355	.5718	.4823
5	.9515	.9057	.8626	.8219	.7835	.7473	.7130	.6806	.6209	.5674	.4972	.4019
6	.9420	.8880	.8375	.7903	.7462	.7050	.6663	.6302	.5645	.5066	.4323	.3349
7	.9327	.8706	.8131	.7599	.7107	.6651	.6227	.5835	.5132	.4523	.3759	.2791
8	.9235	.8535	.7894	.7307	.6768	.6274	.5820	.5403	.4665	.4039	.3269	.2326
9	.9143	.8368	.7664	.7026	.6446	.5919	.5439	.5002	.4241	.3606	.2843	.1938
10	.9053	.8203	.7441	.6756	.6139	.5584	.5083	.4632	.3855	.3220	.2472	.1615
11	.8963	.8043	.7224	.6496	.5847	.5268	.4751	.4289	.3505	.2875	.2149	.1346
12	.8874	.7885	.7014	.6246	.5568	.4970	.4440	.3971	.3186	.2567	.1869	.1122
13	.8787	.7730	.6810	.6006	.5303	.4688	.4150	.3677	.2897	.2292	.1625	.0935
14	.8700	.7579	.6611	.5775	.5051	.4423	.3878	.3405	.2633	.2046	.1413	.0779
15	.8613	.7430	.6419	.5553	.4810	.4173	.3624	.3152	.2394	.1827	.1229	.0649
16	.8528	.7284	.6232	.5339	.4581	.3936	.3387	.2919	.2176	.1631	.1069	.0541
17	.8444	.7142	.6050	.5134	.4363	.3714	.3166	.2703	.1978	.1456	.0929	.0451
18	.8360	.7002	.5874	.4936	.4155	.3503	.2959	.2502	.1799	.1300	.0808	.0376
19	.8277	.6864	.5703	.4746	.3957	.3305	.2765	.2317	.1635	.1161	.0703	.0313
20	.8195	.6730	.5537	.4564	.3769	.3118	.2584	.2145	.1486	.1037	.0611	.0261
21	.8114	.6598	.5375	.4388	.3589	.2942	.2415	.1987	.1351	.0926	.0531	.0217
22	.8034	.6468	.5219	.4220	.3418	.2775	.2257	.1839	.1228	.0826	.0462	.0181
23	.7954	.6342	.5067	.4057	.3256	.2618	.2109	.1703	.1117	.0738	.0402	.0151
24	.7876	.6217	.4919	.3901	.3101	.2470	.1971	.1577	.1015	.0659	.0349	.0126
25	.7798	.6095	.4776	.3751	.2953	.2330	.1842	.1460	.0923	.0588	.0304	.0105
26	.7720	.5976	.4637	.3607	.2812	.2198	.1722	.1352	.0839	.0525	.0264	.0087
27	.7644	.5859	.4502	.3468	.2678	.2074	.1609	.1252	.0763	.0469	.0230	.0073
28	.7568	.5744	.4371	.3335	.2551	.1956	.1504	.1159	.0693	.0419	.0200	.0061
29	.7493	.5631	.4243	.3207	.2429	.1846	.1406	.1073	.0630	.0374	.0174	.0051
30	.7419	.5521	.4120	.3083	.2314	.1741	.1314	.0994	.0573	.0334	.0151	.0042
35	.7059	.5000	.3554	.2534	.1813	.1301	.0937	.0676	.0356	.0189	.0075	.0017
40	.6717	.4529	.3066	.2083	.1420	.0972	.0668	.0460	.0221	.0107	.0037	.0007
45	.6391	.4102	.2644	.1712	.1113	.0727	.0476	.0313	.0137	.0061	.0019	.0003
50	.6080	.3715	.2281	.1407	.0872	.0543	.0339	.0213	.0085	.0035	.0009	.0001
55	.5785	.3365	.1968	.1157	.0683	.0406	.0242	.0145	.0053	.0020	.0005	.0000
60	.5504	.3048	.1697	.0951	.0535	.0303	.0173	.0099	.0033	.0011	.0002	.0000

Table A2.5
Given *A*, Find *P* (pwf)

Period	1%	2%	3%	4%	5%	6%	7%	8%	10%	12%	15%	20%
1	0.9901	0.9804	0.9709	0.9615	0.9524	0.9434	0.9346	0.9259	0.9091	0.8929	0.8696	0.8333
2	1.9704	1.9416	1.9135	1.8861	1.8594	1.8334	1.8080	1.7833	1.7355	1.6901	1.6257	1.5278
3	2.9410	2.8839	2.8286	2.7751	2.7232	2.6730	2.6243	2.5771	2.4869	2.4018	2.2832	2.1065
4	3.9020	3.8077	3.7171	3.6299	3.5460	3.4651	3.3872	3.3121	3.1699	3.0373	2.8550	2.5887
5	4.8534	4.7135	4.5797	4.4518	4.3295	4.2124	4.1002	3.9927	3.7908	3.6048	3.3522	2.9906
6	5.7955	5.6014	5.4172	5.2421	5.0757	4.9173	4.7665	4.6229	4.3553	4.1114	3.7845	3.3255
7	6.7282	6.4720	6.2303	6.0021	5.7864	5.5824	5.3893	5.2064	4.8684	4.5638	4.1604	3.6046
8	7.6517	7.3255	7.0197	6.7327	6.4632	6.2098	5.9713	5.7466	5.3349	4.9676	4.4873	3.8372
9	8.5660	8.1622	7.7861	7.4353	7.1078	6.8017	6.5152	6.2469	5.7590	5.3282	4.7716	4.0310
10	9.4713	8.9826	8.5302	8.1109	7.7217	7.3601	7.0236	6.7101	6.1446	5.6502	5.0188	4.1925
11	10.368	9.7868	9.2526	8.7605	8.3064	7.8869	7.4987	7.1390	6.4951	5.9377	5.2337	4.3271
12	11.255	10.575	9.9540	9.3851	8.8633	8.3838	7.9427	7.5361	6.8137	6.1944	5.4206	4.4392
13	12.134	11.348	10.635	9.9856	9.3936	8.8527	8.3577	7.9038	7.1034	6.4235	5.5831	4.5327
14	13.004	12.106	11.296	10.563	9.8986	9.2950	8.7455	8.2442	7.3667	6.6282	5.7245	4.6106
15	13.865	12.849	11.938	11.118	10.380	9.7122	9.1079	8.5595	7.6061	6.8109	5.8474	4.6755
16	14.718	13.578	12.561	11.652	10.838	10.106	9.4466	8.8514	7.8237	6.9740	5.9542	4.7296
17	15.562	14.292	13.166	12.166	11.274	10.477	9.7632	9.1216	8.0216	7.1196	6.0472	4.7746
18	16.398	14.992	13.754	12.659	11.690	10.828	10.059	9.3719	8.2014	7.2497	6.1280	4.8122
19	17.226	15.678	14.324	13.134	12.085	11.158	10.336	9.6036	8.3649	7.3658	6.1982	4.8435
20	18.046	16.351	14.877	13.590	12.462	11.470	10.594	9.8181	8.5136	7.4694	6.2593	4.8696
21	18.857	17.011	15.415	14.029	12.821	11.764	10.836	10.017	8.6487	7.5620	6.3125	4.8913
22	19.660	17.658	15.937	14.451	13.163	12.042	11.061	10.201	8.7715	7.6446	6.3587	4.9094
23	20.456	18.292	16.444	14.857	13.489	12.303	11.272	10.371	8.8832	7.7184	6.3988	4.9245
24	21.243	18.914	16.936	15.247	13.799	12.550	11.469	10.529	8.9847	7.7843	6.4338	4.9371
25	22.023	19.523	17.413	15.622	14.094	12.783	11.654	10.675	9.0770	7.8431	6.4641	4.9476
26	22.795	20.121	17.877	15.983	14.375	13.003	11.826	10.810	9.1609	7.8957	6.4906	4.9563
27	23.560	20.707	18.327	16.330	14.643	13.211	11.987	10.935	9.2372	7.9426	6.5135	4.9636
28	24.316	21.281	18.764	16.663	14.898	13.406	12.137	11.051	9.3066	7.9844	6.5335	4.9697
29	25.066	21.844	19.188	16.984	15.141	13.591	12.278	11.158	9.3696	8.0218	6.5509	4.9747
30	25.808	22.396	19.600	17.292	15.372	13.765	12.409	11.258	9.4269	8.0552	6.5660	4.9789
35	29.409	24.999	21.487	18.665	16.374	14.498	12.948	11.655	9.6442	8.1755	6.6166	4.9915
40	32.835	27.355	23.115	19.793	17.159	15.046	13.332	11.925	9.7791	8.2438	6.6418	4.9966
45	36.095	29.490	24.519	20.720	17.774	15.456	13.606	12.108	9.8628	8.2825	6.6543	4.9986
50	39.196	31.424	25.730	21.482	18.256	15.762	13.801	12.233	9.9148	8.3045	6.6605	4.9995
55	42.147	33.175	26.774	22.109	18.633	15.991	13.940	12.319	9.9471	8.3170	6.6636	4.9998
60	44.955	34.761	27.676	22.623	18.929	16.161	14.039	12.377	9.9672	8.3240	6.6651	4.9999

Table A2.6
Given *A*, Find *F* (caf)

Period	1%	2%	3%	4%	5%	6%	7%	8%	10%	12%	15%	20%
1	1.0000	1.0000	1.0000	1.0000	1.0000	1.0000	1.0000	1.0000	1.0000	1.0000	1.0000	1.0000
2	2.0100	2.0200	2.0300	2.0400	2.0500	2.0600	2.0700	2.0800	2.1000	2.1200	2.1500	2.2000
3	3.0301	3.0604	3.0909	3.1216	3.1525	3.1836	3.2149	3.2464	3.3100	3.3744	3.4725	3.6400
4	4.0604	4.1216	4.1836	4.2465	4.3101	4.3746	4.4399	4.5061	4.6410	4.7793	4.9934	5.3680
5	5.1010	5.2040	5.3091	5.4163	5.5256	5.6371	5.7507	5.8666	6.1051	6.3528	6.7424	7.4416
6	6.1520	6.3081	6.4684	6.6330	6.8019	6.9753	7.1533	7.3359	7.7156	8.1152	8.7537	9.9299
7	7.2135	7.4343	7.6625	7.8983	8.1420	8.3938	8.6540	8.9228	9.4872	10.089	11.067	12.916
8	8.2857	8.5830	8.8923	9.2142	9.5491	9.8975	10.260	10.637	11.436	12.300	13.727	16.499
9	9.3685	9.7546	10.159	10.583	11.027	11.491	11.978	12.488	13.579	14.776	16.786	20.799
10	10.462	10.950	11.464	12.006	12.578	13.181	13.816	14.487	15.937	17.549	20.304	25.959
11	11.567	12.169	12.808	13.486	14.207	14.972	15.784	16.645	18.531	20.655	24.349	32.150
12	12.683	13.412	14.192	15.026	15.917	16.870	17.888	18.977	21.384	24.133	29.002	39.581
13	13.809	14.680	15.618	16.627	17.713	18.882	20.141	21.495	24.523	28.029	34.352	48.497
14	14.947	15.974	17.086	18.292	19.599	21.015	22.550	24.215	27.975	32.393	40.505	59.196
15	16.097	17.293	18.599	20.024	21.579	23.276	25.129	27.152	31.772	37.280	47.580	72.035
16	17.258	18.639	20.157	21.825	23.657	25.673	27.888	30.324	35.950	42.753	55.717	87.442
17	18.430	20.012	21.762	23.698	25.840	28.213	30.840	33.750	40.545	48.884	65.075	105.93
18	19.615	21.412	23.414	25.645	28.132	30.906	33.999	37.450	45.599	55.750	75.836	128.12
19	20.811	22.841	25.117	27.671	30.539	33.760	37.379	41.446	51.159	63.440	88.212	154.74
20	22.019	24.297	26.870	29.778	33.066	36.786	40.995	45.762	57.275	72.052	102.44	186.69
21	23.239	25.783	28.676	31.969	35.719	39.993	44.865	50.423	64.002	81.699	118.81	225.03
22	24.472	27.299	30.537	34.248	38.505	43.392	49.006	55.457	71.403	92.503	137.63	271.03
23	25.716	28.845	32.453	36.618	41.430	46.996	53.436	60.893	79.543	104.60	159.28	326.24
24	26.973	30.422	34.426	39.083	44.502	50.816	58.177	66.765	88.497	118.16	184.17	392.48
25	28.243	32.030	36.459	41.646	47.727	54.865	63.249	73.106	98.347	133.33	212.79	471.98
26	29.526	33.671	38.553	44.312	51.113	59.156	68.676	79.954	109.18	150.33	245.71	567.38
27	30.821	35.344	40.710	47.084	54.669	63.706	74.484	87.351	121.10	169.37	283.57	681.85
28	32.129	37.051	42.931	49.968	58.403	68.528	80.698	95.339	134.21	190.70	327.10	819.22
29	33.450	38.792	45.219	52.966	62.323	73.640	87.347	103.97	148.63	214.58	377.17	984.07
30	34.785	40.568	47.575	56.085	66.439	79.058	94.461	113.28	164.49	241.33	434.75	1181.9
35	41.660	49.994	60.462	73.652	90.320	111.43	138.24	172.32	271.02	431.66	881.17	2948.3
40	48.886	60.402	75.401	95.026	120.80	154.76	199.64	259.06	442.59	767.09	1779.1	7343.9
45	56.481	71.893	92.720	121.03	159.70	212.74	285.75	386.51	718.90	1358.2	3585.1	18281
50	64.463	84.579	112.80	152.67	209.35	290.34	406.53	573.77	1163.9	2400.0	7217.7	45497
55	72.852	98.587	136.07	191.16	272.71	394.17	575.93	848.92	1880.6	4236.0	14524.	113219
60	81.670	114.05	163.05	237.99	353.58	533.13	813.52	1253.2	3034.8	7471.6	29220.	281733

Interest Tables for Continuous Compounding

The concept of continuous compounding also assumes that cash payments (or receipts) occur once per each of n interest periods, which are usually years. However, the compounding is continuous throughout each such interest period. Thus, with a nominal rate of interest per each of the n interest periods equal to r and interest being compounded k times per such an interest period, the expression for spcaf of Appendix 2 becomes:

$$F = P(1 + r.k^{-1})^{k \cdot n} \tag{1}$$

Note that compounding continuously really means that the value of k is considered to be infinitely large. Therefore, expression (1) should be written as:

$$F = P[\lim_{k \to \infty}(1 + r.k^{-1})^{k \cdot n}]$$

or

$$F = P[\lim_{k \to \infty}(1 + r.k^{-1})^{k}]^{n}$$

Relying on our freshman calculus knowledge we recall that:

$$\lim_{k \to \infty}(1 + r.k^{-1})^{k} = e^{r} \tag{2}$$

where e = the conventional symbol for the number 2.71828 known as the basis of natural logarithms. Thus, expression (2) may be simply written as $F = Pe^{rn}$. The expression e^{rn} for continuous compounding corresponds to $(1 + i)^n$ for discrete compounding. Consequently, $e^r = (1 + i)$ or $i = (e^r - 1)$.

Table A3.1 gives the six continuous compounding formulas that correspond to the six discrete compounding formulas of Table A2.1. They are arrived at by replacing the i of the formulas of Table A2.1 by $(e^r - 1)$.

The acronyms of Table A3.1 have the following interpretation:

cspcaf = continuous compounding, single payment compound amount factor

csppwf = continuous compounding, single payment present worth factor

ccaf = continuous compounding, discrete payment compound amount factor

csff = continuous compounding, discrete payment sinking fund factor

cpwf = continuous compounding, discrete payment present worth factor

ccrf = continuous compounding, discrete payment capital recovery factor

Table A3.1
Interest Factors for Continuous Discounting and Compounding

Find Given	P	F	A
P	1	$cspcaf = e^{rn}$	$ccrf = (e^r - 1)(1 - e^{-rn})^{-1}$
F	$csppwf = e^{-rn}$	1	$csff = (e^r - 1)(e^{rn} - 1)^{-1}$
A	$cpwf = (1 - e^{-rn})(e^r - 1)^{-1}$	$ccaf = (e^{rn} - 1)(e^r - 1)^{-1}$	1

The relation $i = (e^r - 1)$ indicates that, if $i = 0.10$, then $r = 0.094$. Consequently, the difference in answers obtained with discrete and continuous discounting and compounding procedures is a small percentage of the present or final sums of money involved. In addition, we should not be overconcerned about a difference of 0.006 between i = 0.10 and r = 0.094, since it is seldom possible to define the interest rate or cost of capital to be used in investment analyses to the accuracy of the nearest half of a percent. The following example illustrates the difference in answers obtained with discrete and continuous compounding procedures.

Suppose a company procures a machine for $15,000.00, which it agrees to pay in six equal payments, commencing one year after the date of purchase, at an interest rate of 10% per year. Immediately after the second payment, the terms of the agreement are changed to allow the balance to be paid off in a single payment the next year. We are interested in computing the annual payment for the first two years and the final payment with both the discrete and continuous compounding procedures.

Discrete compounding. The yearly payment for the first two years is:

$$A = P(\text{given } P, \text{find } A, i=10\%, n=6)$$
$$= \$15,000 \text{ crf}(i=10\%, n=6)$$
$$= \$15,000(0.22961) = \$3,444.15$$

The final payment is:

$$F = \$3,444.15 + A(\text{given } A, \text{find } P, i=10\%, n=3)$$
$$= \$3,444.15 + \$3,444.15 \text{ pwf}(i=10\%, n=3)$$
$$= \$3,444.15 + \$3,444.15(2.487) = \$12,009.75$$

Continuous compounding. The yearly payment for the first two years is:

$$A = P \text{ (given } P, \text{find } A, r=10\%, n=6)$$
$$= \$15,000 \text{cpwf}(r=10\%, n=6)^{-1}$$
$$= \$15,000(4.2900)^{-1} = \$3,496.50$$

The final payment is:

$$F = \$3,496.50 + A(\text{given } A, \text{find } P, r=10\%, n=3)$$
$$= \$3,496.50 + \$3,496.50 \text{ cpwf}(r=10\%, n=3)$$
$$= \$3,496.50 + \$3,496.50(2.4644) = \$12,113.27$$

The difference in the above F values is $12,113.27 - \$12,009.75 = \$103.52$ or 0.86% of $12,009.75.

It is suggested that the reader solve the example problems of Appendix 2 with the interest tables for continuous compounding. Tables A3.2 through A3.5 give values for the cspcaf, csppwf, cpwf, and ccaf for various r and n values. Values of csff and ccrf are not included, since their use is infrequent. The csff and *ccrf* values may be obtained by taking the reciprocal of the values of ccaf and cpwf, respectively.

Table A3.2
Given *P*, Find *F* (cspcaf)

Period	1%	2%	3%	4%	5%	6%	7%	8%	10%	12%	15%	20%
¼	1.0025	1.0050	1.0075	1.0101	1.0126	1.0151	1.0177	1.0202	1.0253	1.0305	1.0382	1.0513
½	1.0050	1.0101	1.0151	1.0202	1.0253	1.0305	1.0356	1.0408	1.0513	1.0618	1.0779	1.1052
¾	1.0075	1.0151	1.0228	1.0305	1.0382	1.0460	1.0539	1.0618	1.0779	1.0942	1.1191	1.1618
1	1.0101	1.0202	1.0305	1.0408	1.0513	1.0618	1.0725	1.0833	1.1052	1.1275	1.1618	1.2214
2	1.0202	1.0408	1.0618	1.0833	1.1052	1.1275	1.1503	1.1735	1.2214	1.2712	1.3499	1.4918
3	1.0305	1.0618	1.0942	1.1275	1.1618	1.1972	1.2337	1.2712	1.3499	1.4333	1.5683	1.8221
4	1.0408	1.0833	1.1275	1.1735	1.2214	1.2712	1.3231	1.3771	1.4918	1.6161	1.8221	2.2255
5	1.0513	1.1052	1.1618	1.2214	1.2840	1.3499	1.4191	1.4918	1.6487	1.8221	2.1170	2.7183
6	1.0618	1.1275	1.1972	1.2712	1.3499	1.4333	1.5220	1.6161	1.8221	2.0544	2.4596	3.3201
7	1.0725	1.1503	1.2337	1.3231	1.4191	1.5220	1.6323	1.7507	2.0138	2.3164	2.8577	4.0552
8	1.0833	1.1735	1.2712	1.3771	1.4918	1.6161	1.7507	1.8965	2.2255	2.6117	3.3201	4.9530
9	1.0942	1.1972	1.3100	1.4333	1.5683	1.7160	1.8776	2.0544	2.4596	2.9447	3.8574	6.0496
10	1.1052	1.2214	1.3499	1.4918	1.6487	1.8221	2.0138	2.2255	2.7183	3.3201	4.4817	7.3891
11	1.1163	1.2461	1.3910	1.5527	1.7333	1.9348	2.1598	2.4109	3.0042	3.7434	5.2070	9.0250
12	1.1275	1.2712	1.4333	1.6161	1.8221	2.0544	2.3164	2.6117	3.3201	4.2207	6.0496	11.023
13	1.1388	1.2969	1.4770	1.6820	1.9155	2.1815	2.4843	2.8292	3.6693	4.7588	7.0287	13.464
14	1.1503	1.3231	1.5220	1.7507	2.0138	2.3164	2.6645	3.0649	4.0552	5.3656	8.1662	16.445
15	1.1618	1.3499	1.5683	1.8221	2.1170	2.4596	2.8577	3.3201	4.4817	6.0496	9.4877	20.086
16	1.1735	1.3771	1.6161	1.8965	2.2255	2.6117	3.0649	3.5966	4.9530	6.8210	11.023	24.533
17	1.1853	1.4049	1.6653	1.9739	2.3396	2.7732	3.2871	3.8962	5.4739	7.6906	12.807	29.964
18	1.1972	1.4333	1.7160	2.0544	2.4596	2.9447	3.5254	4.2207	6.0496	8.6711	14.880	36.598
19	1.2092	1.4623	1.7683	2.1383	2.5857	3.1268	3.7810	4.5722	6.6859	9.7767	17.288	44.701
20	1.2214	1.4918	1.8221	2.2255	2.7183	3.3201	4.0552	4.9530	7.3891	11.023	20.086	54.598
21	1.2337	1.5220	1.8776	2.3164	2.8577	3.5254	4.3492	5.3656	8.1662	12.429	23.336	66.686
22	1.2461	1.5527	1.9348	2.4109	3.0042	3.7434	4.6646	5.8124	9.0250	14.013	27.113	81.451
23	1.2586	1.5841	1.9937	2.5093	3.1582	3.9749	5.0028	6.2965	9.9742	15.800	31.500	99.484
24	1.2712	1.6161	2.0544	2.6117	3.3201	4.2207	5.3656	6.8210	11.023	17.814	36.598	121.51
25	1.2840	1.6487	2.1170	2.7183	3.4903	4.4817	5.7546	7.3891	12.182	20.086	42.521	148.41
26	1.2969	1.6820	2.1815	2.8292	3.6693	4.7588	6.1719	8.0045	13.464	22.646	49.402	181.27
27	1.3100	1.7160	2.2479	2.9447	3.8574	5.0531	6.6194	8.6711	14.880	25.534	57.397	221.41
28	1.3231	1.7507	2.3164	3.0649	4.0552	5.3656	7.0993	9.3933	16.445	28.789	66.686	270.43
29	1.3364	1.7860	2.3869	3.1899	4.2631	5.6973	7.6141	10.176	18.174	32.460	77.478	330.30
30	1.3499	1.8221	2.4596	3.3201	4.4817	6.0496	8.1662	11.023	20.086	36.598	90.017	403.43
35	1.4191	2.0138	2.8577	4.0552	5.7546	8.1662	11.588	16.445	33.115	66.686	190.57	1096.6
40	1.4918	2.2255	3.3201	4.9530	7.3891	11.023	16.445	24.533	54.598	121.51	403.43	2981.0
45	1.5683	2.4596	3.8574	6.0496	9.4877	14.880	23.336	36.598	90.017	221.41	854.06	8103.1
50	1.6487	2.7183	4.4817	7.3891	12.182	20.086	33.115	54.598	148.41	403.43	1808.0	22026
55	1.7333	3.0042	5.2070	9.0250	15.643	27.113	46.993	81.451	244.69	735.10	3827.6	59874
60	1.8221	3.3201	6.0496	11.023	20.086	36.598	66.686	121.51	403.43	1339.4	8103.1	162755

Table A3.3
Given *F*, Find *P* (csppwf)

Period	1%	2%	3%	4%	5%	6%	7%	8%	10%	12%	15%	20%
¼	0.9975	0.9950	0.9925	0.9900	0.9876	0.9851	0.9827	0.9802	0.9753	0.9704	0.9632	0.9512
½	0.9950	0.9900	0.9851	0.9802	0.9753	0.9704	0.9656	0.9608	0.9512	0.9418	0.9277	0.9048
¾	0.9925	0.9851	0.9778	0.9704	0.9632	0.9560	0.9489	0.9418	0.9277	0.9139	0.8936	0.8607
1	0.9900	0.9802	0.9704	0.9608	0.9512	0.9418	0.9324	0.9231	0.9048	0.8869	0.8607	0.8187
2	0.9802	0.9608	0.9418	0.9231	0.9048	0.8869	0.8694	0.8521	0.8187	0.7866	0.7408	0.6703
3	0.9704	0.9418	0.9139	0.8869	0.8607	0.8353	0.8106	0.7866	0.7408	0.6977	0.6376	0.5488
4	0.9608	0.9231	0.8869	0.8521	0.8187	0.7866	0.7558	0.7261	0.6703	0.6188	0.5488	0.4493
5	0.9512	0.9048	0.8607	0.8187	0.7788	0.7408	0.7047	0.6703	0.6065	0.5488	0.4724	0.3679
6	0.9418	0.8869	0.8353	0.7866	0.7408	0.6977	0.6570	0.6188	0.5488	0.4868	0.4066	0.3012
7	0.9324	0.8694	0.8106	0.7558	0.7047	0.6570	0.6126	0.5712	0.4966	0.4317	0.3499	0.2466
8	0.9231	0.8521	0.7866	0.7261	0.6703	0.6188	0.5712	0.5273	0.4493	0.3829	0.3012	0.2019
9	0.9139	0.8353	0.7634	0.6977	0.6376	0.5827	0.5326	0.4868	0.4066	0.3396	0.2592	0.1653
10	0.9048	0.8187	0.7408	0.6703	0.6065	0.5488	0.4966	0.4493	0.3679	0.3012	0.2231	0.1353
11	0.8958	0.8025	0.7189	0.6440	0.5769	0.5169	0.4630	0.4148	0.3329	0.2671	0.1920	0.1108
12	0.8869	0.7866	0.6977	0.6188	0.5488	0.4868	0.4317	0.3829	0.3012	0.2369	0.1653	0.0907
13	0.8781	0.7711	0.6771	0.5945	0.5220	0.4584	0.4025	0.3535	0.2725	0.2101	0.1423	0.0743
14	0.8694	0.7558	0.6570	0.5712	0.4966	0.4317	0.3753	0.3263	0.2466	0.1864	0.1225	0.0608
15	0.8607	0.7408	0.6376	0.5488	0.4724	0.4066	0.3499	0.3012	0.2231	0.1653	0.1054	0.0498
16	0.8521	0.7261	0.6188	0.5273	0.4493	0.3829	0.3263	0.2780	0.2019	0.1466	0.0907	0.0408
17	0.8437	0.7118	0.6005	0.5066	0.4274	0.3606	0.3042	0.2567	0.1827	0.1300	0.0781	0.0334
18	0.8353	0.6977	0.5827	0.4868	0.4066	0.3396	0.2837	0.2369	0.1653	0.1153	0.0672	0.0273
19	0.8270	0.6839	0.5655	0.4677	0.3867	0.3198	0.2645	0.2187	0.1496	0.1023	0.0578	0.0224
20	0.8187	0.6703	0.5488	0.4493	0.3679	0.3012	0.2466	0.2019	0.1353	0.0907	0.0498	0.0183
21	0.8106	0.6570	0.5326	0.4317	0.3499	0.2837	0.2299	0.1864	0.1225	0.0805	0.0429	0.0150
22	0.8025	0.6440	0.5169	0.4148	0.3329	0.2671	0.2144	0.1720	0.1108	0.0714	0.0369	0.0123
23	0.7945	0.6313	0.5016	0.3985	0.3166	0.2516	0.1999	0.1588	0.1003	0.0633	0.0317	0.0101
24	0.7866	0.6188	0.4868	0.3829	0.3012	0.2369	0.1864	0.1466	0.0907	0.0561	0.0273	0.0082
25	0.7788	0.6065	0.4724	0.3679	0.2865	0.2231	0.1738	0.1353	0.0821	0.0498	0.0235	0.0067
26	0.7711	0.5945	0.4584	0.3535	0.2725	0.2101	0.1620	0.1249	0.0743	0.0442	0.0202	0.0055
27	0.7634	0.5827	0.4449	0.3396	0.2592	0.1979	0.1511	0.1153	0.0672	0.0392	0.0174	0.0045
28	0.7558	0.5712	0.4317	0.3263	0.2466	0.1864	0.1409	0.1065	0.0608	0.0347	0.0150	0.0037
29	0.7483	0.5599	0.4190	0.3135	0.2346	0.1755	0.1313	0.0983	0.0550	0.0308	0.0129	0.0030
30	0.7408	0.5488	0.4066	0.3012	0.2231	0.1653	0.1225	0.0907	0.0498	0.0273	0.0111	0.0025
35	0.7047	0.4966	0.3499	0.2466	0.1738	0.1225	0.0863	0.0608	0.0302	0.0150	0.0052	0.0009
40	0.6703	0.4493	0.3012	0.2019	0.1353	0.0907	0.0608	0.0408	0.0183	0.0082	0.0025	0.0003
45	0.6376	0.4066	0.2592	0.1653	0.1054	0.0672	0.0429	0.0273	0.0111	0.0045	0.0012	0.0001
50	0.6065	0.3679	0.2231	0.1353	0.0821	0.0498	0.0302	0.0183	0.0067	0.0025	0.0006	0.0000
55	0.5769	0.3329	0.1920	0.1108	0.0639	0.0369	0.0213	0.0123	0.0041	0.0014	0.0003	0.0000
60	0.5488	0.3012	0.1653	0.0907	0.0498	0.0273	0.0150	0.0082	0.0025	0.0007	0.0001	0.0000

Table A3.4
Given *A*, Find *P* (cpwf)

Period	1%	2%	3%	4%	5%	6%	7%	8%	10%	12%	15%	20%
¼	0.2484	0.2469	0.2453	0.2438	0.2423	0.2408	0.2393	0.2377	0.2348	0.2318	0.2274	0.2203
½	0.4963	0.4925	0.4889	0.4852	0.4816	0.4779	0.4744	0.4708	0.4637	0.4568	0.4465	0.4298
¾	0.7435	0.7370	0.7306	0.7242	0.7179	0.7116	0.7054	0.6992	0.6870	0.6751	0.6575	0.6291
1	0.9900	0.9802	0.9704	0.9608	0.9512	0.9418	0.9324	0.9231	0.9048	0.8869	0.8607	0.8187
2	1.9702	1.9410	1.9122	1.8839	1.8561	1.8287	1.8018	1.7753	1.7236	1.6735	1.6015	1.4891
3	2.9407	2.8828	2.8261	2.7708	2.7168	2.6640	2.6123	2.5619	2.4644	2.3712	2.2392	2.0379
4	3.9015	3.8059	3.7131	3.6230	3.5355	3.4506	3.3681	3.2880	3.1347	2.9900	2.7880	2.4872
5	4.8527	4.7107	4.5738	4.4417	4.3143	4.1914	4.0728	3.9584	3.7412	3.5388	3.2603	2.8551
6	5.7945	5.5976	5.4090	5.2283	5.0551	4.8891	4.7299	4.5771	4.2900	4.0256	3.6669	3.1563
7	6.7269	6.4670	6.2196	5.9841	5.7598	5.5461	5.3425	5.1483	4.7866	4.4573	4.0168	3.4029
8	7.6500	7.3191	7.0063	6.7103	6.4301	6.1649	5.9137	5.6756	5.2360	4.8402	4.3180	3.6048
9	8.5639	8.1544	7.7696	7.4079	7.0678	6.7477	6.4463	6.1624	5.6425	5.1798	4.5773	3.7701
10	9.4688	8.9731	8.5104	8.0783	7.6743	7.2965	6.9429	6.6117	6.0104	5.4810	4.8004	3.9054
11	10.365	9.7756	9.2294	8.7223	8.2512	7.8133	7.4059	7.0265	6.3433	5.7481	4.9925	4.0162
12	11.252	10.562	9.9270	9.3411	8.8001	8.3001	7.8376	7.4094	6.6445	5.9850	5.1578	4.1069
13	12.130	11.333	10.604	9.9356	9.3221	8.7585	8.2401	7.7629	6.9170	6.1952	5.3000	4.1812
14	12.999	12.089	11.261	10.507	9.8187	9.1902	8.6154	8.0891	7.1636	6.3815	5.4225	4.2420
15	13.860	12.830	11.899	11.056	10.291	9.5968	8.9654	8.3903	7.3867	6.5468	5.5279	4.2918
16	14.712	13.556	12.518	11.583	10.740	9.9797	9.2916	8.6684	7.5886	6.6934	5.6186	4.3325
17	15.555	14.268	13.118	12.090	11.168	10.340	9.5959	8.9250	7.7713	6.8235	5.6967	4.3659
18	16.391	14.966	13.701	12.576	11.574	10.680	9.8795	9.1620	7.9366	6.9388	5.7639	4.3932
19	17.218	15.649	14.266	13.044	11.961	11.000	10.144	9.3807	8.0862	7.0411	5.8217	4.4156
20	18.036	16.320	14.815	13.493	12.329	11.301	10.391	9.5826	8.2215	7.1318	5.8715	4.4339
21	18.847	16.977	15.348	13.925	12.679	11.585	10.621	9.7689	8.3440	7.2123	5.9144	4.4489
22	19.650	17.621	15.865	14.340	13.012	11.852	10.835	9.9410	8.4548	7.2836	5.9513	4.4612
23	20.444	18.252	16.366	14.738	13.328	12.103	11.035	10.100	8.5550	7.3469	5.9830	4.4713
24	21.231	18.871	16.853	15.121	13.630	12.340	11.221	10.246	8.6458	7.4030	6.0103	4.4795
25	22.010	19.477	17.325	15.489	13.916	12.563	11.395	10.382	8.7278	7.4528	6.0338	4.4862
26	22.781	20.072	17.784	15.843	14.189	12.773	11.557	10.507	8.8021	7.4970	6.0541	4.4917
27	23.544	20.655	18.229	16.182	14.448	12.971	11.708	10.622	8.8693	7.5362	6.0715	4.4963
28	24.300	21.226	18.660	16.508	14.694	13.158	11.849	10.728	8.9301	7.5709	6.0865	4.5000
29	25.048	21.786	19.079	16.822	14.929	13.333	11.980	10.827	8.9852	7.6017	6.0994	4.5030
30	25.789	22.335	19.486	17.123	15.152	13.499	12.103	10.917	9.0349	7.6290	6.1105	4.5055
35	29.384	24.920	21.345	18.461	16.115	14.191	12.601	11.277	9.2212	7.7257	6.1467	4.5125
40	32.803	27.259	22.946	19.556	16.865	14.705	12.953	11.517	9.3342	7.7788	6.1638	4.5151
45	36.056	29.376	24.323	20.453	17.448	15.085	13.201	11.679	9.4027	7.8079	6.1719	4.5161
50	39.151	31.291	25.509	21.187	17.903	15.367	13.375	11.787	9.4443	7.8239	6.1757	4.5165
55	42.094	33.024	26.530	21.788	18.257	15.575	13.498	11.859	9.4695	7.8327	6.1775	4.5166
60	44.894	34.592	27.408	22.280	18.533	15.730	13.585	11.908	9.4848	7.8375	6.1784	4.5166

Table A3.5
Given *A*, Find *F* (ccaf)

Period	1%	2%	3%	4%	5%	6%	7%	8%	10%	12%	15%	20%
¼	0.2491	0.2481	0.2472	0.2463	0.2453	0.2444	0.2435	0.2426	0.2407	0.2389	0.2361	0.2316
½	0.4988	0.4975	0.4963	0.4950	0.4938	0.4925	0.4913	0.4900	0.4875	0.4850	0.4813	0.4750
¾	0.7491	0.7481	0.7472	0.7462	0.7453	0.7443	0.7434	0.7425	0.7405	0.7386	0.7358	0.7309
1	1.0000	1.0000	1.0000	1.0000	1.0000	1.0000	1.0000	1.0000	1.0000	1.0000	1.0000	1.0000
2	2.0101	2.0202	2.0305	2.0408	2.0513	2.0618	2.0725	2.0833	2.1052	2.1275	2.1618	2.2214
3	3.0303	3.0610	3.0923	3.1241	3.1564	3.1893	3.2228	3.2568	3.3266	3.3987	3.5117	3.7132
4	4.0607	4.1228	4.1865	4.2516	4.3183	4.3866	4.4565	4.5280	4.6764	4.8321	5.0800	5.5353
5	5.1015	5.2061	5.3140	5.4251	5.5397	5.6578	5.7796	5.9052	6.1683	6.4481	6.9021	7.7609
6	6.1528	6.3113	6.4758	6.6465	6.8237	7.0077	7.1987	7.3970	7.8170	8.2703	9.0191	10.479
7	7.2146	7.4388	7.6730	7.9178	8.1736	8.4410	8.7206	9.0131	9.6391	10.325	11.479	13.799
8	8.2871	8.5891	8.9067	9.2409	9.5926	9.9629	10.353	10.764	11.653	12.641	14.336	17.854
9	9.3704	9.7626	10.178	10.618	11.084	11.579	12.104	12.660	13.878	15.253	17.656	22.808
10	10.465	10.960	11.488	12.051	12.653	13.295	13.981	14.715	16.338	18.197	21.514	28.857
11	11.570	12.181	12.838	13.543	14.301	15.117	15.995	16.940	19.056	21.518	25.996	36.246
12	12.686	13.427	14.229	15.096	16.035	17.052	18.155	19.351	22.060	25.261	31.203	45.271
13	13.814	14.699	15.662	16.712	17.857	19.106	20.471	21.963	25.381	29.482	37.252	56.294
14	14.952	15.995	17.139	18.394	19.772	21.288	22.955	24.792	29.050	34.241	44.281	69.758
15	16.103	17.319	18.661	20.145	21.786	23.604	25.620	27.857	33.105	39.606	52.447	86.203
16	17.264	18.668	20.229	21.967	23.903	26.064	28.478	31.177	37.587	45.656	61.935	106.29
17	18.438	20.046	21.845	23.863	26.129	28.676	31.542	34.774	42.540	52.477	72.958	130.82
18	19.623	21.451	23.511	25.837	28.468	31.449	34.829	38.670	48.014	60.167	85.765	160.78
19	20.821	22.884	25.227	27.892	30.928	34.393	38.355	42.891	54.063	68.838	100.64	197.38
20	22.030	24.346	26.995	30.030	33.514	37.520	42.136	47.463	60.749	78.615	117.93	242.08
21	23.251	25.838	28.817	32.255	36.232	40.840	46.191	52.416	68.138	89.638	138.02	296.68
22	24.485	27.360	30.695	34.572	39.090	44.366	50.540	57.781	76.304	102.07	161.35	363.37
23	25.731	28.913	32.629	36.983	42.094	48.109	55.205	63.594	85.330	116.08	188.47	444.82
24	26.990	30.497	34.623	39.492	45.252	52.084	60.208	69.890	95.304	131.88	219.97	544.30
25	28.261	32.113	36.678	42.104	48.572	56.305	65.573	76.711	106.33	149.69	256.57	665.81
26	29.545	33.762	38.795	44.822	52.062	60.786	71.328	84.100	118.51	169.78	299.09	814.23
27	30.842	35.444	40.976	47.651	55.732	65.545	77.500	92.105	131.97	192.43	348.49	995.50
28	32.152	37.160	43.224	50.596	59.589	70.598	84.119	100.78	146.85	217.96	405.89	1216.9
29	33.475	38.910	45.540	53.661	63.644	75.964	91.218	110.17	163.30	246.75	472.57	1487.3
30	34.811	40.696	47.927	56.851	67.907	81.661	98.833	120.34	181.47	279.21	550.05	1817.6
35	41.698	50.182	60.998	74.863	92.735	115.89	146.03	185.44	305.36	515.20	1171.4	4948.6
40	48.937	60.666	76.183	96.862	124.61	162.09	213.01	282.55	509.63	945.20	2486.7	13459
45	56.548	72.253	93.826	123.73	165.55	224.46	308.05	427.42	846.40	1728.7	5271.2	36594
50	64.548	85.058	114.32	156.55	218.11	308.64	442.92	643.54	1401.7	3156.4	11166.	99481
55	72.959	99.210	138.14	196.64	285.59	422.28	634.32	965.95	2317.1	5757.8	23645.	270426
60	81.802	114.85	165.81	245.60	372.25	575.68	905.92	1446.9	3826.4	10498.	50064.	735103

Cumulative Probabilities of the Standard Normal Distribution Function

d	0.00	0.01	0.02	0.03	0.04	0.05	0.06	0.07	0.08	0.09
0.0	0.0000	0.0040	0.0080	0.0120	0.0160	0.0199	0.0239	0.0279	0.0319	0.0359
0.1	0.0398	0.0438	0.0478	0.0517	0.0557	0.0596	0.0636	0.0675	0.0714	0.0753
0.2	0.0793	0.0832	0.0871	0.0910	0.0948	0.0987	0.1026	0.1064	0.1103	0.1141
0.3	0.1179	0.1217	0.1255	0.1293	0.1331	0.1368	0.1406	0.1443	0.1480	0.1517
0.4	0.1554	0.1591	0.1628	0.1664	0.1700	0.1736	0.1772	0.1808	0.1844	0.1879
0.5	0.1915	0.1950	0.1985	0.2019	0.2054	0.2088	0.2123	0.2157	0.2190	0.2224
0.6	0.2257	0.2291	0.2324	0.2357	0.2389	0.2422	0.2454	0.2486	0.2517	0.2549
0.7	0.2580	0.2611	0.2642	0.2673	0.2704	0.2734	0.2764	0.2794	0.2823	0.2852
0.8	0.2881	0.2910	0.2939	0.2967	0.2995	0.3023	0.3051	0.3078	0.3106	0.3133
0.9	0.3159	0.3186	0.3212	0.3238	0.3264	0.3289	0.3315	0.3340	0.3365	0.3389
1.0	0.3413	0.3438	0.3461	0.3485	0.3508	0.3531	0.3554	0.3577	0.3599	0.3621
1.1	0.3643	0.3665	0.3686	0.3708	0.3729	0.3749	0.3770	0.3790	0.3810	0.3830
1.2	0.3849	0.3869	0.3888	0.3907	0.3925	0.3944	0.3962	0.3980	0.3997	0.4015
1.3	0.4032	0.4049	0.4066	0.4082	0.4099	0.4115	0.4131	0.4147	0.4162	0.4177
1.4	0.4192	0.4207	0.4222	0.4236	0.4251	0.4265	0.4279	0.4292	0.4306	0.4319
1.5	0.4332	0.4345	0.4357	0.4370	0.4382	0.4394	0.4406	0.4418	0.4429	0.4441
1.6	0.4452	0.4463	0.4474	0.4484	0.4495	0.4505	0.4515	0.4525	0.4535	0.4545
1.7	0.4554	0.4564	0.4573	0.4582	0.4591	0.4599	0.4608	0.4616	0.4625	0.4633
1.8	0.4641	0.4649	0.4656	0.4664	0.4671	0.4678	0.4686	0.4693	0.4699	0.4706
1.9	0.4713	0.4719	0.4726	0.4732	0.4738	0.4744	0.4750	0.4756	0.4761	0.4767
2.0	0.4773	0.4778	0.4783	0.4788	0.4793	0.4798	0.4803	0.4808	0.4812	0.4817
2.1	0.4821	0.4826	0.4830	0.4834	0.4838	0.4842	0.4846	0.4850	0.4854	0.4857
2.2	0.4861	0.4866	0.4830	0.4871	0.4875	0.4878	0.4881	0.4884	0.4887	0.4890
2.3	0.4893	0.4896	0.4898	0.4901	0.4904	0.4906	0.4909	0.4911	0.4913	0.4916
2.4	0.4918	0.4920	0.4922	0.4925	0.4927	0.4929	0.4931	0.4932	0.4934	0.4936
2.5	0.4938	0.4940	0.4941	0.4943	0.4945	0.4946	0.4948	0.4949	0.4951	0.4952
2.6	0.4953	0.4955	0.4956	0.4957	0.4959	0.4960	0.4961	0.4962	0.4963	0.4964
2.7	0.4965	0.4966	0.4967	0.4968	0.4969	0.4970	0.4971	0.4972	0.4973	0.4S74
2.8	0.4974	0.4975	0.4976	0.4977	0.4977	0.4978	0.4979	0.4979	0.4980	0.4981
2.9	0.4981	0.4982	0.4982	0.4982	0.4984	0.4984	0.4985	0.4985	0.4986	0.4986
3.0	0.4987	0.4987	0.4987	0.4988	0.4988	0.4989	0.4989	0.4989	0.4990	0.4990

Note: N(d) represents areas under the standard normal distribution function. Suppose that $d_1 = 0.24$. This appendix implies a cumulative probability of $0.5000 + 0.0948 = 0.5948$. If d_1 is equal to 0.2452, we must estimate the probability by interpolating between N(0.25) and N(0.24).

Effect of Delays on the Present Value of a Project

In this appendix we examine the effect of delays in project completion and/or attainment of full capacity production after production has started, on the discounted present value of a project. To facilitate this examination, we introduce the following notations:

V = discounted present value of a project

X = full capacity physical output per unit of time

C = capital output ratio, related to the full capacity physical output X (note that the total planned capital investment CX has a time distribution given by $f(t)$, which is defined below)

P = price per unit of output

d = direct variable operating cost per unit of output; it is assumed that d remains constant at every stage, between the start of production and the attainment of full capacity

D = fixed operating cost per unit of output; it is assumed that D is constant and independent of the output per time period

T_0 = the time at which production starts, measured from the beginning of the investment outlay

T = the time at which production ceases, measured from T_0

j = percentage of investment outlay which occurs before production can begin

r = rate of discount; the continuous compounding of interest–convention is used

$f(t)$ = time distribution of investment outlay; any function depicting this distribution may be adopted. This appendix adopts the gamma density function, which is a flexible and convenient form of $f(t)^2$. Thus, $f(t) = (b^{n+1}/n!)t^n e^{-bt}$; different values of n represent different time distributions of investment outlays. This gamma density function applies when n is an integer. When $n = 0$, the distribution will be negative exponential with parameter b. A "negative exponential" time distribution of investment outlays for projects may be unrealistic, in which case only positive integer values of n should be considered.

$g(t)$ = time profile of output; any function depicting this profile may be adopted. A logistics-type relation is representative of most industrial situations. The following $g(t)$ function is, therefore, adopted in this appendix.

$$g(t) = e^{-a(t-T_0)} \quad \text{for } t \geq T_0$$
$$g(t) = 0 \quad \text{for } t < T_0$$

where a = a given parameter

The terms introduced here represent the input data required for the model. It is evident that the data relative to costs of investment, fixed and variable operating costs, full capacity physical output, price per unit of output, rate of discount, and percentage of investment outlay which occurs before production can begin are all data which are, or at least should be available before any investment decision is made. The functions adopted for $f(t)$ and $g(t)$ also constitute required input data. These data are obtained by means of "goodness-of-fit" tests, which are statistical tests of agreement between a theoretical probability distribution and the distribution of a set of sample observations.

The sample observations relative to the time distribution of investment outlay and time profile of output may be obtained from information about previous investments.

It is emphasized that functions other than the gamma density and logistics-type relation may be adopted. The methodology discussed below can equally be applied to functions such as the unit ramp, unit parabola, triangular, normal, Rayleigh, and Weibull functions. The only reason for taking the gamma density function for the time distribution of investment outlay is that it has a flexible form, by which is meant that its shape can be significantly altered by assuming different values for its parameter n. The main reason for taking the logistics-type relation for the time profile of output is that this shape is representative of most industrial situations.

The above notation enables us to express the discounted present value of a project as follows:

$$V = \int_{T_0}^{T_0 + T} (P - d)Xg(t)e^{-rt}dt - \int_{T_0}^{T_0 + T} De^{-rt}dt - \int_0^\infty CXf(t)e^{-rt}dt \qquad (1)$$

The analysis is simplified by assuming that the salvage value of a project is negligible, as is done in expression (1). In the absence of any substantial salvage value, it is possible that capital outlay can occur even after the production has been terminated. This may, for instance, be the case if capital outlay is required to scrap the production facility or to clean the area in which the facility is located upon termination of production. The upper limit of the third integral of expression (1) indicates the possibility of capital outlay which occurs after termination of production. Introduction of this upper limit also simplifies the following analysis.

Note that

$$\int_0^\infty CXf(t)e^{-rt}dt = \int_0^\infty (b^{n+1}/n!)t^n e^{-(r+b)t}dt$$

or

$$\int_0^\infty CXf(t)e^{-rt}dt = (b^{n+1}/n!)\{e^{-(r+b)t}/(r+b)\}(t^{n-1})\Big|_0^\infty$$
$$- \int_0^\infty (b^{n+1}/n!)\{t^{n-1}e^{-(r+b)}/(r+b)\}dt$$

Note also that this latter expression becomes zero as t approaches zero or infinity (l'Hôpital's rule). Therefore, by successive factoring one gets:

$$\int_0^\infty f(t)e^{-rt}dt = b^{n+1}/(b+r)^{n+1} \qquad (2)$$

The result of expression (2) and the following expressions (3) and (8) is based on integration by parts.

Application of the logistics-type relation for $g(t)$ gives:

$$\int_{T_0}^{T_0 + T} g(t)e^{-rt}dt = e^{-rT_0}[re^{-(r+a)T} - (r+a)e^{-rT} + a]/r(r+a) \qquad (3)$$

for $t \geq T_0$

(Inclusion of the value of $g(t)$ for $t \leq T_0$ in our analysis is of little or no interest.) If we are willing to ignore a term as small as $re^{-(r+a)T}$, which should be very close to zero, then

$$\int_{T_0}^{T_0 + T} g(t)e^{-rt}dt = e^{-rT_0}[a - (a+r)e^{-rT}]/r(r+a) \qquad (4)$$

Using expressions (2) and (4) in equation (1) and computation of the integral containing D in equation (1) results in:

$$V = (P - d)e^{-rT_0}[a - (a + r)e^{-rT}]X/r(r + a) - De^{-rT_0}(1 - e^{-rT})/r$$
$$- CXb^{n+1}/(b + r)^{n+1} \tag{5}$$

It is reasonable to recognize that production may begin after a pre-specified fraction of the investment has been completed:

$$\int_0^{T_0} f(t)dt = j \text{ where } j = \text{the above pre-specified fraction of the}$$
$$\text{investment: } 0 < j \leq 1 \tag{6}$$

Equation (6) establishes T_0, given $f(t)$ and j. Note that the start-up time T_0 must be considered to be a function of the parameters of $f(t)$ and that

$$\frac{\partial j}{\partial b} = \frac{\partial}{\partial b}\left[\int_0^{T_0(b)} (b^{n+1}/n!)t^n e^{-bt}dt\right] = (b^{n+1}/n!)T_0^n e^{-bT_0}\frac{\partial T_0}{\partial b}$$
$$+ \int_0^{T_0}[\{(n + 1)/b\}(b^{n+1}/n!)t^n e^{-bt} + (b^{n+1}/n!)t^n(-t)e^{-bt}]dt$$
$$= (b^{n+1}/n!)T_0^n e^{-bT_0}\frac{\partial T_0}{\partial b} + \int_0^{T_0}[(n + 1)/b]f(t)dt$$
$$+ (b^{n+1}/n!)T_0^{n+1}e^{-bT_0}/b - \int_0^{T_0}[(n + 1)/b]f(t)dt$$
$$= (b^{n+1}/n!)T_0^n e^{-bT_0}\left[\frac{\partial T_0}{\partial b} + T_0/b\right] = 0 \tag{7}$$

since j is a constant. Hence, $\frac{\partial T_0}{\partial b} = -T_0/b$ or $b = k/T_0$ where $k = $ a constant of integration.

The derivation of expression (7) is based on the following result of Leibnitz's rule:

$$\frac{d}{dt}\int_{\alpha(t)}^{\beta t} F(x,t)dx = F[\beta(t), t]\beta'(t) - F[\alpha(t), t]\alpha'(t) + \int_{\alpha(t)}^{\beta(t)} \frac{\partial F}{\partial t}(x, t)dx$$

A value of k may be obtained by expressing the pre-specified fraction of the investment j in terms of this constant of integration and the above parameter n:

$$j = \int_0^{T_0} f(t)dt = 1 - \int_{T_0}^{\infty} f(t)dt = 1 - e^{-bT_0}(bT_0)^n/n!$$

$$- \int_{T_0}^{\infty} [b^n/(n-1)!]t^{n-1}e^{-bt}dt = 1 - e^{-bT_0}(bT_0)^n/n!$$

$$- e^{-bT_0}(bT_0)^{n-1}/(n-1)! - e^{-bT_0}(bT_0)^{n-2}/(n-2)!$$

$$- \cdots - e^{-bT_0}(bT_0) - \int_{T_0}^{\infty} be^{-bt}dt$$

$$= 1 - e^{-bT_0}[(bT_0)^n/n! + (bT_0)^{n-1}/(n-1)! + \cdots + (bT_0) + 1]$$

$$= 1 - e^{-k}(1 + k + k^2/2! + \cdots + k^n/n!) \tag{8}$$

Replacing b by k/T_0 in equation (5) results in an expression for V directly in terms of the start-up time T_0:

$$V = (P-d)e^{-rT_0}[a - (a+r)e^{-rT}]X/r(r+a) - De^{-rT_0}(1-e^{-rT})/r$$
$$- CXk^{n+1}/(k+rT_0)^{n+1} \tag{9}$$

Upon calculation of the value of k with expression (8), we can use expression (9) to assess the impact on the discounted present value of a project, of delays in project completion, and/or attainment of full capacity production after production has started. For instance, values of k for $j = 0.75$, and $n = 1, 2$, and 3, are 2.65, 3.92, and 5.10, respectively.

Let us now examine how we can use the above expressions to analyze the effect of delays in project completion and/or attainment of full capacity production after production has started, on the discounted present value of a project. With the help of the logistics-type relation we determine the correspondence between values of the parameter a and the length of time required to reach a certain percentage of full capacity; this correspondence is in Table A5.1. For example, a value of $a = 1.00$ means that production runs at 70 percent of capacity after 1.20 units of time of operation, or it takes 3.00 units of time to reach 95% of capacity after start-up time T_0.

In order to examine the effect of more rapid project completion and attainment of full capacity production, the units for X and P have been chosen such that the full capacity output per unit of time ($=X$) of a project is equal to unity, and the price of this unit of output ($=P$) is also unity. Thus, capital requirements, discounted present value of the project, and project costs are all expressed in these units. Conversion to units based on the total capital requirements of a project is a simple matter, using the capital-output ratio (C).

The examination is performed for a group of projects with the following characteristics in common:

Table A5.1
Correspondence between Values of the Parameter *a* and the Length of Time Required to Reach a Given Percentage of Full Capacity

	Time Required to Reach g(t) Equal to						
a	40%	50%	60%	70%	80%	90%	95%
1.25	0.41	0.55	0.73	0.96	1.29	1.84	2.40
1.00	0.51	0.69	0.92	1.20	1.61	2.30	3.00
0.75	0.68	0.92	1.22	1.61	2.15	3.07	3.99
0.50	1.02	1.39	1.83	2.41	3.22	4.61	5.99
0.40	1.28	1.73	2.29	3.01	4.02	5.76	7.49
0.30	1.70	2.31	3.05	4.01	5.36	7.68	9.99
0.20	2.55	3.47	4.58	6.02	8.05	11.51	14.98
0.10	5.10	6.93	9.16	12.04	16.09	23.03	29.96

1. The time distribution of investment outlay $f(t)$ is given by $f(t) = (b^3/2!)t^2 e^{-bt}$.
2. The percentage of investment outlay which occurs before production can begin, j, is equal to 80%; hence, $k = 4.28$ [see equation (8)].
3. Capital-output ratio = 1.0.
4. The expected life of the projects is 20 years.
5. Salvage values of the projects after 20 years are negligible.
6. Direct variable operation costs per unit of output, d, are given by $(1 - d) = 0.40$.

Naturally, equation (9) may also be used to analyze the effect of more rapid project completion and attainment of full capacity on the discounted present value of projects which do not have these characteristics in common. Space considerations, however, limit the numerical examples to the analysis of projects with different fixed costs. One may, for instance, wish to examine the aforementioned effect for direct variable operating costs per unit of output, d, given by $(1 - d) = 0.40; 0.50; 0.60; 0.70$ and 0.80.

Table A5.2 shows discounted present values of the projects for combinations of values of the start-up time T_0 and the parameter a: projects with the aforementioned six characteristics, and fixed operating costs $D = 0.05; 0.06; 0.07; 0.08; 0.09$ or 0.10.

The V values of Table A5.2 have been obtained with equation (9) by using a discount rate of 20%. The following conclusions may be

Table A5.2
Discounted Present Value of Projects as a Function of Start-up Time
T_0, **Parameter** a, **and Fixed Operating Costs** D

T_0	a	Value of V for D Equal to					
		0.05	0.06	0.07	0.08	0.09	0.10
2	1.25	.209	.176	.142	.109	.076	.043
	1.00	.170	.137	.104	.071	.038	.005
	.75	.111	.078	.045	.012	−.021	−.050
	.50	.011	−.022	−.056	−.089	−.123	−.150
	.40	−.053	−.086	−.119	−.150	−.186	−.219
	.30	−.143	−.175	−.209	−.242	−.275	−.308
	.20	−.270	−.310	−.343	−.376	−.409	−.442
	.10	−.591	−.533	−.566	−.599	−.632	−.666
3	1.25	1.25	.098	.070	.043	.016	−.011
	1.00	.093	.066	.039	−.012	−.015	−.042
	.75	.045	.018	−.009	−.036	−.064	−.092
	.50	−.037	−.065	−.092	−.119	−.016	−.173
	.40	−.090	−.117	−.144	−.171	−.198	−.226
	.30	−.163	−.190	−.217	−.244	−.272	−.299
	.20	−.273	−.300	−.327	−.354	−.381	−.408
	.10	−.500	−.483	−.510	−.537	−.564	−.591
4	1.25	.058	.035	.013	−.010	−.031	−.054
	1.00	.032	.010	−.013	−.035	−.057	−.080
	.75	−.008	−.030	−.052	−.074	−.097	−.119
	.50	−.075	−.097	−.120	−.142	−.164	−.187
	.40	−.118	−.140	−.162	−.184	−.207	−.229
	.30	−.178	−.200	−.222	−.245	−.267	−.289
	.20	−.268	−.290	−.312	−.334	−.357	−.379
	.10	−.417	−.440	−.462	−.484	−.507	−.529
5	1.25	.005	−.014	−.032	−.050	−.068	−.087
	1.00	−.017	−.035	−.053	−.071	−.090	−.108
	.75	−.049	−.067	−.085	−.140	−.122	−.140
	.50	−.104	−.122	−.141	−.159	−.177	−.195
	.40	−.139	−.157	−.176	−.194	−.210	−.230
	.30	−.188	−.206	−.225	−.243	−.261	−.279
	.20	−.261	−.280	−.298	−.317	−.335	−.353
	.10	−.384	−.402	−.421	−.439	−.457	−.475
6	1.25	−.035	−.050	−.065	−.080	−.095	−.110
	1.00	−.053	−.068	−.083	−.098	−.113	−.128
	.75	−.079	−.094	−.109	−.124	−.139	−.154
	.50	−.124	−.139	−.154	−.169	−.184	−.199
	.40	−.153	−.168	−.183	−.198	−.213	−.228
	.30	−.193	−.208	−.223	−.238	−.253	−.268
	.20	−.253	−.269	−.283	−.298	−.313	−.328
	.10	−.354	−.369	−.384	−.399	−.414	−.429

Note: Characteristics of the projects: $n = 2$; $j = 0.80$; $T = T_0 + 20$; $(1 - d) = 0.40$; $C = 1.0$; and values of D equal to 0.05; 0.06; 0.07; 0.08; 0.09; 0.10. Discount rate = 20 percent.

drawn from an examination of the information presented in Tables A5.1 and A5.2.

1. The effect of delays in project completion on the discounted present value of a project is significantly smaller than the effect of delays in time required to reach a certain percentage of full capacity. For instance, Table A5.2 indicates that the discounted present value of a project with $D = 0.05$, and time profile of output, $g(t)$, with a parameter value $a = 1.25$, reduces from 0.209 to 0.125, or a drop of approximately 40%, if the start-up time T_0 is delayed from $T_0 = 2$ to $T_0 = 3$; the discounted present value of the same project reduces from 0.209 to 0.111, or a drop of approximately 47%, if no delay in the start-up time takes place but a delay of 0.86 units of time in the length of time required to reach 80% of full capacity occurs (see Table A5.1).
2. The smaller the value of the parameter a, or the longer the time required to reach a certain percentage of full capacity, the more sensitive is the discounted present value of a project to changes in the value of this parameter.
3. Increase in the time required to complete a project and/or increase in the time required to reach a certain percentage of full capacity may turn a project from a profitable venture to a nonprofitable undertaking. In fact, equation (9) may be used to determine the break-even point.
4. Generally, changes in the value of the parameter a and/or start-up time T_0 have a stronger impact on the present discounted value of a project if the fixed costs are small.

These types of conclusions may assist management in establishing which project requires special attention after a suspension of construction activities in time of economic recession or after a suspension of activities due to strikes, delays in procurements, prolonged process of decision making regarding essential features of the undertaking, delays due to inadequate control during the preconstruction, construction or production phase, etc.

Equation (9) may also be employed to perform a sensitivity analysis of forecasts of production output. Possible losses due to actual production lower than anticipated as a result of production problems or overestimation of market potential may be examined by assigning lower values to the parameter a.

Conclusions 1 through 4 are drawn from an examination of the information presented in Tables A5.1 and A5.2, which relates to specific numerical examples. It is, therefore, of interest to analyze whether these conclusions are generally true or whether they are only characteristic of the particular values reported for n, j, T, d, C, and D in Table A5.2. Thus, is the effect of delays in project completion on the discounted present value of a project always significantly smaller than the effect of delays in time required to reach a certain percentage of full capacity? To answer this question, we examine the rate of change in the above discounted present value when T_0 and a vary:

$$\frac{\partial V}{\partial T_0} = - e^{-rT_0}(P - d)[a - (a + r)e^{-rT}]X / (r + a) + e^{-rT_0}D(1 - e^{-rT})$$
$$+ r(n + 1)CXk^{n+1} / (k + rT_0)^{n+2} \tag{10}$$

$$\frac{\partial V}{\partial a} = (P - d)e^{-rT_0}X(1 - e^{-rT} - re^{-rT})/(r + a)^2 \tag{11}$$

It is evident that the effect of delays in project completion is only smaller than the effect of delays in time required to reach a certain percentage of full capacity if

$$\frac{\partial V}{\partial T_0} < \frac{\partial V}{\partial a} \tag{12}$$

or if

$$rT_0 + (n + 2)\ln(k + rT_0) < \ln\{(P - d)X[a(r + a) + 1 - (r + a)^2 e^{-rT}]$$
$$- D(1 - e^{-rT})(r + a)^2\} - \ln(r) - \ln(n + 1) - \ln(C) - \ln(X)$$
$$- (n + 1)\ln(k) - 2[\ln(r + a)] \tag{13}$$

Expression (13) may be used to check whether condition (12) is satisfied for a specific problem—that is, for given values of r, P, d, D, n, C, X, k (or j), a and T_0. In other words, the reverse of conclusion (1), or $\frac{\partial V}{\partial T_0} > \frac{\partial V}{\partial a}$, may be found for projects with different characteristics.

Is it always true that the smaller the value of a, the more sensitive is the discounted present value of a project to changes in the value of this parameter if the values of other input parameters are held constant? Yes, since expression (11) indicates that a given percentage change in a affects $\frac{\partial V}{\partial a}$ more if a is small.

Changes in the parameter a do not affect the only term in which the fixed costs D appear in equation (9) while changes in T_0 affect this term less than the third term of equation (9). Changes in the value of the parameter a and/or start-up time T_0 have, therefore, always a stronger impact on the present discounted value of a project if the fixed costs are small.

It is noted that the direct variable operating cost per unit of output, d, and the fixed operating costs, D, of equations (1) and (9) are, for simplicity reasons, assumed to be constant. Equation (1) may be revised to treat these costs as a function of time (t) in a manner similar to the treatment of $g(t)$ and $f(t)$. It is also noted that the first term of equation (1) has to be modified if we wish to evaluate the effect of a suspension in the production, once started, on the discounted present value of a project. Suppose that production is suspended at time T_1 and is started again at time T_2. Both T_1 and T_2 are measured from T_0. Equation (1) is in this case:

$$V = \int_{T_0}^{T_0+T_1} (P-d)Xg(t)e^{-rt}dt + \int_{T_0+T_2}^{T_0+T_2+T-T_1} (P-d)Xg(t)e^{-rt}dt$$
$$- \int_{T_0}^{T_0+T} De^{-rt}dt - \int_0^{\infty} CXf(t)e^{-rt}dt$$

The practical value of the approach of this appendix is in converting such vague questions as "how far off are we," "should we cash in our chips on this one and go to something else," "how can we pull this one out of the hole in time for an acceptable payoff" into quantitative terms that can form the basis for decision and action.

Index

About the Author

HENRI L. BEENHAKKER is a principal economist at the World Bank; adjunct professor, School of Advanced International Studies, Johns Hopkins University; and adviser to the U.S. General Accounting Office. Recently he has also given lectures at the U.S.D.A. graduate school. With professional experience in economics, finance, and engineering, he has assisted industrial and governmental organizations here and abroad in their long-range planning. Dr. Beenhakker has served as Chairman, Department of Industrial Management, University of Iowa, and was also employed by Stanford Research Institute. He is the author of 5 textbooks and more than 35 articles published in leading business and economics journals. His most recent book is *Investment Decision Making in the Private and Public Sectors* (Quorum, 1996).